# THE ULTIMATE RETAIL MANUAL:

## STRATEGIES FOR RETAILERS TO THRIVE & SUCCEED IN THE DIGITAL WORLD

BY

### JEFFREY P. MCNULTY

New Retail Ethos Publications
**newretailethos.com**

Published in the United States by New Retail Ethos Publications an imprint of New Retail Ethos, LLC.

ISBN-10: 1732565414

ISBN-13: 978-1732565418 (Paperback edition)

ISBN: 978-1732565401 (eBook edition)

Printed and bound in the United States of America

For information about special discounts available for bulk purchases, contact New Retail Ethos Publications at jpmcnulty@newretailethos.com or call 844-669-2888

Visit the author's website at www.newretailethos.com

First Edition

New Retail Ethos, LLC
P.O. Box 323
Wrightstown, WI. 54180
Business Contact:844-669-2888
jpmcnulty@newretailethos.com
www.newretailethos.com
www.facebook.com/TheUltimateRetailManual
www.linkedin.com/in/jeffreypmcnulty

ACKNOWLEDGMENTS ........................................................................................................ 1

INTRODUCTION ............................................................................................................... 3

CHAPTER ONE: TALENT ACQUISITION ............................................................................ 10

CHAPTER TWO: BRAND RECOGNITION .......................................................................... 24

CHAPTER THREE: TALENT RETENTION, PART ONE ......................................................... 37

CHAPTER FOUR: TALENT RETENTION, PART TWO .......................................................... 49

CHAPTER FIVE: REVENUE DETERRENTS ......................................................................... 63

CHAPTER SIX: NET INCOME TECHNIQUES TO INCREASE PROFITABILITY ....................... 79

CHAPTER SEVEN: REVENUE GENERATION, PART ONE .................................................... 96

CHAPTER EIGHT: REVENUE GENERATION, PART TWO .................................................. 109

CHAPTER NINE: THE POWER OF ENGAGEMENT, PART ONE ......................................... 127

CHAPTER TEN: THE POWER OF ENGAGEMENT, PART TWO .......................................... 140

CHAPTER ELEVEN: MERCHANDISING CONCEPTS TO INCREASE REVENUE, PART ONE .......... 152

CHAPTER TWELVE: MERCHANDISING CONCEPTS TO INCREASE REVENUE, PART TWO ......... 167

CHAPTER THIRTEEN: STORE ENVIRONMENT, PART ONE .............................................. 181

CHAPTER FOURTEEN: STORE ENVIRONMENT, PART TWO ............................................ 195

CHAPTER FIFTEEN: DIFFERENTIATION, PART ONE ....................................................... 211

CHAPTER SIXTEEN: DIFFERENTIATION, PART TWO ...................................................... 223

CHAPTER SEVENTEEN: ORGANIZATIONAL CULTURE, PART ONE ................................. 237

CHAPTER EIGHTEEN: ORGANIZATIONAL CULTURE, PART TWO ................................... 252

CHAPTER NINETEEN: ORGANIZATIONAL CULTURE, PART THREE ................................. 264

CHAPTER TWENTY: OMNICHANNEL CAPABILITIES, PART ONE .................................... 280

CHAPTER TWENTY-ONE: OMNICHANNEL CAPABILITIES, PART TWO ............................ 293

CHAPTER TWENTY-TWO: INNOVATIVE CONCEPTS, PART ONE ..................................... 303

CHAPTER TWENTY-THREE: INNOVATIVE CONCEPTS, PART TWO .................................. 319

CHAPTER TWENTY-FOUR: INNOVATIVE CONCEPTS, PART THREE ................................. 336

CHAPTER TWENTY-FIVE: CONCLUSION ....................................................................... 356

BIBLIOGRAPHY ........................................................................................................... 362

# **ACKNOWLEDGMENTS**

I wanted to dedicate this book to my wonderful wife, Karlie; for her undying devotion and gentle nudging for me to finally write a book to record all the knowledge that I have acquired during my 30-year tenure in the retail sector. My wife also worked in the retail sector. We first met on the floor of a Home Depot in the Midwest. She worked in the garden department and I was the department manager of the electrical department. As fate would have it, both departments were adjacent to each other, which allowed for multiple interactions throughout the day.

I admired her tenacious work ethic and how she could succeed in a predominantly male atmosphere, despite her limited knowledge in a home improvement environment. She exhibited exemplary customer service, a positive attitude, and a go-geter spirit that was venerated by all her peers as well as the entire management team. I was enthralled by her personality and we started dating after I was promoted and moved to a different store. We have been together for over 24 years now. Consequently, with her mild suggestions, this book is my first foray into sharing my knowledge and retail experiences with the masses.

I would also like to recognize my best friend, Kenneth McDonald, whom I have known for 40 years and have shared some great times together. For the past few years, Kenny would suggest that I write down all the best practices that I was sharing with my friends and colleagues to start formulating my book. I wanted to thank you, Kenny, for your kind words and your honest motivation. You are one of the main driving forces which guided me to delve into this creative endeavor. I am grateful for your subtle, yet persistent, suggestions to share my knowledge and experiences with others.

In addition, I wanted to thank Laura VandenAvond Ph.D., who is an instructor at Northern Michigan University in the Department of Psychological Science. She was my instructor for a developmental psychology class at The University of Wisconsin, Green Bay. She expressed her positive comments surrounding my impressive writing ability which assisted in providing additional impetus for writing this book. Laura is an inspirational figure in my life, and I wanted to articulate my sincere appreciation for your impactful sentiments. Thank you again, Laura, for your inspiration!

## INTRODUCTION

I am currently the Founder & Chief Executive Officer of <u>New Retail Ethos, LLC </u>which assists retail organizations (regardless of size, scope, or niche) with alleviating and addressing common "Pain Points" through all facets of consumer insights, anticipatory intelligence, and retail research across numerous categories. Our company services encompass increasing top-line revenue, addressing operational inefficiencies, providing innovative concepts that proliferate market share, impart a proven system to drastically improve employee/customer engagement, and merchandising concepts that generate increased profitability. I am also the Founder & Chief Executive Officer of <u>New Retail Ethos Publications</u> which assists aspiring authors throughout the entire book publishing process from inception until publication.

When I am speaking with my clients, colleagues, friends, and family I have been informed that they are impressed with the breadth of knowledge and experience I have within the retail sector. They all kept urging me to write a book to share my cacophony of retail knowledge with others.

I am just like any other first-time author; I did not feel like I had any relevant information to offer. Furthermore, I was under the impression that all retail leaders understood the same multifaceted concepts on how to successfully operate a retail store or business as I did. I have always felt that it is better to operate from a place of humility instead of arrogance, while you consistently acquire the necessary confidence and discernment required as you steadily progress through your chosen endeavors. What I gathered from walking and shopping many of the most popular retail stores is the utter lack of basic customer service and employee knowledge

presented. The most shocking of all is the lack of positive engagement in many departments

within their buildings.

During my 30-year career in the retail sector, I worked for: The Home Depot, Lowes, Barnes

& Noble, ShopKo, PetSmart, Toys "R" Us, Publix Supermarkets, and Festival Foods which

encapsulated a comprehensive and diverse number of different retail niches. I progressed through

the following positions: back-up, department manager, key carrier, assistant manager, operations

manager, co-store manager, store manager, district manager in training, assistant lighting

merchant, and district sales support leader. These positions provided a strong and necessary retail

leadership foundation to fully understand the complete gamete of roles and responsibilities

within each organization at the store/district level.

My leadership style has always been to "Lead by Example." I felt that I would have to fully

immerse myself in each position in order to become an effective leader. Thus, I would

earn/garner credibility among the store associates and managers, fully understanding their

predicaments and unique challenges they faced. This would also allow me to express empathy

and compassion, which would start to formulate the foundation for trust and teamwork with my

teams. Henceforth, I understood what is was like to "walk in their shoes." I was extremely

vigilant to constantly remind myself daily to never forget what it felt like with the challenges and

obstacles that each position entails.

I worked in the southeast and Midwest during my tenure which was invaluable to my professional development. This provided the disparate demographic environments to acquire and ascertain how each city could be diametrically different, while also providing a completely new set of challenges. The largest adjustment was the relocation from the southeast to the Midwest and the introduction of the four seasons. This transition drastically impacts the retail stores with the massive planogram changes that come from this seasonality adjustment.

*Throughout my retail career, I started to realize that I had developed a dynamic and proven blueprint that was successful in every retail store regardless of product mix, annual sales volume, or physical location.* I finally had an epiphany during the process of assisting yet another store/district with increasing top-line sales, reducing expenses, maximizing ROI, producing positive net income, and experiencing positive customer and employee engagement. The proverbial light bulb went off. I realized that I was onto something that was transformative and highly portable, yet extremely effective when implemented and executed properly. It was a moment that I will never forget! It became ingrained in my psyche. I kept being informed by my respected colleagues, friends, as well as my clients that I had attained a strong, practical, and impressive retail knowledge acumen and that I should share this knowledge with others.

## WHAT TO EXPECT FROM THIS MANUAL?

As I am writing this manuscript, I am reading *yet another article* about how many major retailers are struggling to maintain their market share, increase top-line sales, and are facing another dismal quarter of "lackluster performance." Some retailers' responses are: "let's close some more stores" or "drastically reduce our payroll." This type of myopic thinking is constricting and is not addressing the **CORE ISSUE IN RETAIL TODAY**. Of course, there is intense competition from digitally native brands and online competition with behemoths like Amazon. However, in business just like life, everything is "cyclical", and the consumer is speaking loud and clear with their wallets. They are demanding a **BACK TO BASICS** approach especially during the Covid-19 pandemic! They are no longer going to accept the apathy that has infiltrated some (but not all) retail stores. The top-tier retailers *(Walmart, Target, Home Depot, Lowe's, Best Buy, Costco, and Kroger)* are doing a fantastic job of adapting to changing consumer preferences.

The core issues in retail today can be broken down into ten main pillars. The pillars that I will discuss are not completely inclusive of every problem within the retail sector. However, the pillars encompass the major economic and pervasive consumer paradigms that affect **WHY** a customer chooses to allocate their hard-earned dollars and their loyalty to certain retail establishments.

Throughout this book, I will dissect each retail theme while communicating the essential information necessary for any leader (department manager up to the CEO) to be wildly successful. When implemented and executed properly, these transformative concepts will assist you in achieving magnificent and proven/tangible outcomes. These ten pillars will transform the look and feel of your retail stores while increasing your market share, establishing rock-solid relationships with your employees, vendors, and customers, improving your top-line revenue, and maximizing your ROI. Each one of these retail concepts has been successfully integrated into the eight different retail companies I worked for during my 30-year tenure while *consistently proving their efficacy.*

The ten pillar retail stratagems have been applied to the following retail sectors: home improvement, department stores, books/media/music, pet retail & pet products, toys & games, apparel, jewelry, electronics, home goods, and multiple grocery stores all with the same stellar accomplishments. These retail concepts are a series of compounding ideas that create an overall advantageous synergistic effect. They generate effectual momentum analogous to The Flywheel Effect (originally coined by Jim Collins author of Good to Great) that Amazon CEO Jeff Bezos incorporates which creates a "virtuous cycle" a.k.a. a positive feedback loop. This translates into a magnetic and interactive shopping environment that is built upon solid foundations, devoted relationships, transparency, and an amalgamation of concrete values that truly serve your customers.

My objective for this retail manual is that it will be a *true leadership guide for the retail/business management segment and will be shared among retailers/businesses, large and small alike.* The most challenging part of this manual for some retail leaders is going to be a "deprogramming of their old archetypes" while apportioning for the assimilation of new (maybe forgotten) ideas that are proven to be effective at completely renovating your stores. **Change is the hardest thing for any person to willingly accept.** However, in our constantly evolving retail environment, we must adapt and modify our behavior while addressing and correcting what is not working regardless of legacy mindsets.

I would recommend assessing your management style and or your corporate culture to ascertain which of the ten pillars need implementation or which ones need some tweaking to increase productivity and drive innovation within your store/s. When implemented and executed properly, these ten pillars will create an inclusive and profitable atmosphere that will increase talent acquisition/retention, improve store morale, and will maximize your net income. Each pillar is its own entity which requires a complete commitment from top-to-bottom, preferably, from the CEO all the way down to the entry-level manager to ensure absolute dedication. Each pillar will build upon the next which creates a cumulative effect that will help propel the next pillar forward and so forth.

"A fish stinks from the head down" is a complete and accurate assessment of how this manual will work for your company/store. The companies I have worked for that had upper management commitment and were totally "resolute in their values and beliefs" regarding these pillars, consistently performed the best across all economic indicators as well as in most human resource metrics. If your organization's upper management will not commit to any of these pillars, then it is up to you and your management team to implement and execute these at the store/district level to the best of your abilities.

When you start blowing your revenue statistics out of the water, are leading your district/region/company in key performance indicators (KPI's) and your consumer feedback surveys are top-notch, then maybe your regional leadership teams will start to take notice. This will create an opportunity for you to showcase the ten-pillar strategy which will thrust your store/district onto a highly visible platform that is congruent with productive and profitable outcomes.

Within *The Ultimate Retail Manual*, I will thoroughly describe in detail how to utilize these concepts in your stores/company. This retail manual was created to assist any new or experienced retail leader (department manager up to the C-Suite executive) with acclimating to the **NEW RETAIL ETHOS** while supplementing and enhancing your existing retail acumen. It is my sincerest aspiration that this book will assist you with increasing your retail IQ, accelerate your retail aspirations, and create a servant leadership style within you that will permeate all your professional interactions, as well as complementing your existing retail knowledge repertoire. I look forward to sharing with you the knowledge, experiences, and best practices I have acquired throughout my 30-year retail tenure. Now that I have whetted your appetite with anticipation, without further ado…

# CHAPTER ONE: TALENT ACQUISITION

**Talent Acquisition** is the **FIRST PILLAR** within the manual and is probably the **MOST** important pillar in which to focus upon. It is often the greatest detriment to any organization because many executives do not place a very high value on "non-tangible" programs, i.e. programs that do not produce revenue or increase profit. The business professionals who are responsible for "talent acquisition" in your company should, adamantly, be completely committed to fostering an inclusive atmosphere that will attract sterling talent. In addition, these human resource employees should be extremely knowledgeable about the company and can build credible rapport with your potential candidates. Acquiring top tier talent is the number one thing you **MUST** do to ensure your company is represented properly. Talent acquisition should be the focus of not just human resource professionals, but the entire management team.

Every strong and viable organization that is top of mind and dominant within their sector, universally, exhibits a fully committed upper echelon talent acquisition program that focuses on acquiring the best and brightest aspirants. The CEO, all the way down to the entry-level manager within the company, are completely devoted to the entire recruitment process. They have been thoroughly trained to interview, assess, and conduct the different types of interviews. These companies fully understand the immediate and long-term ramifications of poor and antiquated hiring decisions that will reverberate throughout the store while permeating the culture of the entire organization. Yes, one bad apple turns into another and so forth, until your stores start reflecting a substandard atmosphere that is contagious. Ultimately, it starts to appear as declining revenue, reduction in your loyal customer base, decreased market share, and diminishing store morale.

At this point, if the issue of horrendous hiring is localized within certain stores/regions, there *can be a short turnaround time to a readjustment period* with a renewed focus on the human resources/leadership teams. If the incompetence is left unchecked for a prolonged period, it can have devastating and irreconcilable impacts on your corporate brand, think (many legacy retailers). In all fairness, the human resource teams are sometimes not properly prepared (through no fault of their own) to handle the monumental task of hiring the **RIGHT TYPE** of personnel to mesh with your culture and your clientele. I have worked with some excellent and outstanding human resource professionals during my tenure. They usually displayed some similar characteristics: strong soft skills, a good judge of character, fully understood each position they were hiring for, were capable of hiring candidates different/opposite from themselves, and were excellent evaluators of talent.

## THE INTERVIEW PROCESS

We are going to discuss the all-important interview process from the employer "point of view" and the components that make up this process:

1. The person conducting the interview should be extremely prepared (read the applicant's resume, LinkedIn profile, and cover letter).

2. Schedule the time for the interview and make sure other managers/peers know, not to disturb you during the interview. This component is the most overlooked, which sends

the message to your candidate that they are not important enough for your undivided attention.

3. **BE ON TIME!!!** Punctuality is the first impression you are sending to the interviewee. How would you feel about the applicant if he/she were 15 minutes late? We feel as employers that our time is valuable, and the aspirant's time is not. I sense a **DOUBLE STANDARD HERE!!!** Remember, the *applicant is interviewing you as well.*

4. Welcome the candidate with a heartfelt greeting, a handshake, and a smile. Make the person feel welcome. Offer them a bottle of water, as they will be talking for an extended period of time.

5. Maintain an empathetic perspective. Always remember that the person is probably nervous and possibly desperate to receive an offer of employment from your company. They could have gone through a plethora of interviews elsewhere already.

6. Please make the candidate comfortable with positive and open body language e.g., not crossing your arms, plenty of eye contact (don't stare), and palms up to relay honesty.

7. Explain the interview process: how long the interview will be, if there will be other managers stopping by, explain the position they are interviewing for and what you are looking to accomplish from this interview.

8. Engage in active listening (a way of listening and responding to another person that improves mutual understanding) by reflecting back what the other person has said, or to clarify their true meaning.

9. Use a structured interview guide to remain consistent and compliant with your questions (hopefully your guide will contain plenty of open-ended questions). These are questions that cannot be answered with a yes or no. There is a myriad of questions you are not allowed to ask e.g., nationality, age, religion, marital status, children, etc. Focus your attention on their resume and cover letter, while engaging in a back and forth open dialogue.

10. Allow the candidate adequate time to ask questions about the company. Too many times the interviewer leaves the candidate with only a few minutes left. As a result, they wind up feeling constricted for time and abandoning their list of questions.

11. The final piece of the interview is the closing remarks from the interviewer. This explains the next step in the process (unless this is the final interview), in addition to the follow-up time for a response from your company. This process is the most egregious from most employers who fail to follow up in the given time frame or do not contact the candidates at all who did **NOT** receive an offer of employment. First and last impressions are paramount to the integrity and character of your company. Remember, **ABSOLUTLEY NO GHOSTING HERE!** Ghosting is when a hiring manager or human resources employee **NEVER** communicates with the candidate again.

12. **FOLLOW UP, FOLLOW UP, FOLLOW UP.** The retail world is very interconnected, and candidates will wind up working for numerous companies within the sector during their lifetime. Lack of follow up on your part will not endear your future aspirants to

apply to your company again. As a result, it will ensure that your reputation is severely tainted. Remember, bad news travels extremely fast. Again, **NO GHOSTING!!!**

## THE GATEKEEPERS OF YOUR TALENT

The individuals who are interviewing and extending offers of employment are considered the "gatekeepers" of the talent that is being supplied to your stores and your organization. These employees can have a tremendously positive impact on your business, or consequently, have a devastating bearing on your company and its future heading. I have worked with a few thousand human resource professionals during my career. There is an enormous crevasse between the inadequate employee and the rock star of talent acquisition.

The most common pitfall for many human resource professionals and managers alike is the propensity to hire people **JUST LIKE THEMSELVES**; i.e., the Type A personality will hire mostly Type A personality individuals. This is a disastrous scenario in the making because of the necessity to provide a diversity of personalities for your customers. Your customers all have unique attributes themselves and will demand the level of service that fits their interaction requirements.

Using the Type A personality (which I was for the earlier part of my career) example, the definition of a Type A is "personalities that are more competitive, outgoing, ambitious, impatient and/or aggressive are labeled Type A" (Wikipedia). I have worked in stores that were heavily slanted towards the Type A's. I can attest that the *atmosphere was extremely competitive and hostile at times, which did not allow for many other viewpoints or perspectives*. It was a totally dominant environment that was centered around results with egoism running rampant throughout the store. For clarification purposes, there is nothing inherently wrong with the Type A personality; however, a more inclusive and accommodating blend of personalities will foster a mutually beneficial and rewarding atmosphere for both customers and associates alike.

The store manager/district manager should be fully engaged in the hiring process, while also being the intermediary for the hiring manager/human resource professional. This will ensure that the candidates who are being hired reflect a diverse group of people, which includes different types of personalities (Type A-Type D). This type of checks and balances system is especially heightened during your hiring season when you will be inundated with a plethora of new hires.

### OFFER OF EMPLOYMENT PROTOCOLS

Now that you have completed the interview process, it is now time to master the art of extending an offer of employment to your chosen candidates. This procedure is often fraught with inconsistencies and is unfair to the applicant. If the candidate is going to be filling an executive position, then the company should be offering a **COMPENSATION PACKAGE.** This can consist of salary, vacation time, stock options, company car, expense account, sign-on bonuses, and relocation packages. An innumerable amount of companies is operating from the time-honored adage of "pay the talent the least amount possible" to save on our bottom line. *However, in the current digital world we live in, candidates can and are, fully aware of the current market value for their services.*

It is like a **GAME** for many (not all) of the hiring managers who are making these employment offers. They want to see how far they can push the proverbial envelope by underpaying and devaluing their candidates with a low-ball offer. I have always believed in "an even exchange of energy" (a common theme throughout the manual) between all parties involved. Let's not forget the law of karma (personally and professionally) that is activated when you **PURPOSELY** attempt to avoid compensating someone for their background and experience. The proper protocol for extending employment offers is to recompense the applicant for "what the position pays" and not for what the candidate was making in their previous jobs. I fully understand there is a tipping point. All companies must account for their controllable expenses (and payroll is the number one controllable expense on the profit and loss statement). At the same time, **<u>FAIRNESS IS THE CURRENCY OF DECENCY</u>**.

Pecuniary flexibility is the oil that lubricates the hiring machine, and the hiring manager should always strive to remain reasonable with their salary offerings. Any company worth its salt should understand that this process is a give and take which is **SUPPOSED** to be a negotiation. It is disingenuous to attempt to demoralize your future employees by offering a substandard salary which should be a collaborative and transparent event that mutually benefits both parties.

I would encourage all human resource professionals or managers that are extending employment offers to "pay the candidate what the position calls for and or pay the applicant what they are truly worth." Employees/managers always find out what other people are earning, and if they are being severely under-compensated, *this presupposes the new person to feelings of inadequacy, diminished self-esteem, and anger.* This creates a disgruntled employee who should be excited and invigorated for their new role; on the contrary, they feel like they have been "duped." This can lead to low morale, excessive absenteeism, and high levels of unproductivity. Not to mention the prevailing negative vibrations this person will emit which will infect those around them. **NOBODY** appreciates feeling like they were bamboozled by their employer!

The hiring manager should also research the benchmark levels within their relative sector to fully understand what their competitors are offering executive leaders on hiring perks like vacation time, sign-on bonuses, and stock options. This type of due diligence will ensure your company is operating from a position of fairness which will reflect in the caliber of candidates your organization can attract and retain.

## THE TERMINATION PROCESS

I wanted to include the termination process within the talent acquisition pillar because this protocol will directly influence your store/company's ability to *attract top-tier talent*. I have witnessed this specific protocol being uncharacteristically abused throughout my tenure within the retail sector because of the <u>glaring inconsistencies in executing this procedure by the book</u>. Many leaders become power-hungry with their positions which are driven by their inflated egos. This can (and will) damage an **ENTIRE** organization by their lack of empathy and cruel behavior when terminating an employee.

Now, many people will say that a terminated person will remain a disgruntled person. While there is some semblance of truth to that statement, a solid company with trustworthy and dedicated leaders will still be able to handle these situations with *class and integrity*. The prestigious organizations are always acting from a place of consistency and character. Both of these traits will usually attract the right type of candidates to their company.

Most companies forget that a terminated employee is **STILL A POTENTIAL CUSTOMER.** They will share their experiences with their circle of influence, either positively or negatively. I have terminated many employees during my tenure. There is a gigantic difference between retailers that handle the situation with empathy and humility and organizations that act unprofessionally and with pretentiousness. The companies from which I departed that acted with humility and kindness are organizations to which I will continue to give my patronage and will sing their praises whenever I can. The retail establishments that treated me with arrogance and egotism, conversely, will never receive my loyalty ever again - even after numerous leadership changes.

The act of termination is a **LIFE-ALTERING EVENT** for most individuals. It should be treated with respect and dignity. Even to those employees that completely deserve their discharge, they are still human beings and should be afforded the decency of a humbled leader/s commitment to ensuring the process is handled with reverence. Many companies have a structured way to terminate employees. This can still be performed with disdain, arrogance, and embarrassment, which is completely unfair to the individual. I completely understand that many leaders feel that the severity of the reason for the termination *should dictate* how the process will proceed. Moreover, I have terminated many individuals who have committed egregious actions/behaviors which resulted in their termination for which I executed the process with compassion, empathy, and professionalism. Unless the individual is attempting to injure or hurt another employee/customer, I would always maintain the same level of professional courtesy towards them throughout the entire termination process.

I remember a time when an assistant manager at a big-box retailer was put in charge while the store manager was at a companywide meeting. This manager had associates lined up outside the manager's office and was pumping them up with positive feedback and praising their work, only to turn around and terminate them on the spot. I was coming in for my closing shift and noticed this extremely unusual circumstance taking place as I was putting on my uniform. I overheard this series of events happening at which I immediately interrupted him and asked the employee to leave the room. I inquired about the authority given to him, pointing out the fact that "only the store manager" can terminate an employee. His response was that our store manager asked him to reduce hours. Therefore, he had selected ten associates to terminate. I immediately contacted our store manager and asked him if he authorized this assistant manager to terminate ten associates.

He responded with a loud *What?!* He explained to me that he clarified to the assistant manager that he wanted to reduce hours for the day, not terminate any associates. This assistant manager was chomping at the bit to get promoted; and, felt like he was the lead dog who was the next manager to be promoted. His behavior that day was a prime example of how power, ego, and arrogance can transform a leader into an infectious entity. Unfortunately, other potential leaders are watching and thinking: *Is this the type of leader I must become to get promoted or be successful at this company which will reverberate throughout the entire store?*

Imagine what would have happened had I not intervened and interrupted this type of behavior that day? This leader was an excellent merchant who displayed exemplary revenue generation talents. However, he was extremely deficient with his soft skills. Consequently, this individual was terminated within a year because of the same pervasive behaviors. The news had already circulated around our district. Subsequently, our store had a black eye for a while with associates and managers shunning our store like the plague. I never forgot that day as it served to heighten my sensitivity to the entire termination process even further.

I had a fantastic store manager who was a strong mentor for me. He pulled me into the office and explained to me that I was going to have to terminate an employee <u>with him as an observer</u>. I immediately became filled with a sense of trepidation while starting to feel nauseous. I asked the proverbial question; why me? He reiterated that I would be a store manager very soon and this part of the job is not optional; so, I needed to practice now to become more proficient and build up my confidence. I had never felt so nervous and scared during my tenure in retail up to that point. Consequently, I fumbled through the termination paperwork and the individual started crying which made things infinitely worse.

This employee had a wife with three kids and was the sole breadwinner in the family. My boss explained that I had to approach this event as a business decision, even though it was torturous in nature. It was a requirement of the store manager position. That day, performing that termination was the best thing for my growth as a leader because it forced me to accept the magnitude of responsibilities placed upon a store leader for which I eagerly embraced to further my ascension. This humbling action also fortified my belief in training future retail managers in their next leadership role, so as to properly prepare them for the nuances of the position. For instance, when my leaders were promoted, they were already comfortable with their next position and its complexities.

I always admired how this boss/mentor approached the termination process with humility and empathy while always allowing the individual to retain their dignity, self-esteem, and pride. He said that losing your job is hard enough, and our mentality is to foster an environment of compassion for them. That advice was poignant and prophetic in nature. I was promoted shortly after that episode and with his tutelage and my continued preparation, I was much more at ease and confident in my ability when I was faced with this treacherous procedure again.

I felt the urge to explain to each employee/leader that this termination is **NOT A REFLECTION** of your true ability and talents as an individual. Therefore, take this incident as a learning lesson to build upon for future growth in your chosen endeavors. I rephrased one of the messages within the book *The One Minute Manager* by Ken Blanchard, Ph.D. and Spencer Johnson, M.D. where you focus on the *behavior of the individual's action/s not the entire person;* i.e., you are a fantastic worker with numerous positive attributes - however, your attendance is not consistent with our standards.

Some individuals could care less about anything you say to them that is positive in nature during the termination process because all they hear is that they are being terminated. I can understand their plight; however, I always felt it was prudent to explain to them the **MAIN** reason/s for their termination for which after the fact, they could reexamine and properly assess their future. I was compelled to give them the opportunity to learn from this situation so that they could correct the necessary behavior/s to prevent this from occurring again in the future. I have encountered individuals that I terminated when I was out shopping and most of them approached me to express their gratitude with the way I handled their termination. Some individuals even thanked me for my honest assessment of their behaviors which forced them to reevaluate their career endeavors.

# **SECTION FOR NOTES**

# CHAPTER TWO: BRAND RECOGNITION

## WHAT IS THE WORD ON THE STREET ABOUT YOUR COMPANY?

Numerous retailers believe that the recruitment process is only about talent acquisition. About 75% of it is just that; however, *people remember your first and last impression.* The retail sector is a very interrelated community of like-minded professionals who network with other managers in their sector. Believe it or not, your organizational reputation is like any other "word of mouth" advertising that exists. Are your new hires raving about your company to their peers at other organizations? Is your ex-employee trashing your hard-earned brand? Are your previous hiring candidates that weren't selected *overly bitter*? Are you losing market share and your most valued customers to your competitors? These questions are paramount to ask and are required to seek honest feedback. Remember, if you think everything is "hunky-dory," then you will not invest your time or energy in the necessary work to recapture your prominence.

## AUDITING YOUR HIRING PROCESS

The rigors and demanding schedule of a retail manager are immensely overwhelming. Moreover, the last thing I wanted to do was to add anything else to my already overflowing plate of responsibilities. When I was a young and inexperienced leader, I felt that trusting my human resource associates (implicitly) was the proper thing to do. I sensed if I became "too involved" with their responsibilities they would perceive my participation as inadequacies on their part. I soon realized the hard way that my involvement was a requirement for ensuring that our store was overflowing with the best and brightest talent available.

I created and implemented a structured auditing system that tracked all the human resource hiring metrics and instituted a level of consistency with all our new hires. At first, the human resource employees/leaders were feeling inadequate, micromanaged, and were not super enthusiastic about this new auditing system. I had a meeting with them to explain why I was implementing this process and how it was **GOING TO MAKE THEIR JOBS EASIER**. I received their *buy-in* immediately when they saw how this auditing procedure was going to streamline the hiring process while ensuring that we were following all state and federal laws.

The audit consisted of the following items: ensure compliance of the structured interview guide, reasonable candidate interview time and scheduling, surprise visits from myself to shadow the interviewer for objective assessments, I-9 & W-4 document inspections (for hired candidates), an inspection of salary pay band adherence, etc. This auditing process was a huge success. Henceforth, I was then asked to assist other stores in the district/region with helping to assimilate the process into their stores. There were numerous *hiccups* along the way, and, on several occasions, I had to provide honest and direct feedback (to many human resource professionals throughout my tenure) that was not congruent with their beliefs.

I had some of my human resource associates/managers that thought **they were above reproach** when it came to their ability to interview and hire new associates. The most common discrepancy was their *inability to notice any red flags* about the candidate's personality that would predispose them as an *improper culture fit for the organization.* A poignant example is this: There is usually a question stating during the structured interview questionnaire, for example, tell me a time when you offered exemplary customer service to a guest. If the individual is having a hard time explaining a situation or is not *describing an example in detail,* then this is a red flag because we work in a heavily dominated customer service environment.

Another example of *retraining the interviewers* is usually centered around the manager not sticking to the interview guide (which can expose your company to possible litigation) and or remaining too rigid or unapproachable. Either perceived behavior is not the "right energy" to project to a potential candidate. The ideal interview situation is a *waltz between both parties,* which can allow the applicant the chance to relax and settle into the interview. When a person is relaxed, they are going to be at their best. This atmosphere will generally showcase their talents through insightful and tangible examples from their prior careers.

In addition, I encountered many managers who wanted to hire "a bunch of mini-MEs" whose style was corresponding with their own specific personality. I repeatedly explained that our store/district must reflect many different personas. Henceforth, we should always welcome those individuals whose temperament is different from ours. The main admonition was that they *fully understood our culture* and how we treat our customers like family, which is a non-negotiable for employment with our company. This specific adjustment required massive deprogramming because of the information they received from previous leaders who surrounded themselves with employees just like them.

The process was arduous and unwelcoming at first. However, after the new procedures were implemented, the leaders began to witness the success of hiring the right people. The results started to matriculate in from the diverse hiring principles I had imparted on my leaders. The store environment started to reflect an inclusive and accommodating atmosphere where **MOST** of the employees started to develop friendships with their colleagues that were established upon respect instead of competition. We were receiving a surplus of compliments from our associates surrounding the hiring process, the quality of candidates we were hiring, and the influx of fresh ideas from the new hires. Overall, the new hiring paradigms were taking hold while producing a conducive arena that was embracing a myriad of varied personalities that reflected our community.

## WHO IS REPRESENTING YOUR BRAND?

The "success or failure" of your organization is most likely attributed to the caliber of talent that your company attracts and retains within your competitive sector. **Bernie Marcus {Co-Founder & CEO of Home Depot} used to say that "he could tell the leadership style of the store manager within 30 seconds of entering any store."** Of course, I was behooved at this incredible feat of prognostication. At the same time, I experienced a sense of inquisitiveness to fully understand what he meant, and how to develop this type of superpower. Bernie was referring to entering the store and having all his Spidey-senses working to interpret the following information: the look and feel of the store entrance, the interaction of the associates with the customers, the sense of urgency surrounding the returns desk area, the cleanliness of customer service areas, the attitudes of the associates, the lines at the checkout, the responsiveness of the managers to customer issues, etc.

He was completely accurate with the wisdom that he shared with me. Moreover, after some intense practice and due diligence on my part, I developed the same type of intuition that had an astronomical level of accuracy. This type of intuitiveness served me very well throughout my tenure in the retail sector, and of course, I was excited about sharing this practice with the entire leadership team. Our customers were **MOST DEFINITELY** able to sense this atmosphere within our store. Subsequently, I wanted to ensure that "all hands were on deck" to facilitate a pleasant shopping experience for all of our guests.

Generally, your store management team is a microcosm of the organizational macrocosm of the "atmosphere" of your company. I always considered my store a *mirror reflection* of what the ideal store should resemble, and it was my ultimate aspiration to achieve this incredible feat. I always sought to create an inclusive environment that presented a polished store that would become a small representation of what our company brand was exuding to our customers.

First, the process of creating an emblematic store that represents your company's core values starts with your salaried leaders which is then subliminally filtered down to your hourly managers. When the **<u>ENTIRE LEADERSHIP TEAM</u>** is operating as a synergistic unit, then you can present a unified and consistent environment for your customers. Your entire management team must - I repeat *must* - all think and behave in the exact same way regarding service, safety, customer complaints, and employee issues. This will establish a store that will exemplify a strong unity where all leaders are "on the same page" about how to represent your organizational brand.

Your store leadership teams are **THE GATEKEEPERS OF YOUR BRAND**. Too many times an inexperienced manager will temporarily weaken your brand which, if left unchecked, could ultimately damage your reputation within your community. I would personally call back every disgruntled customer (even when I did not have to) to ensure that our customers fully understood that whatever the issue or misunderstanding, we were going to reestablish their belief and commitment to continue to shop our store. I was obsessive with responding to customer complaints expeditiously to address their issues and to minimize the *negative consequences from their experience*. Unfortunately, 96% of customers **WILL NOT** complain to you. However, they will tell 15 friends/family about their negative experiences.

We all understand that when a story is repeated, the narrative will accumulate some "embellishments" along the way. This is unfair to the store/company. That is why it is paramount to contact your upset customers swiftly to minimize the potential damage to your brand. It usually results in lost revenue, a diminished loyal customer base, and unflattering social media comments. The problem that existed for me personally was this: *how do I allow my management team the autonomy they require to develop as future successful leaders without damaging our precious yet delicate reputation with our consumers?*

This dichotomy will exist in any retail organization. It should be addressed daily by continued follow-up with your inexperienced managers through role-playing, shadowing of experienced leaders, and an empathetic disposition from the store manager. I would "constantly" remind myself that I was once a young and inexperienced leader. I required *autonomy and time* to learn the retail lessons that would serve me later as I continued to advance in my career. It takes patience, commitment, and empathy from the store manager to foster an inclusive and transparent environment.

This leadership style communicates to the entire store leadership team that mistakes are going to happen, customer complaints are going to be levied and there are going to be "growing pains" for your inexperienced managers. I created a slogan to help alleviate some of the newer manager's anxiety and uncertainty with making so many decisions daily: **BECOME THE MASTER OF THE ONE-TIME MISTAKE.** This translated into learning the lesson and not making that same error again, which dove-tailed into the adage: "it is only a mistake when you repeat the behavior." It now becomes a **LESSON** if you learn from the issue.

Throughout my career, I worked for numerous managers who would literally crucify you for making a mistake. Conversely, they would criticize you for not making your decisions in an expedient manner. I always remembered how I felt paralyzed about making future decisions because I was afraid of the negative and demeaning consequences I would face if they were the wrong choices. I made a personal vow to ensure that I would encourage less experienced managers to embrace their decision-making abilities which I would relay through my **REPETITIVE** slogan of "practice makes perfect." The only way you are going to excel is through repetition.

## SCAFFOLDING TECHNIQUE

I learned to utilize and implement the **SCAFFOLDING TECHNIQUE** which refers to a variety of instructional techniques used to move individuals progressively toward stronger understanding and, ultimately, greater independence in the learning process. This process is usually executed with students attempting to learn new material by "bridging learning gaps." It leads to a better understanding of foreign information; however, I maximized this technique with my entire management team in the stores I managed. One of the main goals of scaffolding is, "to reduce the negative emotions and self-perceptions that students may experience when they get frustrated, intimidated, or discouraged when attempting a difficult task without the assistance, direction, or understanding they need to complete it" (edglossary.org).

Here is a chronological explanation of the scaffolding technique:

1. The leader specifies a certain task to be mastered.

2. The leader and or support staff helps the associate master a task or concept that the employee is initially unable to grasp independently.

3. The leader and or support staff aids with only those skills that are beyond the employee's capability.

4. The leader breaks the task into smaller and more manageable segments for easier assimilation.

5. The leader provides immediate and honest feedback on the associate's progress with the task.

6. Allow the employee to view the execution and completion of the chosen task from an experienced instructor.

7. Facilitate a *dry run* with a smaller intimate team before the major performance of the task, to work out any remaining deficiencies.

8. Schedule the main performance/project and allow full autonomy to be displayed by the associate/leader.

9. Provide encouraging remarks and ensure an environment of positivity ensues.

To provide some previous examples of how I utilized the Scaffolding technique, I will portray my time with The Home Depot as a store manager. The Home Depot is a very large building, typically between 110,000-180,000 square feet. This can create a huge wave of anxiety for employees "expected by customers" to fully understand the 36,000+ SKUs throughout the store.

Let's use the ever-popular toilet installation knowledge that every employee should understand, due to the fact every home is going to have at least one toilet. I would never **thrust** an inexperienced employee/manager into leading the product knowledge class to instruct customers with a hands-on demonstration with a real toilet that is conducted on a platform in the front of the store at 11:00 a.m. on a Saturday morning. Instead, I would slowly increase the individual's relatable knowledge (through e-learning modules, studying product brochures, and shadowing experienced employees) to build their confidence. Then, I would empower specific employees/managers to ascertain the individual's knowledge level to gauge their understanding of the information and provide immediate positive feedback.

We would then afford the associate/leader the opportunity to tackle a hands-on demonstration of a toilet installation within a more intimate group (plumbing department associates only). Thereupon, we would assess the experience level of the person while soliciting feedback from the group through a question and answer segment. At this point, we would establish the individual's comfortability level, then decide if they are ready to move to the big leagues and teach the Saturday morning class for the customers. *This safe zone learning environment was extremely successful at acquiring knowledge while developing strong implementation skills that were transferable to the customers.*

My Home Depot store was a salaried training store for the entire state of Wisconsin. It was a privilege and honor that I took seriously. When an employee is **PROMOTED** to a higher level with increased responsibility, the process for some individuals is overwhelming and unexpected in nature. This is usually because they over-simplify the higher level or were not mentally prepared for the *deluge of responsibilities* they are **NOW** accountable for within their job duties. I would execute the scaffolding technique with the newly promoted salaried leaders which created a successful platform for them to champion back in their store.

As with any newly promoted individual at The Home Depot, there was a training program that everyone was required to complete. Nonetheless, this program was meant as an introduction and provided the main parameters with a strong overview of responsibilities. Reality sets in with real-life scenarios that the newly promoted leader is not yet fully equipped to handle, while they rely heavily on other experienced managers within the store to provide feedback and direction. Another example of utilizing the Scaffolding Technique was the newly promoted employee who is green and starving for the broad range of leadership techniques to allow for continued advancement while bolstering their confidence level.

I was a **GIGANTIC BELIEVER** in the "Buddy System." This system will have the newly promoted employee shadow for 100% of their shift (mirror lunches, break times, schedules, etc.) an experienced leader for the allocated time frame, which would adjust accordingly depending on the position. *This process ensured the inexperienced manager would be afforded the time to learn and grow within an inclusive and productive cocoon which would provide the launching pad for a strong and prosperous future as a leader for the Home Depot.*

After the allocated training period, many store managers, unfortunately, believe the training is over. Henceforth, they would disengage from the individual's progression while expecting the new manager to excel and succeed right away. Their mentality was to **sink or swim** and only the strongest will survive. I adamantly disagreed with this incongruous mentality; therefore, I would continue to provide the necessary culture and inclusive environment for the leader to slowly advance their leadership skill set. This would be established through a plethora of unique employee/customer issues that would arise for which I would seek their feedback and provide valuable lessons to complement their knowledge base.

Too many retailers today underestimate the *power and necessity* of providing a structured and all-encompassing manager training program. Many will easily **DEVIATE OR ADJUST** due to scheduling conflicts, unexpected corporate visits, and personal beliefs or agendas that run contrary to the training program. When this short-change happens to the newly promoted leader, the ramifications can be devastating with reverberating consequences that permeate throughout the entire organization. **I firmly believe in investing in our future leaders and would never undercut their training program to fulfill my objectives or weaken their learning to cater to my own store concerns.**

I approached this philosophy of never shortchanging the management training program candidates with a sense of austerity that was cemented within the bedrock of my integrity. Throughout my tenure within the retail sector, I personally experienced a diluted version of the training programs numerous times because of repetitive store issues that arose during my training. I never felt it was appropriate to involve the newly promoted or newly hired managers with **BEING FORCED** to sacrifice their training because of improper scheduling, inadequate efficiencies of other leaders in the building, and antiquated management beliefs. *There are always going to be unexpected issues that will arise in retail stores.* At the same time, there is an extremely limited amount of time for the new leader to acquire the necessary information to ensure their future success.

We have discussed in the first two chapters the importance of Talent Acquisition and Brand Recognition. Now we will discuss the second pillar, which is Talent Retention.

# SECTION FOR NOTES

# CHAPTER THREE: TALENT RETENTION, PART ONE

Among the ten pillars for a successful retail operation, talent retention is the **SECOND PILLAR** that is usually the most overlooked and undervalued of all the pillars. The other nine are working towards growth, expansion, increased sales, etc. Per visier.com "One third of new hires quit their job after about six (6) months" and "One-third (33 percent) of employees knew whether they would stay with their company long-term after their first week" (visier, 2020). In my experience, some hiring managers, executive leaders, and C-Suite team members will adamantly state that talent retention is important or urgent to their organization. Be that as it may, many of their actions and attitudes are not **SYNCHRONOUS** with their message. There is a cornucopia of retailers who "walk the talk" when it comes to talent retention through their concerted efforts. Unfortunately, they are considered the minority within the retail sector.

This "tongue in cheek" pattern can become detrimental to the long-term success of any company. If left unchecked, it can spark a chain reaction that echoes throughout the entire organization. After talent acquisition, talent retention should remain at the top of the list for any company, not just in the retail sector. If your organization does not retain top-tier talent, your competition will certainly capture those employees/managers that you let **SLIP THROUGH YOUR FINGERS**. Every year in the National Football League (NFL), many coaches are terminated for not winning while the owner always *believes it is the coach's fault*. Sometimes it is their fault; however, if the owner, general manager, and executives continue to draft and employee subpar talented players, the coaching staff can only "coach them up" so much.

There comes a point of diminishing returns when your store/company is chock full of average talent throughout your organization. This dystopian situation will usually reflect in decreased revenue, customer dissatisfaction, poor morale, high management turnover, and declining net income levels. Talent retention must be a mindset that permeates the entire company from the CEO down to the newly promoted Department Head, which generally begins with a stellar onboarding program that is inclusive and exciting.

## HOW IS YOUR ONBOARDING PROCESS?

The onboarding or orientation process in many retail companies leaves something to be desired. Throughout my tenure in the retail sector, I have witnessed some truly outstanding onboarding programs and some completely disastrous ones. With the number of inconsistencies within the retail sector, this can leave the new associate questioning their important decision to join **YOUR COMPANY**. With the eight different retailers I worked for during my tenure in the retail sector, the ratio of successful and engaging training programs was a 50-50 split. Half of the retailers committed to a positive and immersive experience and the other half put forth a disappointing effort. This pillar is imperative in today's digital world where many retailers are scuffling to acquire top-notch talent that is getting progressively harder to attract and retain.

The companies that provided the top onboarding programs had some **common denominators** that were prevalent in each successful onboarding experience:

1. Fully committed to a complex and thorough training program that prepared the associate/manager for their specific roles and responsibilities.

2. Allocated the appropriate amount of time to complete the training program. Managers usually received anywhere from four weeks up to 12 weeks, while associates usually received 40-80 hours with more time allocated for specialized areas within the store.

3. The organization provided superior instructors that garnered credibility through their history and work experience.

4. Scheduled instructors who are thoroughly educated on how to deliver their training materials through all four learning methods (visual, auditory, tactile, and kinesthetic).

5. Assigned instructors who are passionate, yet engaging, with the training materials. At the same time, they felt honored and privileged to be there.

6. Delivered a learning program that was structured and organized which encouraged massive employee interaction.

7. Resources were allocated to complete the program which was never **postponed** or **shortened** due to any circumstance.

8. The program consisted of daily/weekly assessments to ascertain associate/manager retention of the materials.

Now let's dissect each bullet point to fully expand upon the eight consistent paradigms that are shared among successful onboarding programs.

## FULLY COMMITTED TO A COMPLEX AND THOROUGH TRAINING PROGRAM

This first bullet point is where many companies fail miserably by constantly contradicting themselves through their actions and communications throughout the sessions. How many times has an associate completed the onboarding program, yet they do not understand how to make a page over the intercom, explain to a customer any of the products or services offered, and do not know even know where the restrooms are? They are unable to communicate basic store concepts - e.g., ability to inform a customer how to apply for a company credit card, not understanding how much the delivery fee is, or how to order something. At this point, the employee becomes frustrated with their lack of usable knowledge and they start to experience a feeling of being unprepared, which can translate into them questioning their decision to come aboard.

The second part of the equation is the manger's training program with the different levels of commitment expected by numerous companies. I have personally experienced some of the worst manager training programs out there. Conversely, I have had the privilege of partaking in the "Gold Standard" of training programs. There is a <u>wide fissure</u> between the worst and the top-tier programs among the retailers I worked for. The most successful manager training programs all revealed the same **three consistencies** that were pervasive throughout the entire training period:

1. They **NEVER** utilized the manager as coverage in areas of the store, which ultimately, diminishes the integrity of the program, and will shortchange their development.

2. They were extremely thorough with the training materials and never deviating from the curriculum.

3. They ensured the manager **FULLY COMPREHENDED** all the material before moving forward. Remember, the manager was probably a "superstar" before they were hired (external candidate) by your company (which is why YOU hired them). Contrary to this, each organization

is its own entity which has its quirks and uniqueness. It will take the new manager some time to acclimatize as a result.

## ALLOCATED THE APPROPRIATE AMOUNT OF TIME TO COMPLETE THE TRAINING PROGRAM

This second bullet point is the most egregiously abused throughout many organizations. It is where the *disconnect happens for most new associates/managers.* This important allocated time frame must be strongly adhered to. It will ensure that the new employee/leader will receive the appropriate amount of time to fully digest the inundation of new information and start to assimilate into your organization. I fully understand that a retail store is a completely different beast with situations happening every minute, which requires adjustments from the leadership team. Despite this, the training period is "sacred." It is extremely necessary to ensure a proper foundation is established, therefore, setting the individual up to succeed within your company.

## ORGANIZATION PROVIDED SUPERIOR INSTRUCTORS THAT GARNERED CREDIBILITY

This third bullet point is a strong anchor for the successful companies because they make a **CONSCIOUS DECISION** to select instructors who "have excellent credentials." They will immediately connect with their class. How many times have you been through a training class, seminar, webinar, etc. and the instructor had zero to little experience with the materials? This does not bode well for a fully interactive and engaging experience for the students. In addition, this type of atmosphere is providing a disservice to the participants.

Most people desire an instructor who has credibility through their actions, background, or tenure. This facilitates an empathic environment between the instructor and their students. If Michael Jordan is speaking to you about basketball basics, I am sure that you are going to listen! Successful organizations **HAND PICK** their instructors while constantly providing them with constructive feedback from their classes. This certifies that they are providing their employees/managers with a superior training experience that will cement their reputation as a dynamic leader who truly cares about the training for their new hires.

## SCHEDULE INSTRUCTORS WHO ARE THOROUGHLY EDUCATED ON HOW TO DELIVER THEIR TRAINING

This bullet point is a "slippery slope" in some organizations due to the misguided belief that the best instructors are the most knowledgeable instructors. Still, if knowledge is not properly delivered through all four learning methods, the information could be misinterpreted or misunderstood. Successful instructors utilize *all four learning methods*:

1. **Visual learning** through handouts, easels, and PowerPoint presentations.

2. **Auditory learning** through verbal directions, group discussions, and reading aloud.

3. **Tactile learning** through hands-on activities to cement the information through performing the tasks, role-playing with the information, or operating the machines/equipment involved.

4. **Kinesthetic learning** through group pairings, moving seating areas, and switching up who is taking notes, or who is involved in the processes during the classes.

Everyone learns new information in different ways. The top instructors are constantly committed to including all four learning methods. This ensures they accommodate the different **aptitudes** employees have towards learning.

## ASSIGN INSTRUCTORS WHO ARE PASSIONATE AND ENGAGING WITH THE TRAINING MATERIALS

There was always one constant in every retail establishment I have ever worked for that possessed a strong and impactful onboarding program: there was a profusion of dedicated and passionate instructors *who felt honored for the opportunity to impart their wisdom upon the group*. They all exuded an aura of gratitude for the chance to assist in the grooming of the next generation. They approached this process with reverence while fully comprehending the importance of their role in the development of their new hires. Any warm-blooded individual can **IMMEDIATELY** recognize a "paper instructor" who does not embody any emotion, passion, or enthusiasm for the materials or the participants. Subsequently, this is performing a major disfavor to the company and to the new hires.

This major "oversight" by the organization, can have serious consequences on the morale of the store and lay the foundation for an erosion of the store/company talent pool. Moreover, the newly hired employees/managers are not being provided with the necessary information to easily assimilate into their roles. When this happens, it exacts a toll on the more experienced associates who are **ALREADY OVERWHELMED** with their normal daily responsibilities and slowly strains the resources within the store.

It becomes a "double edge sword." In that, it is not the fault of the new hires for their lack of appropriate training they needed. Yet, consequently, the experienced employees realize they are going to have to assume increased responsibilities until the new associates can get up to speed. This can easily become a domino effect within the store and can facilitate the departure of some of your most prominent and productive workers. Remember to **ONLY** assign instructors who are engaging and are prepared to fully commit to providing an immersive and interactive environment for your onboarding programs.

### DELIVER A LEARNING PROGRAM THAT IS STRUCTURED AND ORGANIZED

I have a friend who just started at a highly recognizable retailer as a recruiter. She is utterly amazed at how unorganized the onboarding class is. The instructors just read the PowerPoint slides with zero interaction, blowing through the materials, while leaving no time for any questions. The entire program is not utilizing any employee participation. In addition, she tells me that the program is not structured, the instructors are not knowledgeable about the materials, and they are unable to answer even the most basic questions.

This one friend is a microcosm within our retail sector and this problem is seemingly becoming a major epidemic among the individuals with whom I speak and or know personally. There is a serious "disconnect" between some of the leadership team's perceptions about their orientation/onboarding programs and what is *actually transpiring* within their classes. It appears that the executive leadership team in some companies are believing their own "press clippings" about how they are strong at onboarding. However, they should be reading and following up with each new associate to fully understand how **THEY PERCEIVED** the training from their perspective.

If you hear the same feedback numerous times from different employees, then you have a problem that requires immediate attention. Another persistent theme among the elite organizations that are superior with their orientation programs is that their leadership teams are involved with the feedback and approach this information with humility and a sense of urgency. These very special organizations also react immediately, yet decisively. They implement numerous adjustments, while they *follow up incessantly to ensure the modifications* are being well-received in addition to addressing the concerns the employees provided with their feedback.

## RESOURCES ARE ALLOCATED TO COMPLETE THE PROGRAM

This point is often overlooked due to the overall "greater good" of the store. I have personally been associated with several onboarding programs that were severely shortened due to *staffing needs or knee jerk reactions from the managers.* Their pragmatic reasoning always centered around customer service, completing planograms, or unloading trucks. The message which resonated with me and others in these training classes was that our training was considered inferior to their needs and was justified due to their assessments of how our hours were to be allocated.

I completely understand that, within a retail operation, you are **NEVER** prepared for every possible scenario. Sometimes you must "shift the force" to accommodate an influx of customers; at the same time, it is the store manager's job to set the tone. They must explain to the entire leadership team that **UNDER NO CIRCUMSTANCE** do we ever consider the orientation employees as a viable option to use for our staffing deficiencies or unexpected events within the store. I often utilized the phrase "this is considered a non-negotiable" when discussing certain strict and inflexible archetypes and commitments I felt should always be enforced and followed. This certainly included never viewing the onboarding associates as options for staffing requirements.

## PROGRAM CONSISTED OF DAILY/WEEKLY ASSESSMENTS

Coming back to my friend's onboarding process, her company *does* provide assessments to gauge the associate's grasp of the knowledge. Meanwhile, the scores of all the employees are coming back subpar while they are struggling to retain the information. *It is of supreme importance to ensure* your training instructors are being thorough with the materials while allowing sufficient time to interact with and answer the new hires' questions. Too many instructors breeze through the materials, read the slides **WORD FOR WORD**, and do not ensure the entire class is understanding the curriculum.

The elite companies provide daily/weekly assessments which are extremely observant of individuals not comprehending the training materials. They immediately address the situation. They seek honest feedback and attempt to get to the root of the problem. This usually stems from a "speed racer instructor" who is moving extremely fast while not allocating the necessary time for class participation or active engagement to take place. To reiterate from bullet-point four, everyone learns new information at different speeds and through specific methods (visual, auditory, tactile, and kinesthetic) with superior instructors warranting **ALL** four methods are being implemented.

Another prevalent human behavior trait is that no one likes to look incompetent. Some individuals would rather nod their heads while stating they understand the material when, in actuality, they do not have a clue. This is where the empathetic instructor will avail the class to multiple learning environments that will encapsulate all the participants, thereby, confirming that all associates/managers are feeling comfortable with the materials. I have witnessed an overabundance of instructors who are resistant to changing their methods for evaluating their new hire's retention of information.

In addition, when evaluating employee information retention levels of your classes, it would be prudent for some instructors to consider that some people are not good test-takers. If this is your only method to ascertain their retention, then you could be alienating a good portion of your potential superstars. There are numerous ways to assess the employees' level of understanding of the training materials: one-on-one role-playing, hands-on situations, repeating the information back to the instructor in their own words, and small focus groups. Some introverted people cannot excel in large classroom environments that are rigid with their learning expectations. Yet, they can succeed with the proper learning methods, deviation from legacy standards, and a healthy dose of compassion.

Now we will discuss Talent Retention Part Two in Chapter Four.

# SECTION FOR NOTES

# CHAPTER FOUR: TALENT RETENTION, PART TWO

## THE PERFORMANCE REVIEW PROCESS

We could devote an entire book to the best practices of the entire review process from start to finish. I wanted to share some basic review etiquette techniques that will establish a baseline for your methodology. One of the most powerful progenitors of talent retention is the protocols your retail organization has surrounding the "performance review process." This will determine if your employees/leaders feel inspired, connected, engaged, and are loyal to your organization. This process can run the gamut between an experience with superior professionalism immersed in tangible, credible, and poignant action plans for future growth or an interaction that is fraught with immaturity, massive egotism, unsubstantiated biases, and control issues that will stymie the individual.

The main purpose of the performance review process is to *establish a two-way dialogue* with the individual regarding the different organizational competencies and all aspects of an employee's performance/growth. This includes customer service, engagement, teamwork, reliability, mentoring, planograms, and increasing revenue. Each retailer will have a specific set of key performance indicators (KPIs). There are numerous performance review appraisal forms utilized by retailers for establishing accountability and calculating performance standards with a multitude of different achievement protocols.

The most popular methods are the **numerical measurement** from one to five. One is unsatisfactory, while five is exceptional. The **basic scale** of exceeds expectations, meets expectations or not meeting expectations, the **color scale** of green, yellow or red, and the **simplistic method** of seldom, sometimes, or always. Regardless of each retailer's specific format for tracking performance, the most difficult reference point characteristics to ensure fairness for all employees are consistency, honesty, unbiased assessments, and professionalism. Each one of these behaviors should be intensely scrutinized by the human resources team and upper management to ensure strict adherence.

## HOW TO DELIVER A PERFORMANCE APPRAISAL

Each retailer has its own protocols for how often they require performance appraisals. The most prevalent throughout the retail industry are monthly, 90-day, six months, annual, or a combination of these four methods. Every performance appraisal should encompass all four behaviors (consistency, honesty, unbiased assessments, and professionalism) to guarantee the individual will receive a fair evaluation of their performance. Let's break down each behavior in greater detail to further disseminate the importance of establishing these four critical anchors of integrity.

## MAINTAIN CONSISTENCY WITH EACH PERFORMANCE APPRAISAL

**Consistency** is the first anchor that must be followed to create the optimal environment for the delivery of the performance review. This should consist of *creating a benchmark* for a positive employee experience. This will include adequate allotment of time for the review, zero interruptions during the review, having already scheduled the review with the employee in advance, sticking to the structured appraisal document, creating an atmosphere of two-way communication, and a fair employee action plan for continued growth. There are many leaders who "deviate from the script" or attempt to "wing it" to save time or to cater to their inflated ego.

Some leaders feel that the rules do not apply to them while delivering a performance review. Therefore, they will **CONDUCT THEIR OWN REVIEW** that will be grossly inconsistent with the established company review process. I have witnessed this specific form of *review high jacking* numerous times which has forced me (as a reviewee and as a leader) to reel in the reviewer while steering them back to the standardized appraisal document. This interaction can have severe consequences for the employee which could impede their professional development while creating an environment where superstar talent is being underdeveloped.

I could always perceive a deficiency in the review process when a store I recently took over had a severe lack of bench strength or were burning through qualified individuals. I implemented a "checks and balance system" with every review that was conducted by requiring everyone to assess their interviewer with an evaluation form to determine the consistency of the review process. I would personally review each evaluation form for red flags or bland feedback to discover which leaders might require additional training and or a refresher on how to ensure consistency within their review sessions.

### PROVIDING HONEST FEEDBACK FOR EMPLOYEE GROWTH

**Honesty is** the second anchor which must be adhered to for establishing a credible review process with your employees. There are many retail leaders who abhor giving unpleasant feedback to their employees due to their inexperienced conflict resolution skills, lack of confidence in their review assessment, and their desire to be liked. I completely understand how challenging it is to present an individual with constructive feedback because of the backlash they could experience. At the same time, a disingenuous review assessment will usually inhibit the individual's professional growth and their desired career trajectory within the company.

It is our responsibility as retail leaders (or leaders in any industry) to provide the necessary platform for our associates to excel within their chosen endeavor by providing them with an honest assessment of their strengths and deficiencies. An assessment of an employee's performance should **NEVER** be given *only at their performance review.* Employee assessments should be given on a daily, weekly, and monthly basis to allow the individual an adequate amount of time to address and correct any perceived areas of improvement. I became a huge proponent of giving constant feedback, either positive or constructive when the opportunity was fresh within the associate's mind. You must strike while the iron is hot!

There is nothing worse for an employee than to walk into their performance review only to be "blindsided" with areas of improvement they did not know existed. Many retail leaders keep a scorecard of each associate's mistakes, deficiencies, or shortcomings which they only reveal to the employee during the review process. A leader must accept the responsibility of providing an honest assessment to each associate which could entail subjecting them to the possibility of an intense conflict resolution session.

Most individuals would rather receive constructive criticism and know where they stand than to perceive they are performing admirably only to have the rug pulled out from under them during their appraisal. This part of a leader's role is one of the most challenging to accept because of the *uncomfortability factor that is involved with delivering unpleasant information.* We all know of the sugar daddy/momma leaders at each retail store. We have worked for them because their leadership style is comparable with a popularity contest e.g., will behave in specific ways to garner likeability, bend the rules for the perceived appearance of exhibiting empathy, and showing extreme favoritism for their clique.

To earn the respect of your employees, you must first be honest and transparent with them regarding their performance. Otherwise, you run the risk of ruining their respect for you and your likeability will certainly crumble as well. *As a leader, it is better to be respected than liked.* This should become the mantra of every retail/business leader to establish a strong foundation for their true purpose as a leader. This does not mean that as a leader you cannot have your associates respect you AND like you. Some employees are never going to **LIKE YOU** because you might be the only leader whoever gave them an honest appraisal and or constructive feedback in the store or their career.

I remember a poignant piece of advice that was given to me during the infancy of my leadership career; if you have 80% of the employee's respecting you, then you are performing your job as a leader well. I inquired as to why only 80% and not 100 percent. He said because

there most certainly will be about 20% of the employees that will **RESENT YOU FOR YOUR**

**HONEST FEEDBACK** of their performance, customer service, attitude, and behaviors. He said

the 80-20 rule was a "guideline." The ratio could fluctuate depending on the quality of

individuals your store hired and the dominant leadership style throughout the store; i.e., leaders

who regularly deliver constructive feedback versus leaders who shy away from this behavior.

Whenever I went to a new store/company, I usually (but not always) had to become the

**HAMMER** within the store because of the tendency of *many leaders to shy away from*

*delivering honest feedback to their associates.* I forewarned the "powers to be" before I went to a

new store/company that this leadership style is effective; however, there will be an adjustment

period for the associates/managers which is required to acclimatize to this new method of

accountability. I never enjoyed being called the hammer (my leadership style was **fair and firm**

with the standards set forth by the organization) because of the image/perception you receive

versus the other leaders within the store. I was just performing my responsibility as a retail leader

to adequately prepare each employee/leader to become the best version of themselves or to

improve their career trajectory.

## DELIVERING UNBIASED PERFORMANCE ASSESSMENTS

**Biased behaviors** are the third anchor which can be positive or negative in nature. This is

dependent on the situation, individual, or atmosphere within a retail setting. Human nature

dictates that all humans are biased in nature to their likes/dislikes, childhood experiences, environmental factors, and social groups. Rather than operating as objective observers, people/leaders are prone to perceptual errors that lead to biased interpretations of their environment. Some male leaders have biased perceptions that female workers are inferior to male workers because their societal framework conditioned them through (social networks, exposure to female suppression, male chauvinism mentality especially in specific retail environments, or familial beliefs) to perceive them this way.

First and foremost, these types of behaviors are considered unacceptable. They should be dealt with swiftly and accordingly with proper training, acknowledgment, and through a strong rejuvenation of your organizational culture. Just to be clear, these same biases are prevalent throughout other work environments and are not just confined to the retail setting. They are a litany of biases to contend with within retail stores: racial, religious, educational, geographical, and tenure to name a few. It is our responsibility as leaders to embrace these individuals who express pronounced biases to allow them the time to readjust their perceptions, attitudes, and behaviors to reflect the appropriate culture.

There are some highly unbiased leaders (who are probably considered the minority) within the retail sector. They can certify that their associates are receiving unbiased, fair, and adequate performance appraisals. The *million-dollar question* is: *how do leaders guarantee that their associates are receiving unbiased performance reviews on a consistent basis???* Remember the expression that a fish stinks from the head down? It must start with the store manager leading by example. Having an unbiased attitude can then create a trickle-down effect with the other leaders within the store. The store manager is the *engine that will drive the machine* to ascertain which junior leaders have predetermined perceptions that are susceptible to biased decision-making behaviors.

As a store leader, I would personally review every performance appraisal (before it was delivered) for unsubstantiated biased remarks or assessments regardless of the level of the employee; i.e., everyone except the salaried leaders because I wrote their reviews. This **CONSCIOUS DECISION** increased my daily workload tremendously because, with a store of 300 employees, there are always going to be performance appraisals happening throughout the year e.g., 90-day/new hires, six-month, yearly, or merit increase appraisals to review. *I was fervent about conveying to my junior leaders the supreme importance of delivering an unbiased performance appraisal to their associates.* I approached this subject by tapping into each leader's innate ability to experience empathy (some leaders were a challenge because they did not convey empathy easily or considered it a weakness).

I asked them: *how did you **FEEL** when you received an inaccurate performance review that was grounded in extreme biasness?* This exercise was extremely successful a majority of the time, as it forced each leader to revisit their own unfair experiences throughout their careers. Let's review some of the more prevalent biases within our society today:

1. **Racial biases** surrounding specific races that are unjustified, inaccurate, and unfair to each individual. Certain leaders have a predetermined perception of certain races that must be unlearned to provide an accurate performance appraisal for these employees.

Each store manager must remain vigilant about eradicating these racial biases by reviewing each performance review for discrepancies.

2. **<u>Religious biases</u>** regarding specific religions that create a deleterious environment for other leaders to witness. An individual's religious beliefs have no bearing on that person's ability to perform their role within a retail organization. This form of harassment should **NEVER** be tolerated by any leader.

3. **<u>Educational biases</u>** are running rampant within the retail sector. Essentially, this individual has a college degree and thinks they are smarter than others or this employee has no formal college education consequently, they are not smart enough to work in this environment. Intelligence is a **relative perception** relating to each individual's ability to communicate their *transferable knowledge* within certain environments. We all possess certain innate aptitudes towards specific tasks or situations. Therefore, as leaders, we must understand that each employee has plenty to offer with their unique skill set.

4. **<u>Geographical biases</u>** are another subtle form of inaccurately labeling another employee because of where they are from or where they were born. This type of bias is usually experienced when a retailer is entering a new market which requires an excess of talent to transfer in from established markets. Some of these leaders who transferred into the new market will misappropriate the local employee's performance abilities, i.e. the local associates are inferior because they have not worked for the retailer in the established markets. Therefore, they have not earned their stripes.

5. **Tenured biases** are a legacy method of justifying an employee's abilities within an organization. This form of bias appears to be ingrained in many leaders who were personally immersed in this *anachronistic method* for evaluating or promoting talent. This bias will create discord and disharmony among your retail teams by allowing this propaganda to perpetuate an obsolete paradigm for writing/delivering performance appraisals. It is built upon the foundation that time served within a position/store/company is a superior method for gauging talent than consistent performance levels from each individual.

## PROFESSIONALISM WITH DELIVERING PERFORMANCE REVIEWS

**Professionalism** is the fourth anchor with ensuring each associate receives an accurate performance appraisal. This anchor is the most ubiquitous leadership failure of many retail leaders that I have witnessed throughout my tenure. Unprofessionalism must be expurgated from any manager's behavior when delivering an employee's performance review. Professionalism should be the foundation by which any leader's character and integrity are constructed upon and they accepted when they decided to climb the management ranks. Many leaders feel a strong sense of alacrity when accepting their new position as a leader within the store while cheerfully accepting all the "perks that come with the title." On the other hand, some leaders reluctantly acquiesce when faced with their true responsibilities as a leader e.g., professionalism, integrity, conflict resolution, demeanor, consistency, and honesty.

Many leaders eschew their unpopular duties because they are difficult, unpleasant, and create discord among some employees. Accordingly, true servant leadership requires strong character that will ultimately be tested daily. Professionalism within a review is paramount to setting the tone for the entire encounter. Here are the five most flagrant unprofessional offenses committed by many leaders:

1. **<u>Usage of profanity throughout the review</u>**. Profanity is a surefire sign that the leader is attempting to communicate their expression of emotions such as anger, frustration, or surprise. Some leaders **FEEL** that they are conveying an *honest* (as some articles suggest that individuals who swear are considered more honest) observation, assessment, or opinion when using profanity. Unfortunately, this type of articulation **<u>SHOULD NEVER</u>** be entertained within an appraisal session or within the work environment.

2. **<u>Focusing on situations outside the work environment</u>**. The review process should be fixated on the performance of the individual *within the store environment* and not on the employee's personal affairs (providing they do not interfere with their professional behavior). I have witnessed many leaders who are unable to separate an employee's personal life from their professional one and this behavior usually had disastrous consequences for the associate. I remember a store leader who documented an associate because they accidentally damaged a piece of luggage they borrowed from another employee. The employee **DEMANDED** that the other associate pay for an entirely new set of luggage who had already offered to fix the specific piece of luggage but was unwilling to purchase a brand-new set which consisted of three pieces. This is a "personal

matter" between two associates which had zero impact on the store and should have been kept out of the professional setting.

3. **Lack of respect for punctuality or allowing constant interruptions**. Some leaders feel that the associate and their time are **LESS IMPORTANT** because they are employed with the company. For this reason, they should be more understanding and forgiving. I understand that there are going to be emergencies that pop up. However, they should not be a regular occurrence. Otherwise, the leader has a communication problem, delegation problem, or is not properly training their managers. Every associate is a human being who has feelings. Henceforth, they should be considered when giving them their appraisal.

4. **Scheduling the appropriate amount of time to give the review**. Depending on the type of review (introductory, six-month, annual, etc.) the leader should block off at least 45 minutes to properly communicate and deliver the review. I would always schedule one-hour blocks for each review to facilitate a balanced review process that accommodated a two-way dialogue encounter i.e. provide ample time for the associate to ask questions and assist with any adjustments to their action plan. It is extremely unprofessional to rush through the review and leave the employee feeling confused, angered, and unappreciated. This is supposed to be their time to openly communicate their feelings, desires, and aspirations with their immediate supervisor.

5. **Leaders who are unprepared for the appraisal**. Every leader must properly prepare to deliver their employee's appraisal that is constructed around their true abilities, their past

achievements, previous performance appraisals, and contribution to their team and the store overall. Each leader should have a copy of the employee's previous review (which the associate should be given a copy of as well) to communicate positive and constructive areas regarding growth, behaviors, maturity, professionalism, engagement, and KPIs. With regard to the employee's previous review, this is where the second anchor of (honesty) should come into play. If the previous supervisor did not write an honest appraisal, this could create an assessment filled with conflict and confusion. As a leader, you have the responsibility to deliver an honest evaluation to the employee, even at the expense of the prior supervisor's dereliction of duties.

There is a cacophony of additional unprofessional habits that are being executed within the retail leadership ranks. Be that as it may, if you focus on these five main offenses, you will have a solid foundation to build upon as you become a more professional leader. I always wanted to know the proverbial "pitfalls" that many leaders experienced for which I started working on ahead of time. Because of this, I acquired valuable insight and the courage to seek out the role models and mentors who consistently exhibited professional behavior throughout their careers. I actively sought out opportunities to experience those situations that were littered with unprofessional behaviors. This "proactive approach" afforded me the ability to learn *what to do or what not to do in any given situation* i.e. I created a win-win scenario for my future development as a retail leader.

# <u>SECTION FOR NOTES</u>

## CHAPTER FIVE: REVENUE DETERRENTS

The heart and soul of every retailer/business is revenue generation (or generating sales) which, without this critical component, no retailer or business would survive. Sales are required to pay the rent, staff your stores, stock your shelves with products, pay utilities, and provide a profit (hopefully) to your organization and if public, to your shareholders. Revenue is considered the "lifeblood" of any organization, so why do so many companies fail to succeed with this component? Many (not all) retailers think that if they have products to sell, then they will sell to any customer. Some retail organizations subscribe to the notion of "if you build it then they will come," which for decades was the standard. Nevertheless, this perspective has radically shifted after the recession of 2008, the growth of Omni-channel, the disruption from Amazon, and changing consumer preferences.

The retail sector is a unique animal that requires a specific methodology to entice customers to purchase your products. It is unlike other industries that enjoy the benefit of tailwinds and momentum as their allies. In today's economy, the retail sector has taken a beating. Consequently, it has suffered severe losses (store closures, downsizing, staff reductions, etc.) which are reversible if they understand that the **FUNDAMENTALS OF RETAIL** *will never become passé.* Throughout my retail tenure, I have witnessed some destructive/counterintuitive "themes" permeating the retail sector.

There is an expression that truly sums up my mentality of noticing the commonalities among numerous retailers: **"ONCE A COP, ALWAYS A COP."** When a police officer retires from the force, they do not magically stop observing their surroundings or no longer listen to their

intuition which has served them for decades. They will continue to experience their environment

the same way they did (hopefully without the same intensity) when they were in law

enforcement. Because of these consistent/undesirable behaviors, consumers are deciding to

spend their dollars elsewhere.

## HERE IS A SMALL LIST OF THESE PERVASIVE THEMES:

1.  Allowing customers to leave empty-handed, a.k.a. "Never lose a sale."

2.  Employee product knowledge has taken a gigantic nosedive.

3.  Employees/managers have become the champions of the NO mentality.

4.  Employees/managers do not go above and beyond or even out of their way to assist their
    customers.

5.  Unwilling to meet or beat a competitor's price (online or in-store).

6.  Strict and unforgiving return policies that do not allow positive options for their
    customers.

Every one of these is a **REVENUE DETERRENT** on their own. However, when retailers

start to accumulate these themes, it can become a living nightmare for their revenue streams.

Let's discuss each theme in further detail and provide some deeper understanding of each missed

opportunity for retailers to be able to capitalize on.

**ALLOWING CUSTOMERS TO LEAVE EMPTY HANDED, A.K.A. "NEVER LOSE A SALE"**

This used to be the **GOLDEN RULE** in the retail sector. Yet, what I have witnessed in the past decade is an <u>unsettling lack of urgency</u> from the employee's/managers if the customer leaves the store without making a purchase. This point is most <u>disturbing</u> to me because it sets the tone for the entire culture of a store/company. It should be *a top priority* of each associate/leader in every store. From my experience, when a customer leaves a store empty-handed, that store lost a sales opportunity and quite possibly that customer's loyalty. In today's deprived sales environment, another competitor will be happy to accept that customer's patronage.

The **NEVER LOSE A SALE** paradigm should be filtered from the CEO all the way down to the entry-level associate. This archetype must be strictly implemented daily by every employee, regardless of position and title. When a customer enters your store, it is like the old car salesman adage: "if the customer is on the lot, they are looking to buy a car." It is imperative to instill this in every single employee at your company.

A very tangible example I used to advise my fellow assistant/department managers that were not as passionate about this concept was to count (loss prevention can assist) every single customer leaving your store (through your cameras focused on exit doors) empty-handed (for just one day). Without approaching them, multiply their average ticket by the number of customers. For example, if your average ticket is $60 and you had 300 customers leave your store without a sale: $60 X 300= **$18,000 in potentially lost revenue**. Now, let's take this a step further by utilizing this same formula to calculate your lost revenue for the year.

For argument's sake, let's approach this formula calculating an entire year: $60 average ticket X 300 customers leaving empty-handed X 363 days (assuming each store is closed on Thanksgiving and Christmas). You have a grand total of **$6,543,000 in potentially lost revenue** from a simple calculation. I have always believed in a 50/50 approach (able to compensate for both customers—paying and non-paying). So, let's assume that only half of those customers were going to purchase your standard $60 average ticket. You still have **$3,271,500 in potentially lost revenue**. What retail store on the planet can afford to potentially lose $3,271,500 in revenue per year???

This financial impact can be expanded even further by accounting for all the stores within your retail network. Let's continue with the same $60 average ticket, the identical 300 customers (adjusted to 150 for the 50/50 rule) who left empty-handed with the standard 363 days of business. We are going to plug in 1000 stores to complete the organizational yearly potentially lost revenue. $60 per average ticket X 150 customers X 363 days X 1000 stores= **$3,271,500,000. This is just over $3 BILLION dollars in potentially lost revenue**.

This formula can be even further adjusted for the *conservative financial-minded individuals*. Let's assume that only 25% of people who left your store empty-handed were going to fulfill the $60 average ticket, i.e. only one out of four customers. $60 per average ticket X 75 customers X 363 days X 1000 stores = **$1,635,750,000 in potentially lost revenue**. Most people would agree that, even with the most conservative approach to this calculation (25% of customers purchasing), this pragmatic approach should be a **POWERFUL** wake-up call for *reviewing* your protocols on customers leaving your stores empty-handed. Please let me know of just **ONE RETAIL CEO** who would be fine with losing out on over $1,000,000,000.00 in revenue that they rightfully deserve??? Remember, this was an extremely conservative assessment!!!

### EMPLOYEE PRODUCT KNOWLEDGE HAS TAKEN A GIGANTIC NOSEDIVE

This specific topic is omnipresent among many retailers today. It is one of the main *catalysts for why consumers are fleeing in droves* to other organizations that can educate their customers and win their patronage. **Retailers have a gargantuan advantage versus the online segment because they can connect viscerally with their customers through product demonstrations, putting the item in the customer's hands, and establishing an EMOTIONAL BOND with each consumer.** When I was an executive leader for PetSmart, the most loyal and dedicated customers we had were centered around the adoption of a puppy/dog or kitten/cat at our store. This emotional connection was ingrained and cemented in the customers' psyche. Consequently, they rewarded our store with their loyalty and their pocketbooks.

This **EMOTIONAL CONNECTION** is a very powerful ally within the retailer's arsenal which, if used correctly, can have a monumental financial impact for your store as well as the entire company. The perfect antidote for "showrooming" (customers coming to your store to educate themselves and then buying the item elsewhere, or online) is to foster the environment that will encourage your employees to establish a sincere connection. It creates relationships that are built upon trust, respect, and empathy with your customers. Customers *truly appreciate* organizations that are transparent, yet genuine, which lead by example when it comes to "walking the talk" with building long-lasting and beneficial partnerships with their clientele.

At any rate, to fully succeed with the proper relationship building etiquette, your company must become a **<u>STAUNCH ADVOCATE</u>** for superior employee product knowledge training. This requires an iron-clad commitment from the CEO all the way down to the entry-level manager. Piggybacking on this commitment is the allocation of the *necessary resources* for the stores to fully implement and execute the proper training programs to ensure their teams are staying up to date on the latest and greatest industry information. This will translate into increased revenue, capturing additional market share, improved brand loyalty, enhanced gross margins, positive social media engagement, and "free word of mouth" advertising for your company. How many times have you visited a certain store to become slightly educated on a specific product or item, only to waste your precious time being shuffled from employee to employee, only to become frustrated and finally decide to go elsewhere???

This specific topic could encompass an entire chapter with all the examples and horror stories I have witnessed and experienced throughout my tenure within the retail sector and as a customer. You can attract the best talent, have superior customer service, and have competitive prices. Just the same, if your employees cannot articulate accordingly to your customers on the products you carry, then someone will educate those customers and will happily take their business. The organizations that **CONSISTENTLY SCORE** near the top of best retailers to shop are also, coincidentally, very strong with their employee product knowledge training which is almost an obsession that permeates the entire company.

Technology stores are an example of this type of superior employee product knowledge (Apple, Verizon, and Sprint, etc.). These organizations are being showcased, as this is the lifeblood of their business. They are not afforded the luxury of having 1000s of SKUs that might not require much product knowledge to service their customers. In the home improvement stores, it is imperative to have employees that have a strong knowledge base of the products within their departments as well as their neighboring departments. Most customers are going to be slightly intimidated with the prospect of installing a water heater on their own or attempting to rewire an entire room. They do not want to pay exorbitant fees to have the installation performed by the company. Therefore, these specific customers are going to **REQUIRE** an employee who can properly explain these types of projects to their customers.

By the way, The Home Depot does an **OUTSTANDING JOB** of scheduling a consistent series of "How To, Product Knowledge Classes" on the weekends and during certain nights throughout the week (installing a toilet, installing a ceiling fan, installing ceramic tile, etc.) Customers receive a hands-on demonstration from a knowledgeable associate and can ask questions in real-time. Not many companies offer classes like this *free of charge* to better educate their customers, as they are expecting to capture those installation sales which will increase their average ticket and boost their net income.

## EMPLOYEE'S/MANAGERS HAVE BECOME THE CHAMPIONS OF THE NO MENTALITY

Except for a few retail stores, many retailers have a **NO** mentality with an army of "right fighters" trying to save their company money. In turn, this is severely damaging their reputation and directly contributing to lost revenue and customer defections. As a society, we went from the adage of "the customer is always right" that was a retail slogan and was ingrained into most retailers to an environment that encourages and accepts the NO mentality. In addition, unique customer shopping patterns have emerged, consumer abuses and fraudulent intentions have increased, and retailers are experiencing challenging environments in the current digital age. The proverbial pendulum has swung from one side to the other; we must realign our retail store leaders to utilize improved discernment methods to satisfy the customer.

The **YES** mentality is an accommodating and flexible mindset that gives the employee or manager options to support your customers in a satisfactory way, while also assisting with "deescalating" potential volatile situations. I understand that each organization has a Standard Operating Procedures (S.O.P.) protocol which is in place to provide some structure and guidelines to which their associates adhere to. Nevertheless, in many cases, all a customer wants is for their situation to be resolved in a **NON-CONFRONTATIONAL** manner so that they can move on with their day. Many customers are consumed with anxiety and trepidation about having to explain their situation to a manager, even though 98% of customers are ethical and honest with their intentions.

company they work for by their lack of effort and their ineptitude regarding superior customer service.

The *key ingredient to going above and beyond* for your customers is a strong sense of **EMPATHY** for their situation. I used to have a saying in my mind when I interacted with every customer that helped me stay focused on providing stellar customer service: "treat each customer like they are your grandmother." If I was assisting my grandmother, then I would probably be exhibiting these specific behaviors: extremely polite, friendly, empathetic, personally walking her to each product and answering every question she had. I would be respectful of her plight while ensuring she was the center of my attention and thanking her for her patronage. This mantra forced me to remember what I should be doing with every customer I was assisting. Because of this, I rarely deviated from the appropriate behavior.

## UNWILLING TO MEET OR BEAT A COMPETITOR'S PRICE (ONLINE OR IN STORE)

Technology has altered the way retailers are now inter-relating with their customers. Plus, with the invention of the internet and the mobile phone, consumers are becoming extremely savvy and knowledgeable about their product research. Especially the product pricing available for their specific items. This new-found technology has put many retailers in a "proverbial pickle" as on one side of the economic equation is the gross margin/average ticket conundrum and diametrically opposite is the opportunity to establish your reputation and increase your brand awareness with your consumers. This pecuniary tug-of-war for most retailers usually leans toward the gross margin side, which is slowly eroding the social standing of the organization and is also alienating your core client base.

So, how do you find the perfect balance to interact with your customers? It all starts with a staunch commitment to embrace and evolve with this new technology while *putting out to pasture the old benchmarks that worked in the past but are no longer practical or functional.* The expression of "if it isn't broken, don't try to fix it" is strangling many retailer's abilities to entrench their resources towards **INNOVATION AND ADAPTABILITY**, which is *how* other retailers are combatting this pervasive intrusion. I have always believed that in every situation there is a lesson to be learned. This is extremely applicable to the retail sector. Each company has the option to listen to its customers through their various feedback channels. Then, decide to accept this new challenge while devoting their precious energy and resources to becoming the **PIONEER** in this specific endeavor.

The second critical piece of this puzzle is to ensure that your entire organization completely understands that this is paramount to the future of the company; it explains how each associate/manager can have a positive impact. **Concept-Explain-Commit-Execute-Satisfy** or (C.E.C.E.S.) would be the acronym I would recommend for your company to remember. These five components successfully implement the proper strategy required for a seamless transition from the old way to the new way.

I always preferred the "meet and beat strategy." It created an electric atmosphere for the customers, meaning that the customer was elated with the shrewdness of their due diligence.

*Most customers are willing to spend more money on related accessories* (which are always high margin items) and provides a win-win scenario for both parties. The last thing you want to do is to allow the customer to leave upset and angry. It will foster an array of negative feelings (loss of their time, having to haggle, employee/manager unwilling to meet or beat any advertised price online or from a competitor, etc.) towards your store and ultimately your company.

The strategy of allowing the customer to leave your store should be your last option and only after you have **THOROUGHLY EXHAUSTED EVERY OTHER COMPROMISE**. I understand that "some" customers will attempt to bamboozle you with a similar product that is a lot cheaper. They will try to convince you that the item is not a "refurbished or repaired item and generally challenge the limits of a price match policy. Contrary to this, even in these scenarios, I have always found it successful to explain (without accusing) the customer of the distinct differences in the proposed products and *then offer an incentive for their time to accommodate their determination.*

Maybe you offer a percentage discount, a free accessory, or an extended warranty at no charge. The customers that are belligerent and unaccommodating are uncommon while most shoppers feel incompetent after being educated on the differences of the product. I always wanted to allow these types of customers the opportunity to *save face* by providing them with a collaborative effort between us that provided them with a compromise on my part. Thus, I was creating a positive interaction for both parties involved. Usually, all it takes is some soft skills, empathy, and an attitude of willingness to satisfy most customers. Henceforth, 99% of your customers will have a memorable experience which will also provide your company with some well-deserved positive "word of mouth" advertising.

## STRICT AND UNFORGIVING RETURN POLICIES THAT DO NOT ALLOW POSITIVE OPTIONS FOR THEIR CUSTOMERS

During the long tenure of the retail sector, there has been a major **PENDULUM SWING** with regards to store return policies and the paragons surrounding their execution. In the early 20th century, the rage was all about "the customer is always right." (Marshall Field/ Harry Gordon Selfridge phrases.org.uk) This concept continued throughout most of the 20th century. With the invention of the internet and fraudulent criminals increasing their skill sets, the major brick-and-mortar stores had to evolve and adapt to the new wave of "disingenuous" individuals looking to defraud their stores.

I understand that retailers had to sharpen their return pencils and advance their store return systems to combat these specific individuals. Still, you don't "cut off your nose to spite your face." There has been a severe overreaction with regards to addressing fraud among many of the brick-and-mortar stores which has estranged some of their most loyal customers. *Many customers feel that a violation of trust from a bad return experience can ruin their relationship with the company forever.* The answer here is a healthy compromise that does not disenchant your core customer base to focus on the extremely small percentage of criminals or individuals seeking to defraud your store.

The general estimate is 98% are honest and ethical customers versus 2% that are dishonest and unethical. Consequently, what has happened is many retailers have tightened their return reins so forcefully that they are causing their loyal customer base to flee to other retailers (online or physical space) to satisfy their shopping needs. This knee jerk reaction from retailers is "catering to the 2%" and driving away some of the 98%. As an example, a major retailer used to have a 90-day return policy which was then reduced to 60 days. Subsequently, it was reduced to 30 days and finally ended up at 14 days. Moreover, cashback was only offered up to 14 days with a receipt and, after 14 days, you are basically not going to receive any form of payment/in-store credit of any kind. Most people can accurately guess *what has/is happening to this retailer's sales, profit, and reputation.*

A generous and fair return policy is paramount to a retailer's future. With online juggernauts like Amazon who boast a customer-friendly return policy, this is an area that must be addressed instantaneously. There is **ALWAYS** a happy medium that can be achieved which will track and capture the repeat dishonest offenders. At the same time, it will project an open and accommodating policy that will satisfy 98% of your shoppers. Most customers purchase extra items or are unsure about a purchase and these customers could/will experience buyer's remorse even further with the anticipation and anxiety of having to return their unwanted item.

**ALWAYS SEEK A HEALTHY BALANCE BETWEEN RULES AND SERVICE!!!**

# **SECTION FOR NOTES**

# CHAPTER SIX: NET INCOME TECHNIQUES TO INCREASE PROFITABILITY

In the retail sector today, there is a pervasive issue surrounding increasing sales within stores/companies, while there is also an inundation of newer competitors within the brick-and-mortar space. Additionally, there are a plethora of digitally native (Casper, Bonobos, Warby Parker, Glossier, and Away) participants that are capturing huge chunks of retail sales dollars. The adage of "sales cures all" has never been more aptly needed than in today's challenging economic market for the retail sector. Every day on the evening news or on the internet we hear about another retailer who is closing stores, drastically reducing their personnel, and is filing for bankruptcy protection.

In most cases, these companies were experiencing a severe decline in revenue that persisted for many quarters/years. They were unable to implement and execute a renewed agenda that addressed these concerns. Many companies, when faced with sales deficits and under-performing quarterly/yearly numbers, will hit the panic button and start slashing payroll. I know that it is the number one controllable expense, which is usually explained as *trimming the fat, operating lean, or tightening our belt*. Sometimes this is the most accurate strategy in the short term. However, once this process has gained traction, it becomes the first approach that is revisited the moment sales or profits are not acceptable. It has an unintended consequence of **DIVERTING YOUR ATTENTION** away from the real culprits that are causing the issues.

When it comes to profit/net income, there are usually four different ways to achieve positive numbers: Increase top-line sales, reduce expenses (payroll), decrease inventory, or increase turns (a measure of the number of times inventory is sold or used in a time period such as a year). There are two ways to increase, as well as two ways to decrease with these methods. Each way achieves positive numbers. The most effective and long-term method for achieving positive net income numbers is to address all **FOUR METHODS** and not just one when experiencing under-performing financial data. Again, companies should be focusing their resources on daily accountability for all four methods, which at the store level, is extremely achievable.

The standard calculation for inventory levels is **Cost of Sales Plan ÷ Turnover Goal = Average Inventory Plan**. If a store has excess inventory and is scheduled to achieve an aggressive average turnover of inventory per year, then they are going to have their work cut out for them. In each company, there is a different matrix set up to address each financial metric. So, there is no "one size fits all" formula that we can plug into any company to achieve the exact same result. Despite that, there are standard guidelines that will assist with maximizing profitability.

Each store manager must execute their strategy on a daily/weekly basis to accommodate lower sales number days/weeks to stay on track to achieve their monthly/yearly budgets. *We will address increasing sales techniques in chapters seven and eight (Revenue Generation, Part One and Revenue Generation, Part Two, respectively).*

# FIRST NET INCOME TECHNIQUE

## REDUCING PAYROLL

If a specific day is underperforming in revenue, and you feel you are not going to achieve your weekly budget, then the prudent leadership team will adjust accordingly. This may be accomplished by **reducing payroll**, by asking for volunteers to go home early, or possibly shortening part-time shifts. As always, the team members **SHOULD** be allowed to recapture their hours on a more aggressive revenue day or through other projects throughout your store: store planograms, departmental projects, seasonal projects, and assisting in other areas of the store. By *reacting immediately* to the reduction in-store revenue, each store positions itself to be able to adjust accordingly to remain profitable for the day, week, month, or year.

This method of reacting daily to decreased store revenue is much more labor-intensive; however, it will give the leadership team the time necessary to allocate the proper resources where they are needed while creating an improved outlook on becoming profitable. Many companies react towards the end of the physical week, i.e. Friday, Saturday, and Sunday which, consequently, are the three busiest days of the week for most stores. Lowes, however, is very smart. Their week starts on Saturday, so the first two days of their week are Saturday and Sunday, which traditionally, are the two busiest days of the week. It never made any sense to me why the stores were not addressing their sales budgets daily when the situation is manageable, instead of at the end of the week when drastic payroll reductions were required to achieve positive sales figures.

This ineffective payroll process had a negative consequence that was threefold. It lowered store morale, it decimated the staffing throughout the store, and it severely impacted the customer service levels which had a direct correlation to increased customer complaints, diminished revenue, and derogatory customer surveys. A pro-active store manager will insist that his entire leadership team adopt the daily adjustment philosophy to anticipate and react to underperforming sales days to assure the possibility for profitability.

## SECOND NET INCOME TECHNIQUE

### REDUCTION OF INVENTORY

As previously mentioned, the standard calculation for inventory levels is **Cost of Sales Plan ÷ Turnover Goal = Average Inventory Plan**. Each store has its own parameters set up for its budget allocation and profitability matrices e.g., sales plan, geographical location, foot traffic, new/old store, etc. The second net income technique is to **reduce inventory** when facing dismal sales projections. The key is to **REACT IMMEDIATELY**. I would have each department make a list of their highest inventory items (that were not top sellers, i.e. A or B classified SKUs). Furthermore, I would have each department manager/assistant manager address their department inventory overages. Some viable options are the store transfer system (if applicable in your company), aggressive placement in high-visibility traffic areas throughout the store, vendor buyback programs, store contests, and store events (sidewalk sales, store demonstrations, overhead announcements, etc.).

By reducing your inventory in bloated categories, you are positioning yourself to have an increased opportunity to remain profitable, even though you're experiencing underperforming revenue days/weeks. I personally created a full-time position in my stores (which I mirrored from a store manager of mine from another store who only incorporated it on a part-time basis). This position focused specifically on reducing inventory Monday-Friday. This created the blueprint for operating a "lean and mean" profitable store. *I was laughed at by my peers when I allocated a 40 hour per week position to a non-revenue producing position. Nevertheless, I had the last chuckle when I consistently displayed positive net income numbers on my profit and loss statements.*

I became a pioneer with regard to aggressive and tangible methods to reduce inventory by "thinking outside the box" and taking a chance on creating a *new full-time position* (that did not exist before my mentor implemented the part-time version of it). I essentially addressed a critical profitability metric within my stores. During my tenure in the retail sector, I operated a new store that had an extremely aggressive annual store budget. It was severely over-estimated, and we wound up missing budget by over 57% for the year. Consequently, the next year's budget was more in line with market expectations. However, with the new **LOWER BUDGET**, I was now *three million dollars over in inventory.* This created a gigantic problem relating to profitability and net income levels.

To have any chance of achieving store profit/net income budgets, I had to reduce inventory by three million dollars. WOW, what a monumental uphill battle I was facing. This is when I implemented a full-time position for an employee who was **SOLELY RESPONSIBLE** for reducing inventory. This employee reported to me each week and had a store reduction goal of $75,000 *per week* minimum. They additionally had to meet a monthly goal of $300,000 to be able to consistently sustain drastic reductions to my store inventory levels. I partnered with my district manager and vice president, informing them of my aggressive aspirations; and, they fully supported my agenda. I really had no choice if my store was going to have any chance of achieving positive numbers.

The methods used to reduce three million dollars of inventory in a short span of only ten months were as follows:

1. Contacted the top volume stores in our region for store-to-store transfers (by creating long-lasting collaborative partnerships).

2. Had each department manager locate their heaviest inventory SKUs by category that were C, D, and E sales indicators.

3. Challenged each department/assistant manager to utilize their network to filter their inventory through our "inventory reduction specialist."

4. Established a department of the week to address and execute selected SKUs for in-store demos, sidewalk sales, hot buys, store markdowns, and employee contests.

5. Pursued aggressive vendor buyback programs.

6. Partnered with every merchant to reallocate certain inventory (mandatory home office purchases) to other high-volume stores.

7. Readjusted department planograms (with merchant approval) to allocate increased shelf space for bloated SKU categories.

After I achieved this monumental feat (reducing store inventory by $3,000,000 in only 10 months), I was invited to speak with the presidents/vice presidents for the entire company during their weekly conference call to share my best practices, highlights, achievements, and challenges faced. There were four main factors that contributed to this achievement:

1. A complete mentality shift to "anything is possible" from me down to the entry-level manager.
2. A strong resolute commitment to achieving this goal from everyone in the store.
3. Daily follow-up with all managers and our inventory reduction specialist to gauge our progress and adjust accordingly, if necessary.
4. Implementing creative measures (with full district support) when potentially falling short of expected inventory reduction targets e.g., radio spots to communicate aggressive deals, vestibule signage, enticing signage near major traffic arteries, etc.

After this achievement, our entire store developed a **CAN-DO ATTITUDE** for any future challenges we faced; as a result, most employees displayed a sense of pride for what we could accomplish. It is a beautiful thing to watch most of your associates develop a *new-found energy* that is consistent with achieving anything to which they set their minds upon. According to many individuals, their newly acquired confidence started filtering over into their personal lives with many employees attempting new feats, signing up for experiences outside of their traditional comfort zones, and seeking out new hobbies they were previously afraid to attempt.

## THIRD NET INCOME TECHNIQUE

### INCREASE STORE TURNS

Increase your **store turns** (or turnover) to improve your store profitability. The formula is *cost of goods sold divided by the average investment in inventory for the period*. There are many ways to improve store turns:

1. Negotiate a lower price for the products from your vendors, which will increase customer demand.

2. Reposition or relocate certain slow-moving items to a higher visibility area.

3. In-store marketing initiatives, i.e. BOGO, or buy one get the second ½ off (be careful here, as too many initiatives will erode your gross margin).

4. Strategically implemented store markdowns and store events (sidewalk sales, store demonstrations, overhead announcements, etc.)

Many of these ideas' "mirror" inventory reduction techniques. They have a "symbiotic and synergistic" relationship with one another. Some of the major setbacks to increasing inventory turns could be:

1. Inaccurate on-hand counts. This one is prominent in many retailers.

2. Aggressive store automatic replenishment parameters (that need to be readjusted for historical sales data).

3. Outdated geographical location information i.e. store budget was severely overestimated and certain SKUs/inventory classes require adjustments and SKU reductions (which usually require Merchant approval).

Anyone one of these hindrances can drastically impact your store turns, which will have a negative influence on your store profitability numbers. In my stores, I required each department manager to bring at least two D or E sales class SKUs (a store rating system on how well a SKU sells. A is the best and E is the worst) to our weekly leadership meeting with a **TANGIBLE** plan to address these slow-moving products. In addition, I required the assistant managers to bring at least one vendor to each weekly store leadership meeting that was underperforming and explain what they were doing to address this issue. In this way, all hands are on deck. I ensured that each leader was operating their department/s as a true "owner-operator" that was intimately connected to the outcome of their chosen areas of responsibilities.

The mentality of, if this were my **OWN STORE**: *how would I address these unproductive issues that are eroding my net income and the overall profitability of the store?* This was the message I wanted to communicate to every leader within the building. *When a leader feels like their department/s or store is theirs, they will possess a different mindset that is proliferated with personal ownership, confidence, and creativity that might not have flourished without this mental shift.* I would always approach each leader when they were experiencing revenue issues, service challenges, or merchandising standard concerns with, if this was **YOUR STORE**, what would you do differently?

Just to preface, some leaders would suggest increasing staffing levels while totally forgetting about payroll and how it intimately affects profitability, to which I would respond, let's put our thinking caps on, and generate a more creative plan. Many leaders' first response to most challenges was to increase staffing levels. While in some scenarios this was the appropriate thing to do (seasonal events, department customer penetration increases, or local events), most of the time when I removed this "crutch" the leader would usually concoct an ingenious strategy to rectify their plight. By instilling an **OWNER-OPERATOR MINDSET** within all of my leaders, this created an *effusive ethos within the store where each leader felt compelled and confident to unleash their entrepreneurial spirit that benefited everyone* e.g., customers, employees, vendors, peers, and upper management.

I found that inaccurate on-hand numbers were usually a strong indicator of a SKU showing unproductive store turns. Once the numbers were adjusted for accurate store counts, the SKUs started showing sustained improvement. Another consistent turn killer is product placement, and this is (and always will be) a challenge to address. Only so many SKUs can occupy the "prime real estate" in each department section i.e. waist to shoulders shelf placement for maximum sales volume. I always approached these SKUs with a **CREATIVE MINDSET** that would address the lack of prime real estate available by creatively merchandising them in other departments (cross-merchandising) or strategically throughout the store to fully capture their full sales potential.

## FOURTH NET INCOME TECHNIQUE

### CROSS-MERCHANDISING

**CROSS-MERCHANDISING** is the *unequivocal X-Factor* in increasing your store turns, as well as improving your gross margin while increasing top-line sales. Many of the net income ideas cross over into other sections of sales, gross margin, inventory reduction, and store turns. That is why it is so important to fully understand how each financial metric impacts your store and what you can do, as a retail leader, to completely maximize each category to encapsulate total store profitability. Cross-merchandising is a creative and profitable way to ensure each customer purchases **ALL THE PRODUCTS** they require to complete their project, accessorize their outfit, engage in their chosen task, and can completely achieve their desired results.

Effective cross-merchandising is anticipating all the necessary items a customer will need to address their project. This ensures that these SKUs are prominently placed to allow the customer the opportunity to purchase them. This can alleviate any unforeseen items that will hinder the completion of their projects. The examples below will fluctuate depending on your retail store product mix:

## HOME IMPROVEMENT STORE

1. <u>Customer purchasing a string trimmer</u>. **Potential items required:** Goggles for safety; earplugs for noise reduction; extra trimmer line; shoulder strap for comfort; gloves; extension cord for electric version; gas can; gas additive for stabilization for a gas model; extra battery for a cordless model. First five items for all three different models.

2. <u>Customer purchasing a toilet</u>. **Potential items required:** New supply lines; new shut off valves; toilet seat; new wax ring; Teflon tape; new flange repair ring.

3. <u>Customer purchasing a Chandelier</u>. **Potential items required:** Light bulbs; light bulbs; light bulbs. Nearly every lighting fixture **DOES NOT** come with light bulbs. Customer is upset because their brand-new fixture does not light up after they finished installing. Electrical tape; wire nuts; ceiling medallion; wire cutters; light bulb base lubricant.

4. <u>Customer purchasing ceramic tile</u>. **Potential items required:** Grout; grout sponge; grout sealer; tile spacers; five-gallon bucket; tile trowel; adhesive (for wall tile); mortar (for floor tile); tile cutter.

## ELECTRONICS STORE

1. <u>Customer purchasing a television</u>. **Potential items required:** excellent surge protector; High-Definition Multimedia Interface (HDMI) cables; mounting brackets (if wall hung); external sound equipment (as most flat screens do not have excellent sound quality); batteries for remote; protection plan.

2.  <u>Customer purchasing a smartphone</u>. **Potential items required:** protective case; screen protectors; charge/sync cable; wireless charger; protection plan; insurance.

3.  <u>Customer purchasing a laptop</u>. **Potential items required:** upgraded software; wireless mouse/keyboard; internet security software; upgraded charging adapters; wireless charging pads; laptop bag.

4.  <u>Customer purchasing a digital camera.</u> **Potential items required:** larger memory card; lithium-ion battery; clear lens filter; camera bag for accessories; upgraded lens; tripod.

## DEPARTMENT STORE

1.  <u>Customer purchasing a dress</u>. **Potential items required:** shoes; socks/stockings; hats; jewelry; sunglasses; scarves.

2.  <u>Customer purchasing a suit</u>. **Potential items required:** Belt; shirt; vest; shoes; shoe polish; cufflinks; ties; pocket square.

3.  <u>Customer purchasing a Duvet</u>. **Potential items required:** Sheets; pillowcases; mattress pad; pillows; dust ruffle; foam mattress.

4.  <u>Customer purchasing Luggage.</u> **Potential items required:** Luggage tags; umbrella; passport case; sundries kit; luggage lock; luggage straps.

In addition to these three-store scenarios, I listed the most common add-on accessories that should be located through cross-merchandising in each item's specific store section in a prominent area. This essentially should include easy access to these items. Either when I worked, or have shopped many retail establishments, the most common add-on accessories are

**NOWHERE TO BE FOUND** anywhere near the section. Moreover, 95% percent of the time, the store employee does not mention any of these items. The only time I have encountered an employee suggesting related items is when they are commission-based, and it provides a monetary reward for their performance.

The first thing a new manager should do whenever they come to a new store, in whatever capacity (store manager, assistant manager, department manager, etc.) is to thoroughly walk every section and make a "detailed list" of the areas (where deemed necessary) that do not contain the top four to six common add-on accessories. Then, depending on your position, seek approval to readjust these sections either through renewed planograms, store stanchions, or creative merchandising. The next step is to **TRAIN EVERY ASSOCIATE** in that section through active "role-playing" with a detailed question and answer session. This properly ensures all employees understand the importance of suggesting and selling as many of the top-related accessories as possible.

Some employees will "feel uncomfortable" using these suggestive selling techniques. However, everyone **MUST** understand that they are working in a sales environment. Consequently, most of these add-on products are items that the customers are going to either need and or are going to further enhance their experience with the products. I always approached the suggestive selling techniques as providing stellar customer service to each customer where I felt I was doing a disservice to the customer *if I did not suggest all the items necessary to complete their project, enhance their experience, or provide the proper visceral encounter.*

Another successful tactic for facilitating consistent suggestive selling throughout your store is to explain how each item augments the original item and provides the customer with the proper items that will ensure the customer is completely satisfied. An example during the garden season was when customers purchased garden equipment. The employees understood the **SAFETY RAMIFICATIONS** with operating these products while providing each customer with the proper safety items to keep them safe. Gloves, safety goggles, and earplugs/earmuffs are essential to safeguard against unintended accidents and to guarantee that safety precautions are being taken. It is the associate's responsibility to thoroughly explain to each customer the reason for suggesting these items. After the associate explains the reasoning behind the suggested items, it is up to the customer to discern for themselves if they wish to purchase the specified items.

Empowerment and inclusion are the two key ingredients that will successfully challenge your leadership team to accomplish tremendous feats for which you yourself have never conceived. Also, a solid foundation of encouraging calculated risks (without fear of retribution) will create a vibrant sales culture within your store where your store leaders will succeed and shine. This empowerment culture is extremely contagious and will take on a life of its own. Ultimately, this will foster and facilitate future successful leaders who will operate from a mindset as a merchant, service enthusiast, and as a sales focused leader.

When this happens, you will have created a dynamic sales culture within your store where your leaders will **AUTOMATICALLY** address any revenue deficiencies and react. Accordingly, this occurs without any guidance from you. Instilling a strong sense of autonomy within your store leaders is critical in achieving an inveterate culture that permeates throughout

your entire leadership team.

# <u>SECTION FOR NOTES</u>

# CHAPTER SEVEN: REVENUE GENERATION, PART ONE

## THE BIG SMALL RULE

Now we are going to discuss revenue generation which is the **THIRD PILLAR** in the manual. It is the "lifeblood" of any retail establishment, or for any business in general. Driving sales, increasing revenue, and improving top-line sales are all phrases utilized by different organizations to describe income coming into the company. The expression for most organizations of **SALES CURES ALL AILMENTS** is very poignant which will usually conceal many store/company deficiencies. In every organization I worked for in the retail sector, the number one line on the profit and loss statement was revenue. If this line was positive, we were starting from a strong position to achieve our net income/profitability numbers.

Unless there are glaring operational issues, then a strong revenue stream that is exceeding budget will set the stage for a long and prosperous financial journey. This is *usually the number one precursor necessary to achieve positive net income numbers.* Now we are going to discuss some of my favorite revenue generators from my perspective that was extremely successful throughout my tenure in the retail sector. These "tricks of the trade" per se, will provide a nice refresher course for some leaders and could produce some **epiphanies** for other executives. These methods are tried and true; and, they will work in all retail establishments regardless of size, location, and niche.

The Big-Small rule is a catchphrase that I created to easily communicate to each associate/manager the importance of selling all the related items needed to satisfy the customer. The Big-Small rule simply ensures that whenever you sell a large item/big-ticket item, you **ALWAYS SUGGEST THE SMALLER ACCESSORY ITEMS** to complement the sale. The main reason for this is because the large item/big-ticket item generally does not provide much in the way of gross margin. Contrary to this, the smaller items usually provide a much higher gross margin penetration in each department.

The two should go together to balance each other since the large item provides the influx of higher sales dollars (improved average ticket) and the smaller item/s capture the much larger gross margin percentage. Conversely, this percentage will positively impact your overall net income dollars. When you sell a lawnmower, you are not capturing a large gross margin percentage with just that purchase. However, when you add on a gas can, pair of safety goggles, and an extra can of engine oil to the sale, then you have just increased your gross margin opportunities exponentially.

I continued to notice in stores that I transferred to that the gross margin in **MOST DEPARTMENTS** was not meeting expectations. I found that out when I "thoroughly" explained the Big-Small Rule to all associates/managers. The store walk report (each company has a different name for this report) started showing massive gross margin increases across the board in every department. Now, to be fair, I was a certified **MANIAC** with ensuring that every individual, regardless of position, was implementing this rule when interacting with customers.

The Big-Small rule was easy for all associates/managers to understand; and, it could be applied in any department with tangible success. Another tactic I utilized to properly ascertain that the rule was being followed in all the stores in which I worked was to peak into each customer's shopping cart. I would quickly scan their items to see if they had all the items necessary to complete their project e.g., (ceramic tile with no sponges or spacers, a chandelier with no light bulbs, and a toilet with no wax ring or toilet seat). Countless times the customer would have responses such as: *Oh, I did not know that I needed that; I forgot to grab those items;* or, *thank you so much for suggesting those items.*

The absolute last thing you want as a retail establishment is for your customers to arrive at their home and feel disappointed that you **DID NOT SUGGEST** all the items necessary to complete their project, installation, or venture. When this scenario happens, the customer will most definitely purchase those remaining items from a competitor or another retail establishment that is more convenient and or closer to their home. In addition, you have lost the incremental sales from those items which generally possess high gross margins, while possibly losing a **GOLDEN OPPORTUNITY** to cement a relationship with your customer.

Relationships should be built upon a solid foundation of trust, communication, and transparency. When the customer realizes they are not adequately prepared to tackle their project because your employee failed to mention the specific add-on items, then, they could feel like they are just a number to your store. Some customers will not allow you to have a *second chance* for their patronage when they have put their trust in your store/employees, only to be disappointed.

In every store in which I worked, there were *always reservations* with following the Big-Small rule:

1. Employees/managers feel like they are pressuring customers to purchase additional items.

2. Some individuals did not feel comfortable with suggestive selling because they are more introverted and lacked the confidence to sell the additional items.

3. Individuals did not understand how to handle customer objections properly.

4. Associates/leaders did not possess sufficient product knowledge necessary to answer customer questions.

Let's discuss each bullet point in further detail to address these employee reservations and provide tangible solutions for many of their misconceptions.

## EMPLOYEES/MANAGERS FEEL LIKE THEY ARE PRESSURING CUSTOMERS TO PURCHASE ADDITIONAL ITEMS

This perception was the number one "hang up" with most individuals not readily accepting the Big-Small rule. I would usually address this concern through role-playing techniques, store meetings, one-on-one interactions, and leadership meetings. I would explain to each employee/manager that they were not pressuring the customers because they are **PROVIDING EXEMPLARY CUSTOMER SERVICE.** They are certifying that the customer has purchased the necessary SKUs (unless the customer already possesses the items at home) to adequately

finish their project or achieve their aspirations.

I explained that it is what we are supposed to do as a "trusted source" of information and to

guarantee each customer is provided with the information and products (not all customers will

purchase the necessary items). However, it is our responsibility to at least make them aware of

the necessary items to complete their tasks. I asked my team: *how would you feel if you slaved*

*for hours/days on your project and, right towards completion, you were unable to finish because*

*you were lacking a certain product?* I call it **future empathy** that we are offering to each

customer because we are not just trying to sell the customer items they do not need.

## SOME INDIVIDUALS DID NOT FEEL COMFORTABLE WITH SUGGESTIVE SELLING BECAUSE THEY ARE MORE INTROVERTED

In every retail establishment, you are going to encounter all the different types of

personalities. It is still your responsibility as a leader to establish an environment of

**INCLUSION** to accommodate everyone. Furthermore, it is still a sales atmosphere and you do

not have to be a Type A personality to succeed. I would suggest for everyone to "be themselves"

while I would assist them in finding the middle ground through role-playing exercises and

having them fully understand the *future empathy concept*. Confidence in any area of life usually

is attained through repetition and mastery, both of which take time to achieve. I would

communicate that each customer is another opportunity to improve your confidence. Once you

build confidence in **ANY AREA** of your life, it will transfer to other areas in your life as well.

My expectations were always to strive for continuous improvement while seeking out feedback from mentors/peers whenever necessary. A retail establishment should be considered a strong family unit that protects and supports all family members.

## DID NOT UNDERSTAND HOW TO HANDLE CUSTOMER OBJECTIONS PROPERLY

I learned a long time ago that when a customer says NO, *it usually means that you have not given them a reason to say yes* - **YET.** Most customer objections are an opportunity to answer their questions while alleviating any of their concerns (price, customer technical ability, or installation offerings available). It's a chance to *effectively communicate the reason for each item.* I would always relay to each employee/manager that nobody wants to be sold (as we have all seen the sleazy pitch men claiming remarkable results with XYZ item and have all witnessed some kooky infomercials).

Unfortunately, we cannot control the perceptions that other individuals have created. However, it is our duty to ensure that when each customer leaves your store, you have suggested all the items they needed to complete their project or achieve their vision. From my experience, most customers just want to understand how each suggested item will enhance/improve their experience. Because of this, it is our responsibility to accurately explain this process.

## DID NOT POSSESS SUFFICIENT PRODUCT KNOWLEDGE NECESSARY TO ANSWER CUSTOMER QUESTIONS

This is where the rubber meets the road. It is usually the second most popular reservation (and, deservedly so). Who wants to sound/feel incompetent or stupid when attempting to explain their justification for suggesting the additional required SKUs? Unless an individual possesses a passion for a specific area or has previous experience in a certain field, they are going to need continuous product knowledge training. This is something that should continue indefinitely regardless of their knowledge expertise. I always instructed my leadership team to provide a learning opportunity at each morning/evening huddle, store meetings, leadership meetings, department walks, merchant visits, and on their daily employee interactions. Most people have heard the ABC phrase of Always Be Closing. Well, I created the phrase of ABT or Always Be Teaching. Product knowledge and confidence are usually intertwined. When an individual feels confident explaining the intricacies of a product to a customer, then they will be much more inclined to suggest those necessary items. I would often surprise employees by asking them to explain their reasoning behind a certain suggested SKU where I would reward them for their effort (merit badge, soda/candy bar coupon, or positive recognition, etc.)

Although I created the Big-Small Rule while at a home improvement store, you could easily change the name to the Big Ticket-Small Ticket rule to accommodate retailers in fashion, jewelry, electronics, furniture, home goods, etc. To a customer purchasing a dress, for instance, suggest the jewelry; to a customer purchasing a couch, suggest the fabric cleaner; to a customer purchasing a big-screen television, suggest the surge protector; or, to a customer purchasing a watch, suggest the watch cleaner. The Big-Small rule is another technique to increase top-line sales, grow your average ticket, build positive gross margins, and improve your net income metrics for your store.

## THE NO-LIMIT CONCEPT

I stumbled upon the No-Limit technique while I was attempting to drastically increase the sales in some slow-moving categories in multiple departments. I literally, "struck gold" with this technique. I was flabbergasted with how sales quadrupled or more in almost every situation. The No-Limit concept is a psychological perception where people want what they cannot have, which is the nucleus of the supply and demand debate throughout our retail sector. Exclusivity creates market demand for consumer goods products and sustains the price the market will bear for certain products. I completely understood that if you were selling a one-of-a-kind item you could charge an exorbitant price to your customers for the privilege of owning a unique and rare item. However, the No-Limit technique works successfully on your everyday SKUs that **ARE NOT EXCLUSIVE OR IN DEMAND IN ANYWAY!!!**

The No-Limit concept started "germinating" while I was grocery shopping. I noticed all the advertised sale items had a **LIMIT ATTACHED**. For example, a limit of two per customer, limit four with a $25.00 purchase or more, etc. I also started noticing that many of the membership clubs also had limits built into their advertisements or flyers while I started observing the "excitement surrounding these items." *THAT IS WHEN I HAD AN EPIPHANY.* I decided the very next day to test out this theory in my store. I was a store director at this point, and I asked my operations manager to purchase a lot of the neon psychedelic (pink, orange, yellow, etc.) starbursts from the local office supply store. I then addressed the entire leadership team (while communicating this concept to my district manager as well) in our weekly manager meeting. I explained the No-Limit concept with how I was going to pick several SKUs from the electrical department to run my test. If successful, we would expand to the other departments after the initial pilot was finished.

My initial criteria were to select items that were **ALREADY ON SALE.** We would then test the No-Limit theory on an exact scenario basis, just like I witnessed while shopping the other stores. My first SKUs were in the electrical department and were your standard 40-watt, 60-watt, 75-watt, and 100-watt soft white incandescent light bulbs. I pulled the previous sales numbers/data for these four SKUs each time they were on sale for the exact/almost identical price from previous years to establish my benchmark criteria. Now, just to preface this experiment, all I did was to attach the neon starburst signs to the large price banner that said in capital letters **"No-Limit."** That was the only adjustment that was altered.

NO LIMIT        NO LIMIT        NO LIMIT

On these four SKUs, the advertised lower price was to remain on sale for the entire month; then, I would check the sales data every day (usually 6 days per week) during the beginning of my scheduled shift. The numbers started spiking upwards **IMMEDIATELY** and I was starting to think that I was on to something. I was excited about my *creative idea* to start producing results. The first week's sales number stated that three of the four SKUs (40w, 60w, and 75w, as 100w is always the slowest selling of the four SKUs) were selling double to triple over the previous year's sales numbers. I thought: *Wow!* I shared my exuberance with the leadership team while showing them the historical sales numbers on the overhead projector.

At the end of the advertised lower price period of four weeks, the three most popular SKUs (40w, 60w, and 75w) were now selling quadruple to six times more in units, compared to any time during the benchmark period of two-years (the 100w bulbs fluctuated between double to triple in increased sales). Now I wanted to expand the experiment throughout the store for which I solicited suggestions from each department on two SKUs on which the department managers wanted to try this technique. Some of the SKUs that were selected were: bicycle hooks from hardware, soils/mulches from garden, caulking from paint, and anything that was on sale that was an accessory item. These were either a commodity item or a grab and go item. I never used the No-Limit concept on large items that most individuals would never require more than one of for their homes, i.e. tractors, air compressors, water softeners, etc.

To further expand upon the original success of the No-Limit concept, I then started using the No-Limit starbursts signs on "impulse buy items located at the checkout lanes, vestibule area, wing stacks, end caps, and throughout the "racetrack" of the store for maximum visibility. The results were **TREMENDOUS** every time, provided we *followed through* with creatively merchandising the items in high traffic areas of the store, were commodity SKUs, and ensured the items were impulse buys. I utilized the No-Limit concept at pet stores; apparel stores; electronic stores; books/music/media stores; and toy stores where the results were extremely similar each and every time. This technique will literally transform your revenue-generating capabilities throughout your departments and, if used properly (not overused on too many items which will **DILUTE THE EFFECT**), it will allow you the opportunity to increase incremental sales in all areas of your store.

The No-Limit technique will work in any store concept and in any retail sector with fantastic results that can be replicated throughout different store formats. After I tested this theory, my district manager wanted to share my results with the other stores in our district, as well as with his fellow district managers. I started receiving numerous calls from other stores in our district, and from other districts in other states inquiring further about the No-Limit technique.

At first, I was hesitant when my district manager wanted to share my latest success story. However, I immediately realized that **I WANTED OTHER STORES TO SUCCEED.** We were all part of the same company because each time another store experienced increased incremental sales I felt a strong sense of pride and accomplishment for assisting my company to grow its revenue. I also thoroughly enjoyed seeing the excitement in the eyes of my store leaders and associates when they succeeded with the No-Limit technique.

Another added bonus of the No-Limit technique was the gigantic increase in gross margin dollars the departments/store generated with the additional incremental sales achieved. Most of the time, this technique swung a department that was underachieving with their gross margin numbers and catapulted them into positive gross margin territory. In addition, with most of the departments throughout the store surpassing their gross margin metrics our profit and loss statements were reflecting massive increases in profitability for our store.

I would highly recommend that you test the No-Limit concept in your stores (judicially) because I know that it will surprise even the most hardened critics with its simplistic nature and ease of implementation. There can be too much of a good thing. I would caution everyone to be careful with going "hog wild" with this concept. **DO NOT** saturate your store with No-Limit starbursts. Otherwise, you will diminish the customer impact by engaging in "overexposure of the concept" while contributing to sign pollution within your store i.e. don't go to the well too often! I would be extremely surprised if your store/district did not excel with this technique. *This one specific concept has been one of my most successful achievements throughout my career.*

# **<u>SECTION FOR NOTES</u>**

# CHAPTER EIGHT: REVENUE GENERATION, PART TWO

## CREDIT FOR LARGE PURCHASES

In chapter seven *(Revenue Generation, Part One),* we covered the Big-Small Rule and the No-Limit techniques to increase revenue. Now we are going to discuss a couple of additional procedures to radically improve revenue generation. The next revenue generation method is to become a *fanatic about ensuring your entire store team completely understands the full "soup to nuts" credit program your organization employs.* This topic is similar to the topic of suggestive selling and you most certainly will encounter similar reservations from your store team. Let's discuss some of the most prominent concerns you will experience from your store staff. Then, we will delve into each point with suggestions on how to address:

1.  Employees/managers feel like they are pressuring the customers to sign up for a credit card.

2.  Some individuals did not feel comfortable with discussing credit programs because they are more introverted and lack the confidence to engage the customer.

3.  Employees/managers do not understand how to handle customer objections properly.

4.  Employees/managers do not possess enough adequate/tangible knowledge to answer customer questions.

## EMPLOYEES/MANAGERS FEEL LIKE THEY ARE PRESSURING THE CUSTOMERS

In every store that I have ever worked in, the perception surrounding pressuring the customer has **ALWAYS BEEN PREVALENT**. It is usually the first hesitation most employees/managers have regarding offering credit programs to their customers. As previously discussed in chapter seven *(Revenue Generation, Part One)*, the reservations surrounding offering credit programs is usually a deep-seated, unwarranted fear that paralyzes most individuals from even asking the customer. The most effective method to overcoming and mastering these oppressive fears is to utilize the "scaffolding method" (like we discussed in Chapter 2) while bringing each person along according to their learning curve.

The number one most successful technique for combating this fear is through "Role Playing" with the individual where I would allow them to represent the customer while I articulated and explained to them as the associate/leader the different credit programs available. This system of role-playing has achieved the highest success rate among the numerous methods that I had attempted and was fantastic with dramatically increasing their confidence level. **<u>CONFIDENCE IS BUILT, NOT GIVEN</u>**. This was an expression that I coined to effectively communicate to all individuals that your confidence level will be in direct proportion with your effort, persistence, knowledge, and consistency towards your endeavors.

The role-playing method can be executed in all situations (one-on-one interaction, group setting, peer setting, live customer example, etc.) Moreover, whenever I was mentoring or training any individual, I would seek their opinion on the most effective learning style for them. Some people become **OVERWHELMED** in a group setting. Despite that, they can flourish in a one-on-one setting. Others will thrive on the excitement or attention received in the group setting environment and will rise to the occasion. They will blossom while taking their confidence to another level. It all comes down to thoroughly understanding your team and tapping into **EACH INDIVIDUAL** to understand their personality and the way they "prefer" to learn new information.

An inclusive and servant leader should understand their employees while having a solid grasp of their preferred learning environments and what motivates or demotivates them in various learning atmospheres. Armed with this knowledge, you can more accurately predict and prepare for multiple learning environments and be able to schedule accordingly to accommodate these individuals. It always shocked me whenever I came to a new store and witnessed the plethora of individuals (employees and managers) who were not being "tapped into" by their leaders. *This major oversight by the leadership team will most assuredly limit the person's growth and severely diminish their potential.*

Another phrase that will help alleviate the individual apprehension for offering the different credit programs is the fact that **you are providing the customer with exemplary service by bestowing upon them all the available options to purchase their items.** Conversely, you would be providing the customer with a *major disservice* if you do not actively explore all of the credit programs your organization has to offer.

## INDIVIDUALS WHO ARE INTROVERTED AND LACK CONFIDENCE

The second concern of many employees/leaders is their lack of confidence and introverted behaviors that can become barriers for your employees/managers to suggesting the credit programs. As a leader, it is our responsibility to maintain what I call a "fair and firm" management style. In this situation, I would explain to the introverted individuals that it is okay to be more laid back and quiet. However, it is our job to adequately offer the credit programs available to each customer. I would label these situations as **NON-NEGOTIABLES** (something that is not open for discussion) which is a "requirement" of any position within the retail store to provide superior customer service.

I would explain to the more reserved individuals that it does not matter **HOW** you communicate the credit programs to your customers. So, choose whatever way is effective for you. I remember working for managers who **DEMANDED** that I follow their specific selling style and it was the only style that was considered acceptable. I became a huge proponent of fostering an atmosphere of allowing everyone to "be themselves" with regard to suggesting credit programs because inclusive environments removed many of the trepidations and anxieties among the store team. The only caveat was that your style had to be **EFFECTIVE AND COMPLETE** without any shortcuts or misgivings. It had to pass muster and meet our credit standards.

Depending on the store products we offered, there are always certain SKUs that would usually automatically require the individual to offer the different credit programs available (because of the higher price points). Examples include tractors, hot tubs, hardware tools, fish tanks, music collections, high ticket apparel, electronics and/or patio furniture. The SKUs were more optional in some stores because of the diverse products offered that were predominantly lower price points. I would constantly carry at least five or more credit card applications on me to guarantee that I always had the necessary brochures handy. Likewise, I would always "highly suggest" that every individual carries a couple of credit applications on them as well. Sometimes the customer does not want to wait while you leave and track down a credit card application because the timing could ruin the opportunity. I would communicate to all employees that most customers are time-constrained, which requires each individual to proceed with the credit process smoothly and seamlessly.

**EMPLOYEES NOT TRAINED ON HOW TO HANDLE CUSTOMER OBJECTIONS**

The third most common reservation from individuals is not understanding how to address and respond to customer objections. This pattern was usually addressed through a multitude of methods (role-playing, peer interactions, mentoring, and one-on-one question and answer sessions). This was the most challenging of the four reservations because of our innate nature to retreat from objections, while also seeking areas that will provide acceptance and approval. Most people instinctively abhor rejection while adamantly avoiding those situations at all costs. Nonetheless, once you adequately communicate to your team (through rigorous training) that most rejections/objections stem from having to **OVERCOME THE STEREOTYPICAL SALESMAN** and their gregarious behavior, many individuals will become more proficient.

Human nature dictates that no one wants to be taken advantage of or wants to be sold something which they do not want or need. Unfortunately, this unwarranted perception affects anyone working in the sales industry which must be overcome to be successful. I would always explain to these hesitant individuals that the most effective method to combat this stereotype is to establish an environment of trust, honesty, and transparency while allowing the customer to view your suggestions as an alternative option for their purchases. When you properly inform your customer on the advantages of your credit programs and answer all of their questions, you have then provided the customer with an informative experience that affords them all the information they need for them to make an educated decision for their situation.

Another informational tidbit that I would cover with the associates is that it becomes an excellent situation when a *customer expresses an objection.* An uninterested individual won't have a reaction or show any interest at all regarding your offering. This is giving you the opportunity to further explain to the customer the advantages of the credit programs and provides you the option to continue providing stellar customer service to your guest. I used to say all the time that when a customer says **NO** it is because they do not have all the information **[YET] TO WANT TO SAY YES.**

### EMPLOYEES DO NOT POSSESS ENOUGH KNOWLEDGE

The final objection that most individuals have is: They do not possess enough adequate/tangible knowledge to answer customer questions. This reservation can affect anyone in any situation and is one that takes time and persistence to master. Product/services knowledge is critical to have when you are using a suggestive selling technique. If an employee does not have sufficient information, then they will usually give up after the first customer objection.

I can personally attest to this fear! When I was a store director at The Home Depot, I was "afraid" to walk down the pipe fitting aisle in the plumbing department because there is **ALWAYS A CUSTOMER** that requires assistance. I avoided this aisle like the plague until one day I decided to *confront my fears*. I started learning basic knowledge from some of my plumbing experts. I needed this knowledge to be able to assist the customers with their questions. After a couple of weeks, I started feeling much more confident. I would work in that aisle every chance I had to practice my newly acquired skills. It worked beautifully as I no longer had any hesitation about walking a customer over there or passing through to another part of the store.

My leadership style has always been hands-on and to lead by example, so, when it came to offering credit to our customers (in any store in which I worked), I knew that I had to become an expert. I would then be able to confidently teach others as well as to become a shining example of how to "walk the talk" in my stores. Another method to enhance your knowledge is to **INVITE THE CREDIT VENDORS TO YOUR STORE TO TEACH YOUR ENTIRE TEAM HOW TO SPEAK CONFIDENTLY ABOUT THE DIFFERENT CREDIT PROGRAMS.**

This technique was always my first choice. After all, the credit vendors loved to travel to the stores to educate my team of the benefits and to provide real-life customer scenarios that would complement my "role-playing" sessions with my team. I would then follow up unexpectedly with store associates/managers and immediately **REWARD CORRECT ANSWERS** to some credit questions (merit badges, free soda/candy coupons, and raffle tickets to store giveaways, etc.) *This shock and awe technique provided me and other store leaders the opportunity to gauge and assess how well the associates were retaining the information. I would then be able to immediately adjust accordingly to address any prevalent deficiencies.*

If you want your team to consistently execute superior behavioral standards, it must become a **high priority for you as a leader.** The associates/leadership team (depending on your position) must understand that your expectations are considered non-negotiable and must be implemented always. Setting the expectations in your store/s is something that must happen from day one. As a leader, your team will be watching you fervently to ensure you are leading by example. After your team realizes that you are the epitome of consistency, they will either fall in line and start performing the job responsibilities or have to face the consequences for their actions. Remember, fair and firm leadership style!

Whenever I was transferring to a new store, or I was joining a new organization, I would always ask the human resources manager & district manager how they wanted me to approach the store team in the early stages; i.e., **COME IN LIKE A LION OR A LAMB?** Depending on the nature of the store and its reputation, I would always seek my superiors' input. I would then mentally prepare to execute my strategy. I was asked on numerous occasions to go in like a lion because the store had: morale issues, human resource challenges, financial challenges, staffing issues, poor customer interaction results, and unethical/immoral behaviors present.

When this management style was requested, I immediately prefaced my superiors with the immediate to short term consequences (three-six months) that would ultimately occur. I explained that it will have to get worse before it will get better (just like in the movie Roadhouse with Patrick Swayze). If I was asked to go in like a lamb, I would understand immediately that the store only needed some superficial corrections (consistent leadership, improved training programs, basic morale boosting techniques, mentoring programs, mild people development, and minor succession planning efforts).

In each scenario, the store teams understood instantly that I would have numerous non-negotiables that consisted of exemplary customer service, credit programs, safety, effective selling techniques, following policies and procedures, respect for all people, and having empathy for your teammates. Credit was **ALWAYS ON THE LIST** of non-negotiables because I completely understood the financial ramifications of consistently executing this selling tool, in addition to the positive impact it directly had on our overall store revenue. I would highly suggest to all retail leaders that are reading this manual to have a set of non-negotiables that are effective, compliant, and customer-friendly, which should be aligned with your organization's corporate culture/values for your teams to execute consistently on a daily basis.

### UNASSISTED VERSUS ASSISTED CONVERSION RATE

The one definite technique for increasing revenue in your stores is to ensure that the execution of **ASSISTED CUSTOMER SERVICE** is happening to near perfection. That is if you really want to maximize your average ticket. I would scour every customer survey I received as a store manager while personally speaking with each disgruntled customer. The identical complaint that kept receiving the lion's share of attention was where are your associates? In speaking with each customer, I learned a valuable lesson that became a simple, yet logical blueprint, that I would continue to follow throughout the remainder of my career in retail. Many customers wanted **TO BE ASSISTED WITH THEIR PURCHASES AND WANT TO HAVE THEIR QUESTIONS ANSWERED.**

This concept dovetails nicely into one of our previous chapters of becoming a **YES** company while taking care of your customers. When you are satisfying your customers, they will spend more in your stores. As a result, your top-line sales will increase when this behavior is compounded. If your associates are selling the entire project (all related items required or add on accessories), gross margins will increase exponentially as well. *This is a serious issue going on within the retail sector, for which I have rarely seen any major big-box retailer perform this selling technique consistently and across the entire breadth of the company.* Smaller independents are much better at this specific sales technique, as they must maximize every available customer to effectively compete against the larger brick and mortar stores.

Depending on the retail niche in which I was working, the average customer would always want to be assisted and when they were, the standard conversion rate would skyrocket along with a very impressive bump in average ticket amount. I would explain the products when I personally assisted customers; in addition, I would suggest the add-on items and convey the information in an easy-to-understand matter (as I was not an expert on every SKU in the store). I started to grasp another *epiphany moment.* The customer would cheerfully purchase most of the items I suggested, and it did not feel like "high-pressure salesmanship" on my part or to the perception of the customer.

This selling technique is part of the customer service offering, however, in order to fully maximize this process, there must be a customer hand-off between each associate when they do not contain the necessary knowledge or expertise in a specific area. Let's use the example of a customer who just adopted/received a new cat. They are so excited about their new furry friend; however, they are not thinking logically (about the plethora of items required) at this moment. If left unattended, they will probably leave the store without all the necessary items they need. I found a new dog/cat checklist that the company had in one of their brochures and I copied it onto a full-size piece of paper. Then, I *added numerous items* to the checklist to cover all the bases (not just the bare essentials).

I now had a **POWERFUL SELLING TOOL** to utilize with each customer who adopted/received a new animal that I would use to always instruct all of my associates/managers. This list could then be referenced to aid the sales associate as they walk the customer around the store and personally assists them with their shopping list. The customers were "ecstatic" because an associate/manager was taking the time to ensure they had all of the items they needed to prepare their home for their new bundle of joy. The adoption checklist for each customer **WHEN THEY WERE ASSISTED** was quadruple the amount of the average ticket in the store. Conversely, when they were left unassisted, the amount was still around double. However, when that happened (unfortunately, some people do not want to be assisted), the customer would still purchase more items then they would have without the checklist.

In the home improvement stores, I would create checklists for the major items in each department to create structure and consistency for the associates and for the customers. Let's use the scenario of a customer purchasing a tractor. If left unassisted, they will probably **NOT PURCHASE** most of the items to fully maximize their gardening/lawn experience. Though, when the customer is assisted, and the associate/manager has the tractor checklist in their hand, the atmosphere is light, and the customer does feel pressured. This will create a free-flowing conversation (and the proverbial rejection walls will slowly come down). Idealistically, this will foster the type of environment that will allow the associate to explain all of the additional items to the customer.

Another benefit will be the enhanced/personal customer experience without the stereotypical high-pressure sales environment. The customer will become more receptive and accommodating to the additional items e.g., gas can, goggles, pull behind cart, tractor cover, and additional attachments. The *unassisted* customer process will not usually result in the same experience and the customer will most certainly **NOT PURCHASE THE ADDITIONAL ITEMS** without being assisted by an associate/manager. This type of personalized customer service harkens back to the original days when retail establishments waited on their customers' "hand over foot" while treating them like family.

The assisted conversion rate will still increase dramatically, even without a checklist, provided that the associate explains the process and is able to allow the customer to glimpse the future results from their suggested selections. When was the last time you, as a customer, experienced an associate (not on commission) stay by your side every step of the way??? It is a "bonding experience" for most customers that really creates an emotional connection to the brand and if properly attended to, will cement the customer's loyalty to your company.

I keep seeing more and more retailers thinking that customers want more **SELF-SERVICE KIOSKS**. Some customers actually prefer this process. On the other hand, deep down, *most customers want to be treated like family and want their experience to be top-notch.* When a customer is in your store and they have questions or concerns about an item, they are going to feel relieved when an associate/manager walks them around the department/store to answer their questions while suggesting the additional add-on items to complement their experience. I have rarely witnessed an assisted customer with a knowledgeable associate not increase their suggested purchases when provided with this personalized attention.

Some customers will prefer and demand self-service areas and are not concerned about receiving assistance from anyone. That is the beauty of the retail sector because not everyone wants to receive personalized attention. Some customers already **KNOW WHAT THEY WANT** or just want to be left alone while being able to make their own decisions without any assistance. This beautiful dichotomy provides your sales associates *the resources to allocate their time to the remaining customers who really want the assisted service levels that you will* *provide.* Remember, you do not know until you ask, which customers will want/need assisted

customer service from the ones that do not require the personalized service. **By greeting all your**

**consumers while offering assistance, you will experience a capture rate of 100 percent.**

Thereby, you are catering to both types of customers (those who require assistance versus those

who do not). Therefore, they will reward your store/company with their dollars and their loyalty.

## ASSUMING/ASKING FOR THE SALE

The concept of "assuming the sale" is analogous with the bullet points throughout this

manual, relating to lack of confidence, introverted personalities, and not wanting to pressure the

customer. Let's walk through the required steps that preface asking the customer for the sale.

1. The associate has *asked* the appropriate questions to ascertain the customers' needs and
   desires, i.e. pre-qualified the customer.

2. The associate is guiding the customer through the sales process in a positive and
   enthusiastic manner.

3. The associate "steers clear" of hard/pushy sales closing techniques.

4. The associate provides a **LOW-PRESSURE** environment with the attitude that the
   customer is going to purchase the item/s.

5. The associate establishes trust through honest and transparent communication with the
   customer.

6. The associate has thoroughly *answered* the customer's questions regarding the
   item/service.

7. The associate maintains a professional demeanor throughout the sales process.

8. The associate has explained the appropriate credit programs and or financing options.

9. The associate finalizes the interaction by asking for the sale.

If we dissect this concept from the ground up, we will notice that the associate has **ALREADY PERFORMED ALL THE NECESSARY LEGWORK** to assist the customer with their inquiries. As a result, the associate has "already" established a foundation of trust.

At this point, the associate has completed all the necessary stages while all that is left is to *ask the customer for the sale*. Some of the most successful phrases for asking for the sale are: *Let me get you a cart for that? Can I ring that up for you? What delivery time will work for you? When would like to have that installed? I will walk you up to the register*. In most retailers, I have noticed that most of the employees **DO NOT ASK FOR THE SALE**. They will go through some of the preliminary stages to educate the customer by answering their questions. Yet, when it comes to closing the sale, they severely whiff on the final and the most important part - asking for the sale.

During my retail tenure, and even when I am out shopping the major retailers, I still notice (like they say, once a cop always a cop, well once a retail manager always a retail manager) the missed sales opportunities because the employee does not follow through with assuming the sale. I coined a phrase during my retail tenure… "we have an overabundance of supremely educated customers who walk out of our store empty-handed." I became extremely passionate about certifying that all my associates/managers *were fluent in speaking the language of assuming the sale.*

I had to fervently address this specific concern in every retail store in which I worked. Most employees feel uneasy or lack the confidence to ask for the sale, even though they are spending an inordinate amount of time educating each guest on the products. I had to create an atmosphere where many of the associates/managers had to be "deprogrammed from their prior selling techniques" so that they could embrace and accept the appropriate methods for closing the sale with our customers. I would highly recommend that as a department manager all the way up to the CEO, you emphatically attest that your team/s are completely committed to this specific technique.

Leaders must teach their teams to grab the low-hanging fruit which is rightfully theirs. I would explain to my teams that they are putting in the necessary work, and so now they should reap the rewards for their efforts. *Consequently, the underperformance of this one method could be responsible for more lost revenue than out-of-stocks, pricing issues, or competition combined!* I became aware throughout my duration in retail that many retail organizations will overlook this key component while devoting most of their resources to increased marketing, social media campaigns, omnichannel, and advertising.

From my experience, every store that I worked in dramatically increased their revenue when every leader became obsessed with mastering this concept. I am not advocating abandoning the necessary resources for the other segments. At the same time, your time will be well-spent

conquering this specific selling technique.

## **<u>SECTION FOR NOTES</u>**

# CHAPTER NINE: THE POWER OF ENGAGEMENT, PART ONE

## PROMOTING THE RIGHT LEADERS

The power of engagement, which is interacting with your customers/employees/vendors, is the **FOURTH PILLAR** within the manual. It is the pillar that is often talked about profusely by the executive leadership team. Nonetheless, it becomes a more "tongue in cheek" approach within many organizations. The truest measure of how well your engagement is working in your stores is to **ASK YOUR CUSTOMERS.** The customer will give you honest and unfiltered feedback on their customer experience within your stores. Therefore, this information should be treated like gold. The raw and emotional information the customer relays to your stores is the unequivocal benchmark your leadership teams should be using to educate their employees and for the implementation of corrective measures to address the areas of improvement.

This mortises into our first main point related to the power of engagement. Promoting the right managers/leaders is becoming a lost art form that is creating havoc within the retail sector. The age-old adage is ringing loud and true: **EMPLOYEES LEAVE BECAUSE OF BAD MANAGERS!!!** This statement is severely disrupting the retail sector and is starting to become a runaway train. I still have numerous connections in the retail sector that communicate horror stories about their egotistical, unempathetic, and abusive leaders which are escalating to unhealthy levels. The process for promoting future leaders is universally broken within many retail organizations. Most retailers are "sticking" to the concept of, if she/he is a hard worker and gets things done e.g., packing out freight, finishing planograms, or achieving stellar financials, then they **MUST** be the right person to promote. This is the pitfall most (not all) companies are falling into every day.

*The number one tangible/essential quality a leader must possess before being promoted is to have a strong set of soft skills or people skills.* This indispensable behavioral characteristic is the **MOST IMPORTANT QUALITY** a leader can exhibit while most of the other outstanding qualities can be taught or learned over time. Let's discuss some ways to ensure a potential leader has the necessary leadership attributes for promotion to any level within the company:

1. Interact with the potential candidates' teammates while asking open-ended questions about his/her leadership style.

2. Ask other associates throughout the store/district about the interactions they have had with the leader.

3. Ask other managers their opinions about the future leader.

4. How do they perform under pressure?

5. How do they resolve customer/employee issues?

6. Review the individual's last three performance appraisals.

7. How do they handle conflict resolution?

8. Do they possess strong financial acumen?

9. Do they exhibit strong moral and ethical behavior consistently?

10. Are they a solid team player or are they just focused **SOLELY** on their area/s?

<u>You noticed that only one out of ten attributes were related to financial acumen while the other nine were regarding human interactions.</u> The **OLD-SCHOOL METHOD** was to promote the individual who <u>got stuff done!</u> *This standard has completely shifted 360 degrees. Our culture is now "demanding" from our leaders the ability to have compassion, empathy, integrity, character, and devotion to their team/s.*

I received some very good advice early on in my retail career and I still remember the words; *when you are finally promoted, you will have already been performing the new role and it is the people who will get you promoted.* At first, I did not grasp the entire message as I left my performance review, confused. I had several follow-up questions pertaining to the advice I had been given. How can I perform a role that is above my current managerial level? How can the people get me promoted since I thought it was up to me to ensure my promotion? Do I have to avail myself to the entire store's employees and make sure they all like me? The answer to these pertinent questions became clearer to me as I started studying other managers who were being promoted while I was noticing a prevalent pattern that was becoming apparent.

The first common denominator successful servant leaders all possessed was a set of strong and consistent people skills. These leaders were always speaking about any situation (whether they agreed with it or not) in a **POSITIVE LIGHT**. They never ever spoke with ill-will about the company. The second similarity was that they were highly motivating individuals who commanded great respect from their teams, which was coming from a place of genuine passion about their position as a "role model" for the employees. The third behavioral aspect I noticed was they had developed a *total-store attitude* and were thinking about the entire store (not just their department or assigned areas). The fourth piece I surmised was they were all excellent with human interactions relating to conflict resolution (employee or customer).

Now, in the four examples above, I never mentioned financial accountabilities. However, running a profitable department/store is crucial to the overall success of the store. The financial acumen (of which they should have at least a basic understanding) should not be a required prerequisite to being promoted since this essential knowledge **CAN BE TAUGHT AND LEARNED**. Whenever I was ready to promote any individual, I usually looked *at how well they interacted with people and how they were with conflict resolution. After all, these two leadership qualities will encompass over 75% of the issues that arise in your store/s.*

I developed a "blueprint" that was successful with promoting future leaders. It was considered a radical style at the time because most of my peers/colleagues were promoting the individuals who achieved stellar numbers or who could knock out the planograms very quickly. I would promote the individuals who possessed superior character, stellar integrity, exemplary people skills, strong work ethic, and who were outstanding coaches/mentors. I found out the rest **I COULD TEACH**. Consequently, *I noticed that the people skill train takes a long time to come into the station.* I would focus heavily on conflict resolution with my future leaders and have them "shadow me" while I was speaking with an irate customer. Or, I would have them listen while I spoke with a vendor about shipping issues, etc.

**My number one responsibility as a store manager was to prepare future leaders for the company**. I would be doing these potential leaders a *major disservice* if I did not properly prepare them for the unpopular side of being a leader. Anytime I noticed an opportunity to share a teachable moment about an associate issue or a customer complaint, I did not hesitate. Understanding how to communicate with a very upset and angry individual is an art form that requires practice, patience, empathy, and time. My mindset was to always train the potential candidate for the next level e.g., the backup like a department head, the department head like a key carrier, the key carrier like an assistant manager, and the assistant manager like a store manager. With some of the leadership levels, I was unable to share some confidential information or certain aspects about employees (wages, appraisals, or documentation, etc.) due to confidentiality concerns. On a different note, most of the situations were considered a strong training atmosphere that was conducive to learning.

I would receive numerous phone calls from individuals who worked for me at all eight companies and were promoted to other stores/regions expressing their **GRATITUDE** for my training style and high hopes for them. They stated that because of my fastidious expectations, they were extremely prepared and felt comfortable in these high-pressure situations. My leaders were prepared for most of the problem areas for newly promoted leaders because *I purposely subjected them to these high problematic situations ahead of time while providing them with plenty of "dry runs" to harvest their experience. They had a safe space to practice and learn!*

I wanted to allocate the *proper space* regarding this specific topic of promoting the right leaders, due to the superfluity of employee/customer complaints that will arise from just **ONE** improper promotion for your store/company. I never forgot the adage that states: employees leave because of bad managers. It is the responsibility of the executive leadership team to perform their "due diligence" to ascertain if their chosen candidate is prepared and ready to take the next leadership step. *It is infinitely better to promote someone with superior people skills that has mediocre financial acumen skills, while bringing them along slowly, then, promote someone who is solid on the acumen and financials, when they have inferior soft skills.*

When most retail leaders hear the word "engagement," they immediately cast their attention to the customer side, and rightfully so, they should. On that note, one of the largest opportunities of engagement is for leaders to be put into a position that will foster their growth and allow them to interact with the employees with empathy, compassion, and a genuine sense of caring for their teams. Promoting the wrong leaders can have irrefutable consequences for your store/company because of the "domino effect" they can have on your reputation, brand, and credibility with future candidates. Remember, one bad apple can ruin the bunch. Certain clichés have existed for centuries because they contain valuable information that should be heeded.

### MANAGE BY WANDERING AROUND A.K.A. M.B.W.A.

The second piece of engagement is tailored to the leadership team which is something I learned a long time ago. Manage by Wandering Around succinctly stated, is defined as an *unstructured way* for leaders to walk around the store without an agenda. They make their presence known by interacting with their associates/customers. This process is a fantastic method for engaging with your team/customers and is also an awesome way to display your hands-on leadership style by showing your team that you can walk the talk. M.B.W.A. was a heavily used tool in my leadership toolbox that I would utilize every day unless my day was chock full of meetings and I was unable to get out on the floor.

There are numerous advantages to utilizing the M.B.W.A. style:

1.  You can increase your "visibility" throughout the store.

2.  Creates an environment for positive/constructive feedback for your associates.

3.  Improves your knowledge of departmental strengths/weaknesses.

4.  Motivates your team because their leader is "shoulder-to-shoulder" with them in the trenches which fosters an atmosphere of camaraderie.

5.  Provides the opportunity to engage with your customers while affording you the chance to solicit their positive or constructive feedback.

I thoroughly enjoyed the time when I could practice M.B.W.A. in my stores. I would insist that my salaried leaders practice this daily habit as well.

I also wanted to instill the message that store managers/assistant managers must be willing and able to work side-by-side with their teams while disintegrating the perceived illusion of managers never being on the floor. When I was coming up the ranks, I would rarely witness my store manager on the floor (except for David Lofreddo and Chad Wojcik who exemplified the way it should be done by perfectly balancing their schedules for maximum exposure). This was, of course, unless there was a merchant visit, or a vice-president walk, etc.

The only time many of my previous store leaders ever came out of their offices was when they went to lunch or the bathroom. That perception created a burning passion within me to ensure that I never allowed myself to **SEPARATE OR DISTANCE MYSELF** from the associates because of my title. I overheard many store/assistant managers bragging about their promotion while saying, "I made it and I can hang out in the office or back room most of the day."

Now, there is a fine line between being a leader that is on the floor with their teams and understanding that there is only **ONE OF YOU**. There are certain requirements/commitments as a store manager that will consume your schedule while severely reducing your availability to interact with your associates. However, these specific times are diminutive in nature. *The higher you go within an organization, the less tangible your results become.* This is something I struggled with early on in my store management career. There is something exciting about building an endcap, completing a planogram, or packing out freight.

The reason for this is because it is **TANGIBLE AND IMMEDIATE**; therefore, it is very satisfying. I noticed immediately that the hardest thing for me about being promoted was that an increasing amount of my day was spent on "intangible events" (instead of tangible moments that provided immediate gratification). Henceforth, I shifted my behavior to focus on my newfound satisfaction which came from creating seminal moments with individuals. These moments would blossom and become fully realized in the near future e.g., promotions, improved conflict resolution skills, increased soft skills, superior mentoring skills, and exemplary leadership behaviors.

I concentrated more on coaching/mentoring younger managers/associates, assisting with the creation of succession plans, role-playing with individuals, leading group discussions, motivating others to achieve their aspirations, and spending more time with customers. I started noticing that although these events were less tangible, they were ultimately more gratifying and longer-lasting because I was becoming a leader while moving away from being a manager. There is a **GIGANTIC** difference between being a manager and a leader. A manager turns keys, opens, and closes the building while performing the perfunctory requirements of operating a store. Contrary to this, a leader inspires, coaches, mentors, and shares a vision about the company to the future leaders within the store/company.

A leader has a genuine passion for assisting others in achieving their dreams and aspirations which will create an environment that will permit the associates (with the necessary passion) to fully accomplish their desired outcome. A leader will always have "your best interests" at heart while sacrificing their own success to ensure you are protected. They will not allow their employees to deviate from their chosen destination. *True Servant leaders will make a lasting impact on your career and your life. Moreover, leaders become an inspiration to the people around them.*

We all have had these special leaders come into our lives and they are like a shining star which gleams brightly for all to see. I have noticed that there is a massive shortage within the retail sector of impactful leaders in the brick and mortar stores. One final suggestion for taking advantage of the M.B.W.A. technique is to adjust your times and routes when you start your walks. Many leaders have preset times and destinations that employees can figure out while "gaming the system" e.g., beginning of shift, after lunch, or ending of shift. I would have my teams constantly guessing as to when and where I was going to pop up throughout the store, thus instilling the habit of being customer-ready **AT ALL TIMES**. In addition, after my wandering around, I would spend some time working in a different department each day to further enhance my visibility while establishing solidarity with my associates.

### RUNNING OUT OF PROJECT KILLER SKUS

A very important piece of the engagement puzzle is ensuring that you are in-stock on your most important SKUs. These special SKUs are called "project killers" or "abandon cart syndrome items" which when you are out of stock on, will kill the project or disrupt the theme of what a customer is attempting to accomplish. At the home improvement stores, there are a surplus of these types of SKUs: 2x4 studs, 4x8 drywall, OSB plywood, 40-watt light bulbs, tile mortar, concrete, mulch, topsoil, and white paint. Each one of these products is the **LINCHPIN** or the **NUCLEUS** of specific projects. Without these items, the customer's project or aspirations will not come to fruition.

In every retail store, there are numerous products that must be available to the customer. This guarantees that they can purchase these items to complete their project. How many times have you visited a store for one item, or a ton of items and they are out of stock on certain key items which forced you to walk out empty-handed and the store lost the sale??? In grocery stores, these items are milk, eggs, bread, sugar, flour, and bananas. *If they are not in stock on these staple items,* this can perpetuate a feeling of anger and disappointment within you, which, ultimately, can lead to your departure from that store forfeiting any possible revenue for the company.

In every store I worked in as an associate or manager, the number two customer complaint expressed (only behind lack of personnel) was from an out-of-stock situation. Usually, the customer was extremely disappointed and angry for the waste of their time, the gas spent driving to the store, and the disruption of their day. As a manager, there are only a limited amount of options that you have at your disposal when you are out-of-stock on certain items. These precarious situations will test your resolve and ingenuity to provide an alternate solution e.g., offer to transfer the item and provide free delivery to their home or markdown a more expensive item if applicable.

The "silver lining" during these unfortunate issues is the golden opportunity to create a lasting relationship with your customer because of your **WILLINGNESS TO FIND A SOLUTION**. Alas, there are times when you are helpless as a leader to provide an acceptable alternative solution. The customer winds up leaving your store frustrated and disappointed. Because of the potential situation for unflattering organizational exposure, unacceptable customer service, and lost revenue, I became zealous with demanding that our department heads ensure that we **NEVER** (or almost never) disappoint our customers by always safeguarding the appropriate quantities for these specific SKUs.

There were frequent situations where I had to personally call the merchant over a certain department and request an increase in product allocation for my store or become extremely "proactive" with upcoming seasonal/demographic occurrences for certain items. In every store, and in every city, there are always certain items that will sell "erratically." If this is a newer store, there will not be any seasonal/historical data to utilize which is used to prepare your allotments. In today's digital world, unlike bygone eras, retailers are not afforded the luxury of their consumers having the patience or effusive attitudes regarding out-of-stocks. They are expecting when they drive to your establishment that the products they desire are in-stock, especially on the staple SKUs to complete their projects.

I remember an old mantra for ensuring that at least 50% of your customers are potentially going to be satisfied with your store; 50% of your customers want to know where it is (the implication is the item is in-stock) and how much it is (the item is priced properly). I was also told that if you can accomplish these two basic feats, *the items are in-stock and properly priced* on a consistent basis, then you can provide stellar customer service to the remaining 50% of your customers that truly require assistance. I can *corroborate this mantra* firsthand within the retail sector. While percentages are not exactly 50-50, they are closely estimated.

## **SECTION FOR NOTES**

## CHAPTER TEN: THE POWER OF ENGAGEMENT, PART TWO

### THE LOSS LEADER PROGRAM

The loss leader program is usually apparent in every brick and mortar store. It is defined as SKUs that the company usually **LOSES MONEY ON**. In spite of this, they are considered staples and will create strong footfall for your stores. To illustrate this program, we are going to preface in advance that we are not insinuating anything related to the "bait and switch" programs out there. The bait and switch program are an unethical and illegal program instituted by sellers where certain retailers **PURPOSELY** only have a *limited supply on hand* of sale priced or flash sale items to increase their store revenue. The intention of these retailers is to sell inferior or reduced quality items (which they run out very early) and suggest that higher-priced SKUs are purchased instead of the advertised product.

The loss leader program is a legitimate program that each retailer is committed to providing its customers with certain staples that will force the retailer to incur a loss (below purchase price) to provide superior engagement and to win customers' loyalty. To operate this program effectively, there are certain *selling protocols* that must be in place to guard against unethical concerns:

1. Management must closely monitor certain customers attempting to purchase massive quantities while attempting to resell those items.

2.  Safeguard against competitors buying large quantities of these SKUs to reduce their oppositions in-stock condition (which dovetails into the previous Project Killer SKU section.)

3.  Ensuring your store is closely monitoring the gross margin levels throughout the departments. Specific SKUs can create a pervasive pestilence for your gross margin that could negatively affect the entire store's profitability.

At the home improvement stores, the commercial customers would attempt to purchase massive quantities of OSB (Oriented Strand Board), 2x4 studs, concrete, drywall, PVC pipe and fittings, garden mulches, and soils. We had certain quantities built into the program that would require a manager's approval to proceed with the transaction as a "gross margin precaution" to protect against eroding the store's profitability levels. To approve such quantities, most leaders would ask what else the customer is purchasing in order to ascertain the intention of the customer. Furthermore, they would only inquire whether they were going to purchase other items (with a higher gross-margin) to offset the loss leader gross margin occurrence.

In most retailers, there is **A LIMIT ON (remember the No-Limit Concept in Chapter Seven)** certain items to protect against the customers who want to purchase *exceedingly high quantities* of these loss leader SKUs. This shields their highly volatile profitability numbers while also providing the opportunity for other customers to purchase these items on sale or that are reduced in price. There are practical and financial reasons that stores enact a limit policy on certain items within their stores. In the retailers without a "stated limit" on their loss leaders, it is usually at the management's discretion on the number of items that a customer can purchase. The loss leader program is an effective method to establish credible and transparent relationships with your customers while fostering the atmosphere of *dependability and reliability* for customers to always be able to purchase these SKUs.

## CULTIVATING AN ATMOSPHERE OF EMPATHY

Empathy is defined as *the ability to understand and share the feelings of another individual*. Cultivating an atmosphere of empathy in your stores/company is one of the highest achievements to which you can aspire. This monumental task must originate from the CEO and remain "unfiltered and unaltered" all the way down to the store level where the associates/customers can notice and feel this environment. The benefits of establishing a culture of empathy in your stores is a *win-win* for everyone:

1. Improved employee happiness/satisfaction.

2. Employees feel valued and their opinion matters.

3. Associates/managers feel connected with their teams.

4. Employees learn to treat others with respect and dignity.

5. Individuals experience an open and inclusive environment.

6. Associates/managers feel accepted and are encouraged to reach their full potential.

7. Individuals experience enhanced levels of personal empowerment.

8. Employees no longer feel alienated from others.

9. Drastically improves conflict resolution.

Now we are going to delve into each bullet point for further clarification.

## IMPROVED EMPLOYEE HAPPINESS/SATISFACTION

Establishing an environment where empathy is allowed to flourish will cultivate an atmosphere of happiness, and ultimately, it increases employee satisfaction. Empathy is about connecting with your customers, associates, and leaders while listening to their ideas, concerns, and questions. How many times has a misunderstanding or disagreement happened in your store/life where the core issue is one or both parties involved are strongly expressing their dearth of being understood? *Most individuals just want to be heard or understood. When empathy is being practiced, the conflict is usually diminished, thereby, allowing a solution to be offered.* I have had the pleasure to work in an empathetic retail environment where I can personally vouch for the increased employee happiness and improved satisfaction levels that are experienced by this inclusive atmosphere.

## EMPLOYEES FEEL VALUED AND THEIR OPINION MATTERS

An atmosphere of empathy is created through employees/managers listening to others and making them **FEEL** like a valuable member of the team. Leaders are creating an open environment where the associates are "encouraged" to express their opinion without fear of embarrassment or retribution. The easiest way to allow employees to feel valued is to **ASK THEIR OPINION** on particular topics. If their ideas or suggestions are warranted, give them the freedom to explore their passions. I worked for a leader who established a loyal following from his team. Fortunately, he shared his secret with me; whenever an employee/manager came up with a great idea, he encouraged the individual to take **OWNERSHIP** and run with the idea. This creates massive "buy-in" from the individual and it now *becomes their baby* which, ultimately, creates a strong indication of their value to the team.

## ASSOCIATES/MANAGERS FEEL CONNECTED WITH THEIR TEAMS

Whenever you study the most successful teams in *any setting,* they always possess a strong connection with their craft and other members of the team. Empathy is the precursor to establishing an environment of trust and transparency with your teams. This will increase exponentially, due to the ability of your teams to feel connected. Feeling "a part of something" bigger than you is a potent actuator for cementing an environment of confidence and commitment among your associates/managers. Whenever I felt connected with my store or team, I always desired to give 100% with whatever task I was working on. In this sense, I genuinely recognized that I was involved with an organization that truly cared about me and my future. Empathy can inspire loyalty among your teams!

## EMPLOYEES LEARN TO TREAT OTHERS WITH RESPECT AND DIGNITY

When there is a strong culture of empathy being displayed among the team members and the leadership team, it provides the blueprint for everyone to follow. The most effective way to learn something is for the behavior to be modeled by others. Within an atmosphere of empathy, the associates feel compelled to treat each other with respect and dignity. Essentially it **PERMEATES THROUGHOUT THE ENTIRE STORE.** Whenever an associate was involved in a personal situation and the leadership team responded to their issue from a place of deep, sincere empathy, the employee wanted to return the favor by emulating the kindness that was given to them with other employees and customers. Remember, employees will mimic the behaviors they see or behaviors to which they are exposed to from the leadership team.

## INDIVIDUALS EXPERIENCE AN OPEN AND INCLUSIVE ENVIRONMENT

Leaders that have an empathetic nature within their management style are capable of developing an atmosphere of openness and inclusion among their teams that has a far-reaching effect which is prevalent and contagious. *Inclusion could be considered a synonym for empathy because of the nature of understanding what it "feels like to be excluded" and treated as an outcast in their store.* An empathetic leader can intuitively sense when an associate is feeling disregarded or rejected (for whatever reason) and will immediately seek to understand while reassuring them that they are an important and valued member of the store team. Empathy and inclusion have a harmonious relationship in which the employees and customers throughout the store can feel it's comforting effects.

## ASSOCIATES/MANAGERS FEEL ACCEPTED AND ARE ENCOURAGED TO REACH THEIR FULL POTENTIAL

Acceptance and encouragement are friendly neighbors with empathy. When your superiors display a sense of compassion and empathy with their teams, this environment accelerates the confidence levels of all associates. It fundamentally provides a "launching pad" for individuals to take chances and reach for the stars. Whenever an individual feels accepted and supported, this will set in motion a series of events that can propel them to achieve their highest aspirations.

Looking back on my finest business achievements, there were a couple of common denominators involved: I felt accepted, was encouraged to make mistakes, and I received a strong level of confidence and support from my bosses. This catapulted me to achieve some pretty impressive accomplishments. Without their belief in my abilities or the opportunity to learn some valuable business lessons (without serious consequences), I would never have achieved those remarkable results.

## INDIVIDUALS EXPERIENCE ENHANCED LEVELS OF PERSONAL EMPOWERMENT

Whenever there is an atmosphere of empathy exuding from associates and leaders alike, there is genuinely a strong platform available for employees to enhance and improve their own levels of personal empowerment. Empathy "permeates" an individual's psyche and provides the foundation required for a major transformation to develop within the individual. This new-found energy can compel people to eliminate preconceived fears while encouraging others to attempt new challenges. Individuals start to believe in themselves; as a result, their confidence level increases. This creates an "I can do this type of mentality" that is the first building block to higher achievements.

## EMPLOYEES NO LONGER FEEL ALIENATED FROM OTHERS

Empathy has a unique way of bringing people together while establishing an environment of inclusion. I always remembered how **I FELT** when I was able to work with associates and leaders who were fantastic at showing and developing empathy among their teams. I felt connected to my teammates because there was a strong sense of bonding within the building and the employees were extremely productive and happy. Alienation happens because of the lack of empathy among people to really "understand" an individual, their challenges and/or life circumstances. Having empathetic associates and leaders will create lifelong friendships and partnerships. I cannot overstate the concept of empathy with the fact that this basic emotion is disappearing from our retail stores while being slowly "phased out" of our culture.

## DRASTICALLY IMPROVES CONFLICT RESOLUTION

As previously stated, most conflict arises from one or many individuals **NOT UNDERSTANDING** the other person's viewpoint or perspective on a particular issue. There are numerous sayings about empathy: when you walk in my shoes, don't be too quick to judge, etc. "When you show deep empathy toward others, their defensive energy goes down, and positive energy replaces it, that's when you can get more creative in solving problems." (Covey, 2020). One powerful tool in the proverbial toolbox for "de-escalating any conflict" is showing a commitment to extending the other party some common courtesy and a heavy dose of empathy.

## SHOWING EMPATHY TOWARDS YOUR EMPLOYEES

When most people hear the word "engagement," they immediately direct their attention towards the customer side and do not readily acknowledge that this is only 50% of the equation. Engagement with our associates/managers is the other 50% of the puzzle which is most often neglected by many executive leaders. I completely understand that without the customers **NO BUSINESS** would succeed. However, I have always believed (and shouted from the rooftops) that the employees, managers, and vendors are just as important, if not more so, because without the employees, *who would assist the customers*?

In many retail stores that I worked in, the executive leadership teams mainly focused 90% of their energy on the ubiquitous catchphrases: satisfy the customer, listen to the customer, value the customer, etc. I never **UNDERSTOOD** why the employee, or the manager, or the vendor was perceived as inferior or unimportant when compared to the customer. I always believed that **THE CUSTOMER, EMPLOYEE, VENDOR - AND YES - THE MANAGER** was equally essential. Each should be respected and treated exactly the same. We need to radically change this unfavorable paradigm and start realizing that all of the individuals involved in the retail sector (customer, associate, manager, vendor, etc.) are equally significant. Everyone should be able to co-exist synergistically for the greater good with every individual being treated like family.

Showing empathy towards your associates is one of the cornerstones of engagement and is becoming a "lost art" within the retail sector. How many times has a very good employee started falling off from their normal productivity and the manager immediately desires to terminate the employee? We are all human beings that experience the trials and tribulations of life and no one escapes completely unscathed. The first thing I would do when confronted with a long-term high performer who had suddenly started acting "out of character" was to speak with the individual while seeking to understand what was happening in their personal life.

This can become very uncomfortable for some associates because of the embarrassment or shame relating to the situation/s in which they are experiencing. They might not be willing to share their innermost personal details with their store manager. I have always worked on my approachability as a leader while establishing a reputation for being trustworthy, honest, and transparent (whenever I could) with all my associates. This consistent behavior usually afforded me the opportunity to listen and assist the associate whenever possible. I was never a leader that "rushed to judgment" because I was seeking to understand the associate's viewpoint. If I was unable to assist the associate because the problem required a more professional assessment e.g., doctor, counselor, attorney, etc. I would exhaust every resource to ensure they received the best options available.

Depending on the circumstance, there was usually an excess of solutions available to aid the associate. We can accomplish miraculous things when we approach the situation from a place of empathy and compassion. If an associate was going through a divorce and was attempting to establish a visitation schedule with their children, I would ask the individual to provide me with an acceptable work schedule that would accommodate their situation. If an associate was having financial issues, I would attempt to provide them with some overtime, work on a promotion (if they were qualified and were close to the next level) by expediting the training process or provide them a more predictable schedule so that they were able to pick up additional work to supplement their income.

If the individual was involved in a domestic issue, we would put them in touch with our

employee "hotline" that would be able to provide additional resources to accommodate their

situation. In most cases, the associate just wanted **SOMEONE** to show empathy and compassion

towards them while being there to listen and offer constructive solutions. When I was an

associate or inexperienced manager, I was always appalled when I noticed a store manager

attempting to "flex their ego muscles" by plotting to terminate the previous high performing

associate without ever seeking to understand what was going on in their life. These incidents had

a highly emotional impact on me, and I vowed to never become this type of leader. In the next

chapter, *Merchandising Concepts to Increase Revenue,* we are going to dive headfirst into the

concepts of merchandising and how to maximize the space you have.

## **<u>SECTION FOR NOTES</u>**

# CHAPTER ELEVEN: MERCHANDISING CONCEPTS TO INCREASE REVENUE, PART ONE

## THE SILENT SALESMAN

We are going to discuss merchandising in this chapter, which is the **FIFTH PILLAR** within the manual. I am going to share some of the best practices that I have discovered which, when utilized correctly, will greatly assist with generating increased revenue and provide stellar customer service for your patrons. Every retail establishment that I have ever worked for or shopped at has always had their "own way of merchandising." In some cases, their method was effective and appropriate. However, in many cases, the merchandising is spotty at best and leaves much to the imagination. With outstanding merchandising, you will find that the products are grouped within a theme, segment, or category to augment the store's selection while allowing the customer to locate items that will complete their project or satisfy their needs.

The entire retail sector is famous for the indulgence of items within their stores, which is a result of the unique, and sometimes innovative methods, in which they display their merchandise. The **SILENT SALESMAN** is a method utilized to facilitate a positive customer experience when they are shopping a section which contains an exorbitant number of SKUs. This can appear confusing and overwhelming to many customers. As we previously discussed, 50% of customers want to know where an item is located and how much that item costs. The silent salesman will provide the customer with an *easy-to-understand process* of locating their specific

SKUs within a section with ease, therefore, allowing that customer to bypass the requirement of finding an associate.

Now let's take a look at an example of a locator system within the faucet aisle of a home improvement store:

| BATH FAUCETS DISPLAYS | BATH FAUCETS DISPLAYS | KITCHEN FAUCETS DISPLAYS | KITCHEN FAUCETS DISPLAYS | SHOWER FIXTURES DISPLAYS | SHOWER FIXTURES DISPLAYS |
|---|---|---|---|---|---|
| LABEL-A2 | LABEL-A4 | LABEL-A6 | LABEL-A8 | LABEL-A10 | LABEL-A12 |
| LABEL-A14 | LABEL-A16 | LABEL-A18 | LABEL-A20 | LABEL-A22 | LABEL-A24 |
| LABEL-A26 | LABEL-A28 | LABEL-A30 | LABEL-A32 | LABEL-A34 | LABEL-A36 |
| LABEL-A40 | LABEL-A42 | LABEL-A44 | LABEL-A46 | LABEL-A48 | LABEL-A50 |
| LABEL-A52 | LABEL-A54 | LABEL-A56 | LABEL-A58 | LABEL-A60 | LABEL-A62 |

As you can see, the locator system **PURPOSELY** and strategically left out the odd numbers. When you must add-in a new SKU, you have **ALL THE ODD NUMBERS** available to utilize. *The locator circle is always positioned to the right of the product label and should be fastened onto a blank price label for consistency.* I have witnessed some hodgepodges during my tenure with locator systems. Moreover, they usually deviated from the "original" planogram. Consequently, this occurs from the insertion of numerous SKUs that altered the locator system. Henceforth, the locator system begins to **MORPH** into different versions (here is where you do not need to reinvent the wheel; just stay with what works).

With a pre-meditated and effective locator system in place wherever possible throughout your store, your customers are going to experience an interactive, immersive, and satisfying retail shopping excursion. This system, when implemented and maintained properly, will severely reduce the anxiety and frustration of customers with purchasing products on their trip. Whenever I asked a customer how I could assist them, one out of two customers (usually) would want to know where a certain item was and then they would inquire (mentally or aloud) how much is this specific product.

The "Silent Salesman" was a proverbial goldmine that I stumbled upon and fell in love with immediately. The initial rollout within my stores consisted of explaining to the associates/managers the huge advantages contained within this remedial yet targeted system that would drastically reduce one of the major customer's **POINTS OF FRICTION**. This consisted of finding the products for which they were searching for and then ensuring our labeling system was flawless. I would thoroughly enjoy "role-playing" with the employees while enacting some real-life customer scenarios to further illustrate the seamless process. In turn, this created a much more pleasurable shopping experience for the patrons.

After the initial rollout, I would then challenge each department manager/assistant manager to thoroughly walk every 4-foot/8-foot section within their departments to determine where it would be suitable to execute the silent salesman program. The first thing that I needed to address was the increased office supply expense (which I had already received approval from my district manager) that was necessary to stock up on the required locator labels. Once that was accomplished and we received our supplies, it was then critical to ensure the timely execution of the silent salesman program within each department.

One critical component that was considered a "Non-Negotiable" was that it was mandatory that I personally visited and signed off on every 4-foot or 8-foot section to maintain absolute consistency throughout the entire store. This level of accountability was instituted because there are always a few **MAVERICKS** running around attempting to reinvent or readjust the system to suit their specific agendas or styles. The silent salesman program, in its current form, does not require any further enhancements to make it more effective. When it is implemented and executed properly, the customer will experience a pleasant shopping trip. They will leave your store much more satisfied with an increasing willingness to return.

After the initial meetings, rollouts, and approvals of the silent salesman program, I started noticing numerous positive trends that were occurring within our store:

1.  Customer satisfaction survey metrics were trending upwards.

2.  We were receiving a reduction in customer complaints.

3.  Our average ticket was steadily increasing.

4.  Our overall store revenue was increasing from week to week.

5.  Our profit and loss statements were reflecting positive net income statistics.

6.  We were attracting new customers while retaining our existing customer base.

7.  The overall store morale was improving due to the reduction in upset customers.

Now we are going to dissect each bullet point to further elaborate on the advantages of implementing the silent salesman program.

### CUSTOMER SATISFACTION SURVEY METRICS WERE TRENDING UPWARDS

In every store which I worked for, there was always some type of customer satisfaction survey or method to track and record the customer's perspective of our customer service skills. After implementing the silent salesman program throughout the entire store, our customer satisfaction metrics were "steadily increasing" every week. Shortly after, my store ranked number one in the district and in the top five in the entire region (over 300 stores) for overall customer satisfaction. I was inundated with calls from other store managers from other states and throughout the region on how I drastically improved the customer service metrics. Our customers were consistently reporting that our service was exceeding their expectations.

### WE WERE RECEIVING A REDUCTION IN CUSTOMER COMPLAINTS

Another obvious correlation we were experiencing was a **NOTICEABLE** attenuation of customer complaints, as this was a direct connection with the customers being extremely satisfied with their visits to our store. Again, in referencing the perspective of *50% of the customers want to know where the item is, and how much the item costs*, this system will pragmatically reduce your customer complaints significantly. **I would be remiss if I did not mention, that to take full advantage of the silent salesman program, your store MUST PRESENT A VERY HEALTHY IN-STOCK CONDITION**. Otherwise, it won't make much of a difference if the customer is unable to purchase their desired items. Having a silent salesperson program without a strong in-stock condition is counterintuitive to providing exemplary customer service.

## OUR AVERAGE TICKET WAS STEADILY INCREASING

In direct association with the silent salesman program, we begin to notice our "average ticket" creeping up each week. And, after a couple of months, it had risen substantially. The accumulated data was reflecting that customers were increasingly satisfied with their store visits. Consequently, they were then purchasing more items because of their lack of frustration that would naturally occur during their store visits. At first, I opined that the increase in our average ticket was an anomaly. However, upon further inspection, I ascertained that after numerous weeks of average ticket increases, I was unable to ignore the obvious numbers. I scoured all the revenue reports, the out-of-stock reports, the customer feedback surveys, and the plethora of ancillary information until I discovered that I was certain it was *mostly in response to the silent salesman program.*

## OUR OVERALL STORE REVENUE WAS INCREASING WEEK TO WEEK

As to be expected, our overall store sales were increasing in direct connection with our average ticket improving; this symbiotic relationship would continue for quite a while. I started performing "exit interviews" with customers of different age groups/nationalities e.g., couples versus individuals or residential/commercial customers on multiple days while ensuring I captured all departments to begin dialoguing with the customers to discuss their shopping experiences throughout the store.

I asked the customers for a few minutes of their time for which I offered them a $10 gift card. I asked scripted "open-ended" questions to understand their feelings about the departments they shopped, asked how we could improve their experience that day, and sought feedback on sections they shopped that displayed the silent salesman program. I received overwhelmingly positive responses from the customers who shopped the sections with the program while most stated that the store exceeded their expectations. The correlation is, *happy and satisfied customers* will **ALWAYS** spend more in your store.

## OUR PROFIT AND LOSS STATEMENT WAS REFLECTING POSITIVE NET INCOME STATISTICS

While I was dissecting our P&L statement, I began noticing that our specific department gross margins were increasing, and our overall profitability was trending upwards. After further inspection, I surmised that our customers were purchasing additional higher gross margin items that were "strategically" located within the sections that contained the silent salesman program. This program was causing a domino effect throughout my store; an increased average ticket, store revenue was steadily rising, and overall profitability was improving across the board. I started wondering: *can all these measurable metrics **REALLY BE IMPROVING** because of a simple locator system program??? And the answer is a resounding YES. It really is this uncomplicated and mundane system that is augmenting and impacting every aspect of our store while resonating with our customers.*

## WE WERE ATTRACTING NEW CUSTOMERS WHILE RETAINING OUR EXISTING CUSTOMER BASE

Another residual effect the silent salesman program was having on our store was an uptick in new customer transactions with the added advantage of a strong retention environment of our existing customer base. Our word-of-mouth advertising was spreading like wildfire from our satisfied customers. Henceforth, we were starting to attract customers from our strongest competition throughout the area. We have all experienced a dissatisfied and unpleasant shopping trip more than once. When the opportunity is shared with you about a competitor who is clicking on all cylinders, most individuals will give the alternative retailer a chance.

When you receive brand new customers to your store and you are able to wow them with your in-stock condition, superior customer service, fantastic engagement skills, and the experience of locating their products fast and accurately, you will have succeeded in capturing a new and loyal customer. They will shop your store while singing your praises to their friends and family thus, perpetuating the proverbial cycle of positive organizational advertising while affording you the opportunity to continue to win their patronage. A satisfied customer is generally a loyal customer.

## THE OVERALL STORE MORALE WAS IMPROVING DUE TO LESS UPSET CUSTOMERS

Another supplementary effect that was permeating the store was that the store morale was drastically improving due to the reduction in upset/impatient customers which the store team was experiencing. At first, I thought the store morale improvement was just the *luck of the draw* for that day. However, after further introspection, speaking with the entire store over the course of three weeks, and having one-on-one conversations with the associates, it was abundantly clear that customers were less upset and more patient throughout the entire store. This realization translated into the creation of a positive and peaceful environment for the associates.

After witnessing the drastic improvement of store morale, I realized that I had stumbled onto something so incredibly simple, yet so impactful across the board (increased revenue, improved gross margins, higher profitability metrics, an increase in customer satisfaction, and improved store morale). One of the major lessons that I learned from working in the retail sector for an extended period of time was that the most impactful and rewarding concepts are extremely rudimentary in nature. When they are implemented and executed to near perfection, the results will be astounding and profitable for your store. **CONSISTENCY IS THE KEY!!!**

### HOW TO IMPLEMENT THE 80/20 RULE TO INCREASE REVENUE

The 80/20 rule is the fact that generally 80% of your store sales are achieved from <u>ONLY</u> 20% of your total store SKUs. Now, this number can slightly fluctuate up or down depending on the specific niche you're in or time of year for your business. However, the math creates an opportunistic attitude which, if completely understood, can propel you towards achieving exponential sales increases and improved customer loyalty. The 80/20 rule dovetails into Chapter Fives's *(Revenue Deterrents)* "Never Lose a Sale" concept and Chapter Nine's *(The Power of Engagement, Part One)* "Project Killer SKUs" information which gives you some critical insight and clarity with which to structure your store sections to accommodate "rate of sale" holding power.

With this highly tactful information, it is paramount to walk each and every 4ft/8ft section throughout your store. This guarantees the SKUs that **PRODUCE 80%** of your total store revenue is *prominently featured* and has the holding capacity to accommodate unforeseen sales spikes throughout the year. I used to communicate to the department managers, assistant store managers, and the buyer/merchants that these SKUs are to be viewed as "<u>we can never be out of stock on these specific items.</u>" Now, I will tell you that there is a gigantic difference between the eight different retailers I worked for in their perspective and execution/planning surrounding the 80/20 rule. Ultimately, it was my responsibility (as a store manager) to guarantee that we never ran out-of-stock on these specific SKUs.

To certify that we were consistently in-stock on the "must-have SKUs" in each department, I instructed each department manager to put a yellow dot in the upper left-hand corner of the shelf label/store sign. This became a staunch reminder for each associate/manager of the supreme importance of these mandatory SKUs receiving 100% in-stock status at all times. I would personally walk one to two departments per day with the list of "must-have SKUs" to properly determine their status and to view their space allocation. In the stores where I did not receive the luxury of having buyers/merchants who properly allocated the necessary planogram accommodations for these critical SKUs, I would have to implement store planogram changes on a case-by-case basis to confirm the allocated space was sufficient to handle the accurate rate of sale.

The effective method to verify proper space allocation for the 20% of SKUs that generate 80% of your store sales is to confirm that each store within a district has received an *accurate revenue classification code* e.g., AA store, A store, B store, C store, etc. If a store reflects an inaccurate revenue classification, it will obstruct and cripple the store's ability to receive the necessary product to fulfill their customer demand. One of the first phone calls I would make (after partnering with my district leader), whenever assuming responsibility for a new store, was to the lead merchant for our district/division to deduce if my store had an accurate revenue classification. Correcting this minor oversight can and will allow you to bypass a long and hard road to achieving your store's full potential in regard to revenue projections/commitments while also delighting your guests with your in-stock condition.

## EMPLOYEE AWARENESS OF 80/20 RULE

One of the largest pitfalls to the proper execution of implementing the 80/20 rule within your store/s will ultimately be the success or failure of ensuring that **ALL OF YOUR EMPLOYEES** fully understand and are extremely knowledgeable on these precious SKUs. Each associate/manager must comprehend the importance of these critical SKUs while taking precautionary measures to protect these items from running out of stock. In addition, each employee must be able to articulate to the customer the reason to purchase each SKU i.e. why should the customer purchase this SKU? These specific SKUs usually have a strong track record of reliability, quality, and satisfaction which must be communicated to everyone.

There are also specific times throughout the year where there can be several weak links in the proverbial 80/20 rule chain. The first area of concern is usually surrounding seasonal hiring campaigns since your store is being inundated with an influx of new associates. *These new associates are not yet fully aware of the importance of the 80/20 rule* (even though it was/should have been completely covered in the on-boarding process). During this initial stage, it is paramount to educate the new hires expeditiously on the best practices surrounding the 80/20 rule with their specific role in the process.

Remember the old adage "it only takes one bad apple to ruin the bunch." This is how the slow descent of disruption can commence within a store. First, it is one associate and then a second, which if left unchecked, can spread exponentially throughout your store. I have personally witnessed this phenomenon unfold within a store. It will result in a major decrease in overall store revenue, massive customer dissatisfaction, and potential loss of your loyal customer base.

The second time of year to remain vigilant is around the holidays, as there are numerous vendors who take "extended time off." This transition can and will create havoc on your in-stock conditions, especially on your 20% SKUs if you are not prepared. I would always implement a thorough on-hand SKU count to be executed one or two months in advance. I would also communicate with the merchants to fathom if there were any **FORESEEN ISSUES** that were out there to fully understand the consequences of these issues. The reason I chose one or two months in advance of the holiday season was to create a "buffer system." This afforded me the necessary time to adjust and react to any foreseen issues regarding certain categories/SKUs.

I know some of you might be questioning the simplicity of the timing for auditing the on-hand SKU count or the mentioning of contacting the merchants as there is no way they would not "communicate" any issues regarding in-stock conditions. However, I can promise you that the level of communication is drastically different at each company I worked for. I want to reiterate that the purpose of this manual is to prepare you for any occurrence, albeit, simple or complex, and to ensure that you are aware of the huge discrepancies that exist from one employer to the next. For some of you, this might be a nice refresher course while for others with less retail experience it might be an eye-opening experience of epic proportions. *It would be imprudent of me to leave out some information that was considered remedial or elementary.*

If I were to put on my <u>pragmatic cap</u> right now, I would be questioning the validity of the importance of the 80/20 rule. I would not be able to comprehend how this would not be properly addressed by the buyers and merchants for every organization, considering the drastic revenue implications. I would also question the employee awareness element because if these SKUs are generating 80% of the revenue throughout the store then they must be able to sell themselves without the interference or assistance of employees. In my early adoption of the 80/20 rule, I posited that this rule and all its essence were fully understood by the powers to be.

Although during my tenure with different retailers, I experienced a "rude awakening" and had to endure numerous encounters surrounding this concept. *Buyers/merchants can easily become overwhelmed, just like within the stores with major vendor issues, staffing issues, or shipping concerns.* I would approach each merchant with a strong level of empathy and compassion while seeking out creative methods to assist them whenever I could. I had to create a laser-like focus on overseeing every possible detail to ensure that my store was positioned to be profitable. Please do not overlook this concept within any of your retail stores. Please remember that you can **NEVER OVERCOMMUNICATE!!!**

# SECTION FOR NOTES

# CHAPTER TWELVE: MERCHANDISING CONCEPTS TO INCREASE REVENUE, PART TWO

## PLANOGRAMS TO ACCOMMODATE RATE OF SALE

The basics of merchandising 101 are planograms, store layouts, shelf allocation, SKU allocation mix, and product accommodation area. Depending on your company and your exact store designation - big box, market store, satellite, or specialty - you will generally receive a blueprint for each planogram throughout your store. It will describe in detail where each SKU is shelved and how many facings each SKU will have. Some store managers are proactive, and they will understand if and when a planogram is unaccommodating to their clientele or is inadequate with the necessary holding power to satisfy their customers. However, some stores will not react as fervently while continuing to run out of products and disappointing their patrons.

The merchant team at any organization is inundated daily with new products while constantly attempting to strategize and implement the perfect planogram layouts for each store within their region. Unfortunately, there are some stores/planograms that remain stagnant with regards to their updated planograms/store layout configurations. This is where the meticulous managers (department, assistant, or store manager) must react immediately and communicate with their merchant team to remedy the situation.

If there is an extended period of no communication from the merchant team and you have exhausted all formal channels to rectify the situation, it then reverts back to the management team (after collaborating with your district manager) to address and correct the deficient planograms swiftly. You must remember that the customer can be "unforgiving" when your store is constantly not meeting their expectations, especially regarding not being able to purchase the items they desire.

Now, I must preface this behavior in stating that I am not condoning actions that are borderline "dissident" in nature. I am not saying that each store manager should personally adjust each planogram to their liking because that is how inconsistencies in merchandising arise and can quickly damage the integrity of the organization. I am also asking each manager to have performed their *due diligence* in reviewing the sales data reports while confirming they have already personally viewed the section that requires an adjustment *before attempting any corrections*. What I am advocating for is that each store manager has their **"finger on the pulse of their business"** every day. It is their responsibility to at least meet, if not exceed, the expectations of their guests by maintaining a strong and healthy in-stock condition.

In reality, each store is a snowflake in nature. No two stores are alike, even if they are only eight miles apart. I have personally experienced two stores that are only eight miles apart in the same city with the consumer shopping patterns being drastically diverse in nature. Consequently, the product assortment shelf allocation required continual tweaking to accommodate the customer's needs. With that being said, I have **NEVER WORKED IN A STORE** that did not require planogram adjustments to address their customer's concerns.

As an example, I was the store manager of one of these stores that were eight miles apart for which I continued to receive requests for additional "Rustic Lighting" options, even though we were able to special order these items. Unfortunately, the customers did not want to wait for the items. They were planning to purchase their selections immediately and wanted to start on their project that day. I partnered with my lighting merchant to become a pilot store for the "Lodge Collection" and the results were phenomenal with revenue increasing dramatically. In fact, because of my store's huge success, the Lodge Collection was implemented in 300 stores across the region. Conversely, when the other store (again, only eight miles away) received the Lodge Collection SKUs, their sales were not as impressive (though they were experiencing increased revenue) - even though their store volume was 40% higher than mine.

In retail, each store and each department within the store can have unique store specific peaks and valleys with certain product lines. It is up to the associates and the department managers to communicate these targeted customer nuances to the management team. In reality, most of the planogram adjustments usually only require a *minor change to the shelf allocation.* One SKU is going to require three facings instead of two, or another SKU is going to receive one facing instead of two. Depending on the company you work for and the criteria they have in place regarding planogram alterations, this will determine the latitude and autonomous authority you will have as a store manager to implement planogram adjustments.

In most retail companies, a store manager will receive a medium amount of autonomy to react to customer buying patterns and make minor modifications without requiring district or regional approval. However, in almost all planogram changes, the executive leadership team would expect you to be able to explain your decision-making process with proper empirical and statistical data to support your decisions. The minimum expectations are that you have examined the sales data reports, performed an audited SKU on-hand count, and have already discussed alternative solutions before making the planogram changes. My philosophy was that, whenever in doubt, communicate your desires/conclusions to your district leader to establish a partnership. Remember, as a store manager, you **KNOW YOUR STORE BETTER THAN ANYONE.**

## SEASONALITY WITH SEAMLESS TRANSITIONS

In every retail store, there are going to be seasonal merchandising adjustments that are going to require planogram changes with substantial alterations to your departments (especially in the states that are exposed to the four seasons). There are some retailers that have mastered the transition from one seasonal product mix to the next and they experience a "seamless" transition. Contrary to this, in most retailers, this process is inconsistent (throughout the country) at best and untimely (playing catch up) at worst. In each retailer, there is a **"preview window"** that will plant the seed within the customer's mind to start thinking about and planning their shopping needs for the upcoming season. The timing of this window will be determined by your specific niche i.e. department stores, apparel stores, home improvement stores, etc.

The seasonality transition should encompass advanced planning. Hopefully, your store will receive detailed instructions from your corporate office (instead of having to wing it, which is where decreased sell-through of merchandise and diminished revenue occur). Expectantly, you should have informative guidelines from last season on the major successes and pitfalls to appropriately guide you. During these seasonal transitions, it can be a stressful time for the associates and the customers. A strong leadership team will have a "critical path" to follow with deadlines for each planogram while not exposing the customer to major disruption (within reason) for their regular shopping needs.

What do you do if you are working in a new store that does not have access to prior data? I have experienced this nightmare before, which created an inconsistent and chaotic guest experience throughout the year. I had to rely on data from a different store that did not have the same customer demographics, average ticket, or seasonal timing. Throughout that year, I was frustrated, overworked, and uncomfortable (flying blind) because I did not receive the appropriate seasonal timelines in which I adhered to. My recommendation is to locate a store within your district/region that has comparable realistic data to support your transitions. Again, each retailer is inimitable with how they handle/communicate seasonal information at the store level.

The specific timing of your seasonal merchandising assortment must be perfect in order to maximize and capture proportionate sales of the categories that **ARE STILL IN SEASON**. There are plenty of renegades out there who are operating their own seasonal agenda e.g., snowblowers in July, sweaters in June, and ice fishing endcaps in July. There is an interdependent dance that needs to occur to ensure your stores are capitalizing on every sale within your current season. You want to be the first in line to snag the premature seasonal sales from customers who usually shop very early for their seasonal items. At the same time, you don't want to do this at the expense of missing additional sales from the in-season SKUs.

Accurate seasonal planning leads to increased revenue, higher customer satisfaction levels, decreased surplus stock at all levels of the supply chain, diminished risk of running out of high-demand SKUs, and fewer markdowns. Long-range planning is intertwined with increased profitability. Another missing element in some retailers is adequately planning of each store's demographics and diversifying customer shopping patterns (different nationalities celebrate other holidays than the traditional ones). As previously stated, *each store is an island* with its own "unique and diverse" idiosyncrasies that require specific merchandising methodologies to cater to their clientele. There were home improvement stores in urban Chicago that were receiving *riding lawn mowers* when the average resident had *little to now grass at all*.

The next critical piece in the seasonality transition program is to accurately plan your exit strategy with markdown cadences and effective "meltdown plans." This will guarantee you are not encumbered by **EXCESS INVENTORY** that will require extreme markdowns and further erode your gross margin while decreasing your profitability. Each retailer has a different set of timelines for executing their markdown cadences. It is always better to exit the seasonal category slightly early while preserving precious gross margin dollars than to attempt to **CHASE THE**

**LAST SALE** and wind up with surplus inventory. Many retailers are establishing a set standard across their stores (cookie cutter) to create a baseline for seasonality, therefore attempting to alleviate any capricious customer shopping patterns.

## VISUAL MERCHANDISING TO INCREASE REVENUE

In every retailer throughout the country, the number one metric for profitability is "sales per square foot." This data will reflect either a positive or negative situation in each retailer. Visual merchandising must be your most productive and fetching salesperson in order to attract and capture additional revenue. Visual merchandising can encapsulate store window displays, store layouts, immersive, engaging, and interactive showrooms, store signage, tables, shelves/racks, endcaps/gondola's, fixtures/props, and vestibules. The main approach to effective visual merchandising is "to tell a compelling story" that the customer can follow which will encourage a receptive and open-minded response from the customer to contemplate purchasing your goods.

One of the first concepts to implement is to assure that your store/departments exhibit a "theme" with which the customer can easily navigate to thoroughly understand the crux of each area. Most retailers utilize color, lighting, music, interactive displays, and store acronyms to illustrate their unique themes in each department throughout the store. A successful theme will usually encompass all of these visual concepts wherever possible to create a fully immersive and inclusive environment that will captivate your customers, while also increasing top-line sales.

Some of the prevalent impediments that occur within the major retailers on the visual merchandising landscape are:

1. Displays not working (damaged or broken displays/products).

2. Accessibility to displays to accommodate peak times/holidays.

3. Outdated displays.

4. Availability of product.

5. Being proactive with underperforming displays.

6. Cleanliness of displays e.g., light bulbs out, dusty product, missing or incorrect signage, and overall unapproachable areas.

Now let's discuss each impediment in further detail.

## DISPLAYS NOT WORKING

The number one frustration among consumers with regards to visual merchandising is displays that do not properly work. Whether I was a store manager or while I am shopping as a customer, nothing creates more annoyance for customers than a display not working or one that does not perform correctly. This specific problem must be addressed multiple times throughout the day, preferably, pre-opening, mid-day, pre-dinner rush, and after closing to guarantee that your store is not succumbing to this situation. In essence, it causes high trepidation among customers. Failing to certify that your displays are working, **CAN AND WILL** result in lost revenue while also severely damaging your brand loyalty among your patrons.

## ACCESSIBILITY TO DISPLAYS DURING PEAK TIMES/HOLIDAYS

Every customer has experienced the anxiety of not being able to access a certain interactive display during peak times or around the holidays. In most circumstances, this problem can easily be remedied through proper planning and the insertion of extra working displays to accommodate increased customer traffic. I am not saying that each retailer must add a ridiculous number of displays; however, the addition of a couple of extra working displays can diminish the agitation among customers during peak hours. Most people understand that minimal wait times are normal during certain times. Another preventative measure is to allocate staffing to the more popular interactive display areas to provide employee support and guidance for your customers during the busier times throughout the day/year.

## OUTDATED DISPLAYS

The timeliness of your visual displays must be congruent within the mainstream flow of your products, which will deliver a message to your customers that you are on "the cutting edge" with your visual merchandising concepts. Nothing screams mediocrity to your customers more than having visual displays that are not showcasing the latest and greatest product assortment for your customers to purchase. In today's marketplace, customers are **DEMANDING** that retailers provide and deliver a rich and interactive experience through their visual displays. They desire displays that compel them to purchase the newest fashion trend, the latest smartphone, or the hottest new lithium-ion battery leaf blower. This critical oversight will usually repel your loyal customers, will open the doors for increased competition from your rivals, and slowly erode your customer's confidence in your effectiveness to satisfy their retail needs.

## AVAILABILITY OF PRODUCT

When a retailer chooses to promote their product through interactive and engaging displays, the customer assumes that when they are ready to purchase their items, the retailer will have enough product on-hand to placate their request. With proper advanced planning and strong communication with your merchant team, running out of stock on your display items should become an abnormality instead of a daily occurrence. Customers will exhibit a small semblance of patience when your store "occasionally" runs out of stock on a particular item. On the other hand, this should be the exception and never the rule. In the digital age, customers are insistent that all retailers have the foresight to anticipate the demand for certain retail segments. In addition, they have a *very high expectation of being able to purchase their items immediately.*

The downside to continually running out of display product is that the customer will usually leave your store and purchase their item/s at a brick and mortar competitor or online. If this unreliable behavior continues, your revenue will diminish, your brand will become tarnished, and you run the risk of alienating your core customers. I was always grateful and appreciative of the disgruntled customers for allowing our store the "opportunity" to address and rectify their issues. This is infinitely better than having them leaving the store while sharing their unpleasant experience with their friends and family. **WHAT RETAILER CAN AFFORD TO HAVE NEGATIVE ADVERTISING FOR THEIR STORE/COMPANY?**

## BEING PROACTIVE WITH UNDERPERFORMING DISPLAYS

With the golden metric of "sales per square foot" being the litmus test for how effective a retailer is with their retail space; the most profitable retailers remain vigilant about reacting to underperforming or unprofitable displays by implementing corrective procedures immediately. A successful retailer will track and record the revenue data received from their display merchandise. This revenue should be **SIGNIFICANTLY HIGHER** than your normal sales throughout the department. In my stores, I used to track the sales data daily to determine if I had the right visual displays front and center throughout the store. If one of these displays was providing disappointing sales numbers, I would immediately swap it out for an alternative product. The key to maintaining profitable displays is to "have your ear to the ground" of each displays performance while instilling your sense of urgency among your store leadership team to react accordingly when the numbers are floundering.

## CLEANLINESS OF DISPLAY AREAS

One of the biggest display faux pas is the lack of fastidious behavior surrounding the overall cleanliness of the display areas. I was a big proponent of the **CAR DEALERSHIP SHOWROOM** example. I took my entire leadership team to a local car dealership to offer them visual cues (after obtaining dealership approval from management of course) as my anchor when explaining to the entire management team how a display area should look at **ALL TIMES**. I would give them poignant and tangible methods from the car dealership environment that must transfer to their display areas.

In the car dealership showrooms, there are no cracks in the windshields, no flat tires, no dirt on the cars, and no stack outs of armor all next to the cars. The cars were being displayed in "mint condition" at all times, without exception. I would then challenge the entire leadership team to thoroughly walk each of their display areas with a fine-tooth comb to address any concerns that we just discussed and implement corrective procedures to refresh these zones. I will be covering this specific concept in greater detail in chapter thirteen, *Store Environment (Part One),* when we will be discussing store environment.

I created a store display checklist for the opening and closing manager to follow while maintaining sterling display integrity throughout the store. The checklist contained the following items:

1.  All light bulbs working.

2.  All displays wiped down for dirt and dust.

3.  All display areas free of trash and debris.

4.  All wire connections are safe and do not provide a tripping hazard.

5.  All displays are in perfect working condition. If not, document the work order number to address and or solution provided i.e. opening associate will address the concern or specific part will be obtained first thing in the morning, etc.

6.  Any suggestions for improvement.

7.  Daily sales data recorded on the checklist.

8.  All signage is 100% compliant.

As the store manager, I would review each opening and closing display checklist each morning/evening to ensure that each list was properly filled out and contained the necessary information. If the checklist was not properly filled out, I would personally address it with the appropriate manager to determine the reason. I was a fanatic about maintaining the consistency of this checklist because I completely understood the ramifications both financially and reputationally regarding display integrity. I would **OFTEN** be approached by leaders inquiring about my fanaticism with this seemingly obtuse checklist. I would proceed to thoroughly explain my reasoning behind the checklist and its purpose, at which point, each leader would have a revelation and would then completely understand its paramount importance.

I could probably devote an entire chapter to this concept because of the utmost importance of this subject. Many retailers scantily pay any attention to their display areas unless there is a customer complaint, or one has been damaged. The cleanliness of displays will merge nicely into our next chapter where we are going to address your store environment.

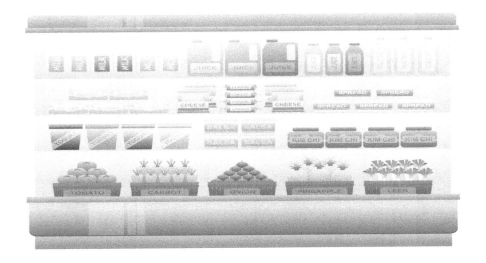

## **SECTION FOR NOTES**

# CHAPTER THIRTEEN: STORE ENVIRONMENT, PART ONE

## IMAGE-PERCEPTION-REALITY CONCEPT

Store environment is the **SIXTH PILLAR** within the manual which is extremely crucial to your entire organization as it will set in motion a blueprint that can generate successful and profitable stores. Contrary wise, it can create a shopping atmosphere that is littered with problems, erratic sales, customer complaints, and morale issues. I developed the *Image-Perception-Reality Concept* to teach and train my employees/leaders about the paramount importance of how a customer <u>mentally</u> perceives your **ENTIRE STORE**. The process is unassuming at first glance. It is something we all do anytime we enter any environment; customer views an *image* (an endcap, a section, etc.) which creates a *perception* in their mind (positive or negative); and, from this information, accurate or not, becomes the customer's *reality*.

The image-perception-reality concept is heavily influenced by the *first impression* cognitive assessment we all make when we encounter anything for the first time. It is also one of the main principles of *Feng-Shui* which is how energy interacts with and moves through space i.e. your physical store. The concept took years to understand and consisted of three basic principles: performing merchandising experiments, adjustments of cleanliness standards, and manipulation of customer traffic flow patterns (for minimal periods) in multiple stores/companies throughout the country. After rigorously testing these principles, I began to fully comprehend the elementary, yet extremely impactful effect, of this concept.

We have **ALL** experienced walking into a space and "immediately" felt an uneasiness or comfortable feeling associated with the space e.g., a friend's home, store, or a spot in nature. In our digital society, *many people do not question their feelings regarding energy within a space and how it makes them feel.* Subsequently, when we enter a space, we **INSTINCTIVELY** sense how the environment affects our mood. This intuitive knowing is usually triggered unconsciously <u>without our conscious mind processing the energy</u>. However, individuals are affected (positively or negatively) by these feelings whenever they encounter a pleasant space or a chaotic environment.

I noticed that the departments that were clean, organized, had solid traffic flow, and were maintained meticulously was the same departments that were **CONSISTENTLY** exceeding budget, received the fewest customer complaints, and had the highest morale throughout the store. A coincidence maybe, or perhaps, there was a common thread that was connecting these departments together like some invisible string. The further I delved into this enigma, I started correlating the similarities (which were piling up) among the departments. At this time, I coined the phrase "image-perception-reality."

I started voraciously reading books about Feng-Shui and how to harness this ubiquitous energy for consistently favorable results. In learning a myriad of Feng-Shui principles, I started "resonating" with the concepts. At that moment, I had an **AHA MOMENT**. A light bulb went off as I realized that I had been advocating this message (of how energy flows through an environment either positively or negatively) for a considerable time. However, I was always met with ridicule, indignation, or sarcasm from my superiors. I instinctively understood that the

energy permeating any space could be adjusted to facilitate a more pleasant shopping experience

for the customer. As an entry-level manager, I was not afforded the opportunity to implement

any of my ideas surrounding energy enhancement. Henceforth, I waited until I became a store

manager to execute my well thought out adjustments. During this period, I amassed an enormous

amount of *tangible and effective data* from my experiments that was proven and consistent.

### MERCHANDISING EXPERIMENTS TO TEST MY THEORY

From this point, I wanted to test my hypothesis (after discussing my plans with my district

manager to obtain his approval) and started executing small changes throughout the store in

certain sections to observe customer behaviors. Meanwhile, my colleagues remarked apropos of

the initiative, stating it was a stupid idea. The *first* of the three principles were the merchandising

experiments in which I would take a section that was normally high volume and removed enough

product to make the section look like Swiss cheese. However, there was never a moment when

we ran out-of-stock completely, thus, depriving our store of revenue.

In addition, I would **DELIBERATELY** trash the section and make it look like a hurricane

went through (which was extremely difficult for me because I was so persnickety about the look

of my store). I would then anxiously wait for the sales data to be gathered, customer comments

relayed, and employee perspectives communicated. I would perform these minor experiments

throughout each week for a period of one month. Then, I would thoroughly review all of the data (taking into consideration the season we were in and the time of year it was while equating the numbers to comparable figures).

I would also instruct all associates/managers to communicate to me the customer comments/complaints they were receiving regarding the chosen sections. I would then tally the results every week and communicate this information with the entire store. I would utilize all the communication channels we were employing (morning/evening huddles, all store meetings, communication letters with the paychecks, department meetings, leadership meetings with the entire management team, etc.

*The image-perception-reality experiment was metamorphosing into its own entity and my theories about this concept were starting to crystallize.* Sales numbers were considerably lower in the sections I choose, the number of customer complaints had increased, and the employees/managers reported an increase in "agitated" customers in the departments that had experimental sections. The fact of the matter is that by interfering with the regular energy of a section, I was **disrupting the normal flow of positive "CHI"** which had created disharmonious energy the customers could <u>sense and feel</u>. This, in turn, was causing them to feel "uneasy" which would translate into fewer sales and increased complaints.

During my experiments, I had *rediscovered* (which I had already intuitively understood) that the feeling of a space and how the energy moves in and through a space, will create either a positive or negative response from the people (employees and customers) who are interacting in that area.

**ADJUSTMENTS OF CLEANLINESS STANDARDS**

The *second* of the three principles were the minor adjustments I made to the "normal" cleanliness standards (borderline white glove for me) throughout the chosen sections. I would *intentionally* instruct the associates/managers **NOT TO MAINTAIN AND TO ABSTAIN FROM** the normal cleaning standards that were a trademark of my leadership style. This consisted of a **three-week period** on this specific principle in three separate departments i.e. one week per department with specific sections chosen. This part of the experiment was **extremely difficult** for me to stomach because of the obsequious behavior I have for maintaining a clean and presentable store for our customers on a daily basis.

This process entailed: no straightening of product i.e. no facing or blocking of product to look like a solid wall of product, no dusting of product (which in a home improvement environment is brutal), no attention to detail (except for missing or torn shelf labels and marketing materials, etc.), no cleaning of any kind, and no replacing any burned out light bulbs. I must preface that the employees and managers **ALSO** had a hard time refraining from giving some TLC to the chosen sections. However, they understood the experiment and that we had to allow it to proceed while restraining ourselves throughout the entire three-week timeline.

The reason I had chosen a one-week period per department for this piece was that the cleanliness principle would be viewed multiple times by customers during the week, while we also had to accommodate for the customers "giving us a pass" for an unclean environment the first time. One time is a mistake, but two or more times becomes a pattern. Another excruciating part of the experiment was to *forgo our consistent sales numbers* while subjecting myself and

our store to the disruption of our daily routines. Just like the merchandising experiment, after

each week, I would review all the "numerical data" and communicate this with the entire store

team. I would continue to keep them abreast throughout the process. Meanwhile, I would solicit

their advice, feedback, and opinions to gather further pertinent information.

This specific principle received a plethora of negative feedback from the customers and

spurned additional criticisms about the environment of our store. In addition, this experiment

conjured up questions about our store environment: What is going on in this store? Did you

change management? Are you guys going out of business? This part of the experiment hit us

pretty hard! Furthermore, after I received the customer feedback, I shortened the timeline on this

principle to only three weeks total (originally supposed to be four-weeks), in which, the overall

results were transformative and conclusive. In accordance with the merchandising principle, the

sales numbers decreased; however, this time the numbers *diminished even further* than the

merchandising experiment as the evidence was highly tangible and eye-opening for most of the

employees and managers.

I must convey that when I choose to perform these experiments, I was already exceeding my

yearly budget and I had some "wiggle room" on my numbers to test out my theories. The years it

took to fully understand this concept were intermixed with witnessing this idea in action, **NOT

INTENTIONALLY**, and during my calculated time frames as a store manager.

## MANIPULATION OF CUSTOMER TRAFFIC FLOW PATTERNS

The *last* of the three principles were to purposely adjust the customer traffic flow patterns throughout the store e.g., put large ladders in the racetrack aisles, put big carts in heavily shopped aisles, and forgo addressing any hindrances that would block or reduce any aisle flow. I explained to the department managers and assistant managers that I was going to conduct an experiment for only **ONE-HOUR.** Afterward, I wanted to reconvene to discuss their perceptions and to receive feedback on the customer comments/opinions.

I carried out my pre-meditated strategy by moving the 16-foot ladders to the main aisles, moved the large carts into heavily shopped areas, and I did not address anything that would cause congestion throughout the store. This part of the experiment was also very difficult for me to carry out; at the same time, I started my stopwatch and waited impatiently for one-hour to pass. At the end of the one-hour time frame, I called all managers to the back and asked for their feedback. The comments started coming in "fast and furious" about customers being upset, angered, and argumentative. They specified that it felt like **MOST** customers were "on edge" and exhibited very "little patience" as opposed to normally having more understanding and consideration for an issue or slightly extended wait time. Some customers abandoned their shopping carts and left the store; sales were down for that specific hour when compared to historical data.

Most of my managers were aghast and asked zealously, **WHAT DID YOU DO???** I explained to them that all I did was to severely restrict the customer traffic flow throughout the store. I used the example of **what happens to the mood and behavior of most drivers when a five-lane highway is reduced to two lanes???** The drivers become impatient, are worried about being late, and are angry about having their routine disturbed. Their energy shifts to a more negative pattern, and they are generally upset about the situation. I said, "This is what happens when our aisles are blocked and do not allow customers to move freely around the store."

After this experiment, all my managers **COMPLETELY UNDERSTOOD** why I was constantly moving ladders and carts to more appropriate and less traveled areas throughout the store. They also comprehended why I was *extremely proactive in making sure these issues never arose in the first place.* I discussed with them the horror stories I had witnessed during my career surrounding this topic and how supremely important it is to keep all the aisles open and uncluttered. This affords the customers easy maneuverability throughout the store. In a retail environment (or any environment for that matter), **ENERGY** can be *chaotic or harmonious* within any space. All it takes is to understand a few basic principles of how to keep spaces clean and accessible to allow the energy to flow uninterrupted.

The overall consensus of the image-perception-reality concept was enlightening and very poignant within the retail setting. It reconfirmed my suspicions surrounding how important it is to maintain clean and shoppable sections while making it a top priority to address any encumbrances that will disrupt the flow of positive energy in your store environment. My peers were hoping to experience "Schadenfreude" from my temporary experiment. However, after my district manager asked me to share my findings with the entire district team, half of the store managers were interested to hear more; the other half remained skeptical and cynical

surrounding the findings while continuing along their normal path.

The image-perception-reality concept provided empirical results along with tangible data that

was not achieved through chance, happenstance, or coincidence. This information cemented the

fact that when customers are shopping your stores, they will react accordingly to the store

environment with their wallets and their loyalty. The fact is that <u>revenue decreased each time</u> we

experimented with all three of the principles listed. If these issues are happening in your stores,

haphazardly or unintentionally, your stores will continue to suffer the consequences of

diminished sales and customers choosing to take their patronage elsewhere. In this era of online

and brick-and-mortar competition, we do not have the luxury of not addressing our store

environments. We must react swiftly to **ANYTHING** that will force our customers to go to

another competitor. In conclusion, I replicated these identical experiments at every retailer I

worked for with the same expected results. It did not matter which company I worked for, the

products sold, or the specific niche I worked in; this blueprint is extremely effective,

reproducible, and portable.

### DIRTY DISH SYNDROME

Another component that will address your store environment in a positive fashion is to create

a setting where your customers **WANT TO ADHERE TO YOUR HOUSEKEEPING**

**STANDARDS**. This can easily be achieved by what I call the "DIRTY DISH SYNDROME."

The dirty dish syndrome is a *metaphor* used to describe a situation that will facilitate a desired result when properly executed and maintained. In most cases, when a person is finished with their plate, glass, or bowl and they approach a clean and empty sink, they will usually rinse off their items and place their items in the dishwasher. Or, they will place the items neatly in the sink, already pre-rinsed thereby creating a clean and organized section.

Conversely, if the sink (or retail area) is already overflowing or resembles a disaster zone, the **family member/friend/customer** will follow the designated pattern. Usually, this will affect their behavior similarly. So, the question becomes: *how can a metaphor about dirty dishes assist with my retail store environment???* Identical to the image-perception-reality concept, customers **WANT** to be good neighbors. *They want to play their role in keeping your store environment clean and hospitable while shopping in a well-maintained and visually appealing retail setting.* Let's look at some real-life retail examples that were prevalent with *creating an atmosphere* that helped facilitate customers in becoming good housekeeping consumers. They will become part of your extended retail family and will drastically reduce the time it takes to **RECOVER** your store.

## MISCELLANEOUS ITEMS THROUGHOUT THE STORE

One of the first things I noticed about keeping all the store sections clean and shoppable was the high percentage of customers who **RETURNED THEIR UNWANTED ITEMS** back to their original location throughout the store. As anyone in retail knows, you normally accumulate a surfeit of carts with miscellaneous items misplaced throughout the store. This process requires added resources to return all the items back to their proper location. The dirty dish syndrome channels perfectly into the image-perception-reality concept in that when an environment is clean and shoppable, most (not all) customers will do their part to help maintain that store presentation. Most customers will go above and beyond to perform their duties as a good patron while helping to keep the store clean and presentable.

## CREATING POSITIVE CUSTOMER BEHAVIORS IN DEPARTMENTS

The second thing I began to notice with the dirty dish syndrome was that when customers were shopping in departments throughout the store, *an increased percentage of the time*, they would place items back onto the shelf neatly while they were browsing and making their selections. This is similar to the previous topic of miscellaneous items throughout the store decreasing. It was as if the customers were treating the sections like they were sacred and were following the **MODUS OPERANDI** of the store associates. In addition, I started receiving an inordinate amount of employee comments regarding how "respectful" the customers were behaving in their departments. Moreover, customers were displaying improved patience when they were required to wait for service. Again, the energy of a clean and maintained space is positive and inviting to which the customers will respond accordingly.

## INCREASED EMPLOYEE/MANAGER PRIDE

Another ancillary remnant from focusing on the dirty dish syndrome was that most of the employees/managers were exhibiting heightened displays of pride surrounding their areas of responsibility while exuding this gratified behavior throughout the day with their teams. The customers were intuitively sensing the positive vibrations coming from the employees and this carried over into their behavior while interacting with the associates. Whenever I would visit the employees/managers sections for a "walk-through," they were proud of how their departments looked. This newfound sense of ownership would also translate into increased *self-motivation* to ensure their areas were properly represented with clean and shoppable sections. I was thoroughly pleased with the massive improvement in self-motivation (or intrinsic motivation) from the employees/managers which is one of the most powerful forms of motivation because it comes from **WITHIN THE INDIVIDUAL**. We will discuss the power of intrinsic motivation in chapter eighteen – *Organizational Culture, Part Two*.

These two specific principles can have a profound effect on the overall atmosphere of your store, increase your top-line revenue, and foster an environment where all individuals (employees and customers) feel comfortable working/shopping within your store. I want to reiterate the importance of understanding the transformative implications surrounding energy and how it flows throughout a space. Unfortunately, many leaders do not wish to recognize anything that is not tangible due to their trepidations regarding the unknown.

During these experiments, I felt completely alone because most of my peers subscribed to the paradigm that this **ENERGY CONCEPT** thing was just mumbo-jumbo or pseudo new age mysticism. I realized that the only way to bridge the gap between my theories and their skepticism was to conduct these experiments to provide the necessary ammunition to quell their doubts while also confirming my intuitive information. Even after discussing my miraculous results, it was still a 50-50 split between the believers and non-believers. The non-believers stuck to their proverbial guns while proclaiming statements like it was pure luck, you tilted the results

to your favor, or you can't be white glove in a warehouse. However, **PROOF IS IN THE**

**PUDDING!**

# SECTION FOR NOTES

# CHAPTER FOURTEEN: STORE ENVIRONMENT, PART TWO

## STORE PARKING LOT

It still amazes me that, to this day, when I visit a retail establishment, I can *immediately surmise* which stores completely understand the paramount importance of making a first impression with their customers. The parking lot is your very first chance to make a **great impression** on your customers. This will require a passion from your entire store leadership team to make this section of the store (yes, it is still a section of the store, even though it is located outside of the building) a top priority. The distinguished leaders personally visit their parking lots an average of once per hour, or maybe twice per hour on the weekends to guarantee that their first impressions are going to be stellar.

Speak to anyone who has had their vehicle hit by a stray shopping cart; or, even worse, by a lumber/flat cart at a home improvement store. You will immediately understand while experiencing a sense of empathy with their situation. Nothing, and I mean nothing (barring another vehicle hitting their car) will upset one of your customers more than having to track down a manager to have them fill out a customer vehicle accident report. This will take some time out of their day and, depending on the severity of the incident, they will also have to contact their insurance carrier.

I would recommend saving yourself and your management staff the required resources of addressing these customer issues by instilling a sense of urgency with your leadership team about visiting the parking lot at least once per hour, and twice per hour on Friday through Sunday. I created a "manager on duty" checklist that each manager had to carry with them on a clipboard for their M.O.D. shift, which specifically instructed them on their required **PERSONAL VISITATIONS** throughout the store. They were not allowed to be delegated to anyone else (except if they were with a customer and could not break away). Then, they could ask another manager to assist them.

A good percentage of your customers also experience *vehicle damage anxiety* when they visit your parking lot while they are walking to your front door. They notice all the "stray" carts in the parking lot, which can and will initiate the worrying process about their vehicle being damaged (especially on windy days). You **DO NOT WANT** this type of anxiety running through your customer's minds as they enter your establishment. Your first store impression should put the guests into a confident and enthusiastic mood surrounding their shopping excursion, as this will allow your patrons to remain relaxed and worry-free during their visit.

The potential issue for most retailers is that the "staffing" for the parking lot is usually *bare-bones,* which does not compensate for spikes in business. This can create a vacuum where there are no associates monitoring the parking lot. Most lot attendants are working very hard **AND** in very inclement and demanding weather, not to mention the physical demands of the job i.e. pushing carts, loading customer vehicles, and addressing concerns throughout the day. Some companies do not have the resources to adequately staff this section of the store. As a result, there is zero coverage available when the only lot attendant takes their break/lunch.

## OVERFLOWING CART CORRALS

**ALL RETAILERS** must understand the supreme significance surrounding the parking lot which is the *first and last impression* that the customer remembers during their visit to your store. **Recently, I personally visited eight different retailers during my shopping excursions and only one retailer (Costco) had a prominent presence with their cart retrieval.** Overflowing cart corrals are becoming a major epidemic with many retailers, which is creating the opportunity for carts (of all sizes) to potentially damage your customer's vehicles. This minor oversight can create havoc on your managers' time, in addition to your store's profitability i.e. customer vehicle incident reports directly impact your profit and loss statement. I would personally "lead by example" whenever possible, by consistently calling **CART RUNS** throughout the day, or by asking one associate from each department to assist with a quick cart run. Moreover, I would be the first person out there shagging carts.

This strategy was three-fold: firstly, it sent a very powerful message to the entire store that **I perceived** the parking lot as an important area of the store. Secondly, it was instrumental in quickly cleaning up the parking lot from all carts and debris (it is always quick when you have numerous employees/managers all assisting with cart retrieval); and, thirdly, the most impactful message it communicated was that the lot attendants are **AN IMPORTANT PART OF OUR TEAM**. This supportive advocacy from me conveyed to everyone that our lot attendants were not inferior or peons (I always loathed that word to describe anyone). However, some managers still like to use it when speaking about certain levels of hierarchy within their stores.

Another major issue with retail parking lots is the lack of attention to the garbage bins, which are usually overflowing onto the ground. These will create a nasty/negative first impression for your customers. *In the retail setting, there is a "theme" that is permeating the entire space that is about being clean, shoppable, and detail orientated as this is what your customers demand of their shopping experiences.* It is ironic how many retailers completely disregard the message that they are sending to their customers with their parking lots. Whenever we are going to meet someone for the first time (date, job interview, our superiors, etc.), we always strive to make a fantastic first impression by dressing up, getting our hair done, showering, putting on some cologne/perfume, and displaying our best behavior.

If this identical type of focus and attention were given to the parking lots of all retailers, what a magnificent first and last impression you would cement with your customers. Most of this information is perceived intuitively and unconsciously (unless there is a direct incident and then the impression will become front and center) by the customer. Unfortunately, this data is being processed by the customer as a negative or positive experience. I myself have shopped stores where the parking lot was teeming with carts, the trash bins were overflowing, and there was a lot of debris on the ground i.e. broken glass, soda cans/bottles, and cardboard boxes, etc. I felt uncomfortable shopping at that retailer. Moreover, this negative energy **INFLUENCED** my future decision to shop there.

There are numerous books about focusing on the details in life because the little things matter. I would encourage every retailer not to **OVERLOOK** the minute particulars of the parking lot because most of them will ring true, especially within the retail sector. Most retailers are struggling to stay afloat amid a constant threat of competition from online businesses, competitors' aggressive pricing wars, and increased customer expectations surrounding same day/next day delivery. What is getting lost in the mix is that the retail landscape is evolving and morphing into a different environment where the customer is in control and not the **BIG CORPORATIONS**. This _archetypal shift and loss of control_ are _baffling many retail executives with which they are unsure of what to do to address their issues._

I remember when I was a store manager and how many of my peers thought I was insane. They thought I was off my rocker for paying attention to the parking lot while I was told I should be helping customers instead of playing lot attendant. I was a lone wolf, as they say, regarding my passion for creating and maintaining a strong and positive first and last impression with my customers. Customers are showing retailers "tough love" right now, and their message is that they are demanding more from their businesses for their loyal benefaction. The perception is that if a retailer cannot address their own parking lot, then how are they going to effectively focus on my needs?

Another "extremely overlooked" segment of the parking lot is the actual **CONDITION** of the parking lot surfaces. I notice there is an exorbitant number of retail parking lots where there are large potholes, major crevices, and uneven surfaces which all _contribute_ to the overall look and feel of the outside space. Corresponding with the piece about shopping carts causing customer vehicle damage, potholes and uneven surfaces will also cause damage to your customers' property. In turn, this will not endear your customers to endorsing or praising your store/company. Remember, one store is all it takes for a customer to correlate their anger or dissatisfaction with your **ENTIRE COMPANY**.

The retailers that are exposed to the most parking lot issues are the stores that are located in parts of the country that experience the four seasons. The changing temperatures and extreme weather phenomena all influence the ever-changing conditions of your parking lots. Many (not all) managers pay zero attention to their lot conditions *until* there is a customer complaint or an issue that arises. I have always encouraged my leadership teams to anticipate and become proactive with their awareness while performing their due diligence ahead of time to prevent customer complaints i.e. an ounce of prevention is worth a pound of cure.

We have all experienced traveling on deplorable roads with potholes and uneven surfaces with large dips and gradient issues which have sometimes affected our vehicles. Subsequently, these all require unexpected repairs. However, customers do not expect to have these issues happen in a retailer's parking lot. Empathy is a very powerful emotion to provide the necessary "motivation" to ask yourself: *how would I feel if my car were damaged or required repair from shopping at a particular retailer and how would **I FEEL** about returning to that retailer in the future???* A smart and engaged store manager will inspect every inch of their parking lot to guarantee that their customers are going to be delighted with their shopping experience and will not have to endure any *preventable* issues while visiting their establishment.

## EXTERIOR BUILDING SIGNS

The last topic I would like to discuss relating to the parking lot is the long delay from management in repairing the store signs that are supposed to be illuminated at night which represents your brand. This minor oversight is creating a perception in your customers' mind that your store is **NOT** persnickety in nature. Harkening back to the feng-shui concept we spoke about earlier; every detail of your store is being unconsciously perceived and evaluated by your customers. This image-perception-reality phenomenon can and will affect the feeling of your building, which ultimately will determine how often your customers will visit your store.

Remember, energy can be positive, serene, and accepting. Or, it can be negative, chaotic, and repelling. All it takes are a few subtle lapses to slowly erode all of the hard work your team is achieving in other aspects of your store. *We are living in the digital age and consumers have an overabundance of shopping options that are available.* We need leaders who are going to notice and respond to any potential energy vampires (which drain the positive energy from your store) that exist (outside but are nonetheless still a part of the building).

## VESTIBULES AND FRONT ENTRANCES

We have already clarified that *all customers* are constantly evaluating and observing your store environment. When your parking lot and your vestibules/front entrances are clean and inviting, you are putting your best foot forward with creating a pleasant shopping experience from the start. I always considered the vestibule/front entrance as **AN EXTENSION OF THE PARKING LOT** because it is a continuation of the first impression area which is also the space that can "immediately" wreak havoc on the feng-shui of your store. Some of the major infractions are:

1.  Too many shopping carts blocking the entrance.

2.  Inadequate amount of shopping carts.

3.  Customer returns or customer pick-up items blocking the entrance.

4.  Unsafe conditions e.g., leaning merchandise, slip, trip, and fall hazards, or liquids/rain/snow on the floor.

5.  Excessive stack-outs of product that are narrowing the opening to your store.

### TOO MANY SHOPPING CARTS BLOCKING THE ENTRANCE

If you really want to create an undesirable first impression with your customers, block your store entrance with leftover customer shopping carts. The store entrance is the mouth of your store. Imagine what happens if they cannot even enter your store unencumbered by an overflow of shopping carts? Some retailers will address this situation by being "proactive & smart," staffing this area with a greeter/shopping cart person to ensure that all carts are returned to their designated area, thus, safeguarding that the entrance always remains unobstructed.

Many retailers will consider this preventative planning to be a huge waste of employee resources and will not implement anything remotely effective. The savvy and clever organizations will become masters at preventing these seemingly innocuous issues while committing the necessary payroll for the greater good of their company. *The key to being able to implement and support the staffing needed to address concerns throughout your stores is to guarantee that all employees are prepared to wear different hats of responsibility and can be cross-trained in multiple areas.* Remember, each associate's responsibility does not have to be a **PERMANENT** position within the store. Moreover, the lot attendant position does need to be staffed accordingly through aggressive cross-training and proper planning.

## NOT ENOUGH SHOPPING CARTS

Another widespread occurrence (especially during peak times and on weekends) is the lack of available shopping carts/flatbed carts for your customers. The average ticket increases exponentially when a customer has a shopping cart versus when they have a basket or no cart at all. If you want your customers to shop longer while spending more money within your stores, you must become vigilant about maintaining your shopping cart area. Commit the necessary resources to guarantee your incoming customers always have access to available carts (buggies, large carts, and carts for children) for their shopping excursion. I trained all my employees and leadership team to always ask two questions when approaching customers: *What can I help you find today?* and *Can I get you a shopping cart?* (if they did not have a cart already).

These two questions were well-received by most customers. In addition, after ascertaining what the customer was searching for, 75% of our customers would say yes to our employee retrieving a shopping cart/basket for them. Many stores have "multiple" entrances with some customers entering through the alternative store entrances. Usually, these alternative entrances **DO NOT** have a surplus of shopping carts on hand. Henceforth, they forget to grab a shopping cart and will usually need a cart during their visit. However, some customers are impatient and become frustrated when they are unable to locate a shopping cart nearby and will demonstrably

leave the store because of this issue. In performing exit interviews with customers, I discovered

that some are on a strict schedule which does not afford them the time to look for a shopping

cart. In addition, many customers did not want to walk back to the front of the store to retrieve

one, especially, in large big-box stores that range from 100,000 sq. ft. up to 200,000 sq. ft.

Another preemptive strategy I encouraged was to strategically place shopping carts and

baskets throughout the store in areas that were predominantly merchandised with large, bulky,

and heavy items to aggressively anticipate the customers' requirements. An added anticipatory

tactic I asked all employees to execute was when any associate/leader noticed a customer with

many products in their hands they were required to say: *Let me get you a shopping cart; I will be*

*right back.* Most customers would not disagree with the associate's statement while being

extremely grateful and appreciative for the employee noticing and responding to their plight.

### CUSTOMER RETURNS/PICK UP ITEMS BLOCKING THE ENTRANCE

The main entrances to your store are to be kept 100% unblocked while accommodating easy

access to your building at all times. Far too often, retailers are allowing their front entrances to

be congested with customer returns or are creating a customer "staging area" for pick-up items.

The **KEY CONCEPT** here is to become passionate about ensuring that the first impressions you

are projecting to your customers are positive in nature. These should be top of mind with your

leadership team and this identical enthusiasm must transfer to your entire team. All employees and managers must be in perfect alignment with the understanding that it is *never, ever,*

*acceptable to block the main entrance to your store.*

This synergistic mentality is achieved by creating an obsessive behavior surrounding your

store standards about never blocking the main entrance. Also, installing a system/protocol that

will alleviate any large/bulky return items from the front entrance is important i.e. having the

returns cashier call the relevant departments "immediately" for retrieval. As for customer pick-

up items, your store should already have a designated staging area that does not impede the main

entrance. Consequently, your leadership team should be following up with their M.O.D.

(manager on duty) shifts by patrolling these areas and executing the mandatory store standards.

Let's visualize a viable hypothetical customer situation:

1. The customer enters your parking lot and their car hits a large pothole.

2. The customer parks their car and, as they are walking to the front door, they notice a

   shopping cart hit their car.

3. Next, they slip on some trash overflowing from the receptacle.

4. Now they are being blocked from entering the store because of large items in their way.

5. Finally, after navigating an obstacle course, they enter your store and cannot locate a cart.

Please reread this scenario and now picture that **YOU ARE THIS CUSTOMER!!!** How

would you feel? What is your mood like? After all of that, would you be excited to spend your

hard-earned dollars at this retailer? I know this "hypothetical situation seems far-fetched;"

however, I have had to speak to customers (shortly after assuming responsibility for another store) that have had **ALL FIVE OFF THESE OCCURRENCES** happen to them. These customers are usually flummoxed by the ineptitude of the store leadership team for their sluggishness to react and address these specific issues.

This situation is a real-life scenario for some of your customers (maybe not all five occurrences at the same time, but at least a few). Many retailers are already struggling to capture market share and increase top-line revenue. Consequently, you do not have the resources or manpower necessary to consistently readdress these mundane yet critical components of your business. I have already used the phrase that "A fish stinks from the head down" and this saying has never been more important than in the retail sector today. The store manager is the driving force behind how the store will operate, what the associates will focus on, and how they will behave. **REMEMBER, THAT EVERY DETAIL MATTERS!**

## UNSAFE CONDITIONS AT THE ENTRANCE

For the retail stores that experience winter conditions, snow and ice create additional challenges for stores other than just rain. This cacophony of meteorological phenomena can create very unsafe and hazardous conditions for guests at your front entrance. During the winter months, retailers must become *hyper-vigilant* with their housekeeping standards surrounding the front sidewalk and front entrance. These two places are the most heavily traveled areas, and if your store is not neurotic about customer safety, then you will likely experience an increase in customer slips and falls. These incidents will directly **IMPACT YOUR P&L STATEMENT** concurrent with producing a negative customer perception about your establishment.

Big-box retailers are much better at anticipating and reacting to the weather conditions than the smaller box/independent stores. Smaller stores struggle with labor allocation and available resources. Big-box stores usually have large floor rugs with multiple blowers to dry the rugs out from the wetness and slush the customers are bringing inside. Wet floor signs are prominently displayed as they are salting and re-salting their walkways throughout the day. I have observed that some of the smaller stores are not able to adjust as quickly and can find themselves ill-prepared for serious weather conditions.

Another retail oversight that I witness in the front entrance is unsafe and dangerous product that is creating a slip, trip, or fall environment for their customers. I have observed leaning merchandise that has not been maintained. If a customer were to "graze" with their body/cart, then the product could fall onto them and create an injury. I have seen pallets of product that have been heavily shopped which are now intruding into the walkway of customers and will affect/injure customers who are not paying attention. In addition, stores must be constantly aware of how their merchandise is laid out and stacked in the front entrances/vestibules to anticipate children interacting in that area.

## EXCESSIVE STACK OUTS OF PRODUCT NARROWING THE ENTRANCE

Every retail store has a couple of merchandise "nonconformists" who attempt *to push the envelope* with aggressively stationing excessive products in the front entrance/vestibule area. There is a fine line between capitalizing on seasonal timing versus creating a discombobulated mixture of products that could become unsafe and dangerous after being heavily shopped. Most retailers have planograms for their seasonal merchandising within these areas. Despite this, some individuals can get greedy by circumventing the suggested planograms with their own master plan to increase revenue.

To combat this type of renegade behavior, I would paint yellow lines on the floor, specifically designating the boundaries for merchandise stack outs. This strategy was super effective for most individuals to comprehend but there are always a few stragglers that will slip through the cracks in the name of **DRIVING ADDITIONAL SALES**. I would personally speak to these employees/leaders to reiterate the importance of abiding by the approved vestibule/entrance protocols. I would explain to them that I have seen children climbing (before I could respond) on uneven stack-outs that were injured because they were playing. I would instill in these individuals the following cliché to cement their understanding: **the best kind of injury is the injury that never happens.**

*The key to maintaining safe front entrances is a dedicated and committed leadership/employee presence to put "eyeballs" on these areas around the clock with the understanding that these specific areas (parking lot and front entrance) are to be visited and maintained at all times.* I realized early on in my leadership career that the parking lot/front entrance was the "Achilles Heel" for most stores that I worked for. Moreover, I also noticed that many of the leadership teams **DID NOT FEEL** this area warranted any additional attention. These areas are probably your store's most important zones because they are "setting the tone" for your customer's shopping experience, which can either be positive or negative - depending

on your store leadership team's concentration.

# **SECTION FOR NOTES**

# CHAPTER FIFTEEN: DIFFERENTIATION, PART ONE

## PROPRIETARY BRANDS

In this chapter, we are going to discuss the power of differentiation which is the **SEVENTH PILLAR** within the manual. Its message simply put is "what separates your organization" from your competition??? One of the most effective differentiators is through the usage of proprietary brands within your company's product assortment. Proprietary brands are privately-owned and controlled SKUs that are **EXCLUSIVE** to a retailer's portfolio of products, which are only able to be purchased at their organization. There are *numerous advantages* to a retailer increasing its penetration of proprietary SKUs to supplement their existing SKU allocation product mix. With proprietary brands, **THE RETAILER** is in control of the pricing/cost structure, quality of product, adaptability, exclusivity, and brand loyalty.

## PRICING/COST STRUCTURE

When an organization decides to design and execute their own line of products to establish their niche within the retail sector, the first advantage is their massive control over the pricing and cost structure they are going to pursue. During the economic challenges of the "great recession" from 2008-2011, the average consumer's perceptions and attitudes toward private label brands changed dramatically. Customers **STARTED TO QUESTION** their *blind loyalty* to large consumer brands while starting to become much more receptive to store private label brands. Today, many consumers believe that private label brands and national brands are essentially made of the same ingredients/materials and that they are generally paying more for advertising and packaging outlays.

Consumers are now more discerning about the brands they purchase. Most proprietary brands are equivalent to the same quality of the national brands with, some products "exceeding" the quality and value at a discounted price. With private labels, the retailer has the ability to control pricing and implement its own cost structure, which, in reality, is generally 25-30% cheaper than the identical national brand product. U.S. store private label brand sales continue to increase exponentially despite improving economic conditions. "During the first half of the year (2017), Amazon's private labels accounted for just **two percent** of total units sold, excluding marketplace and subscriptions, but the retailer boosted that figure to **12 percent** during Prime Day" (Perez, 2017). As of May 20, 2020, **Amazon now offers 22,617 products from 111 of its own brands, more than triple the number of items it offered in June 2018.** (Digitalcommerce360, 2020).

## PRODUCT QUALITY

Another advantage of producing proprietary brands is the strong ability to monitor and oversee superior product quality development in "near real-time." With national brands, you are at the mercy of the vendor; plus, you do not possess the same network of accountability as within your circle of influence. With private label products, you are in **COMPLETE CONTROL** over all the ingredients/materials that make up your SKUs while maintaining strict adherence and guidelines for the quality of your merchandise. Private label products are sometimes perceived to be of lesser quality than those of established brand-name retailers. This consumer "perception" is easily overcome with employee product knowledge, proper communication of materials used in private label products, usage of products by consumers, and customer reviews.

Through customer trial and error, private label brands are succeeding while capturing additional market share through understanding consumer purchasing attitudes and behaviors. With customer friendly return policies and aggressive pecuniary savings, many consumers are starting to realize that the proprietary brands are just as good -if not better - than comparable national brands. They are receiving a quality product for a lower price; thus, creating a proverbial win-win for the customer.

## ABILITY TO ADAPT AND BE NIMBLE

Adaptability is an asset of private label products. It provides the retailer with the speed and nimbleness required to "thrust" a new product or line of products into their existing SKU allocation assortment quickly. With increased retailer and manufacturer collaboration, retailers are becoming *proactive* in assortment analytics with their private label products, thus, creating an environment of expedited turn around (from inception to shelf) while avoiding unproductive lag time throughout the process. Depending on your specific retail niche, some retailers manufacture and produce their own private label SKUs while others choose a third-party manufacturer alliance to outsource their products.

Proprietary brands also circumvent obfuscation when dealing with national brands. This, in turn, nurtures a "direct pipeline" with your suppliers and manufacturers that will allow the retailer to retain majority control over the entire process with little interference from outside sources. Proprietary brands can put substantial pressure (speed and sprightly action) on the manufacturers of branded goods and who have to compete against their own customers (the retailers) for market share.

## EXCLUSIVITY OF PRODUCTS

A highly attractive reality of proprietary brands is the allure of product exclusivity which will entice customers to purchase their products. This creates an environment with the understanding that, when consumers enjoy your private label brands, they will only be able to purchase them at your stores/company. Private label branding is a shrewd way to separate yourself from your competition by generating consumer demand for your private label SKUs. Consequently, you will increase overall market share within your retail niche i.e. the more consumers procuring your private-label SKUs, then the further they will shift their purchasing dollars to your company.

*Many companies are dramatically expanding their proprietary/exclusive brands:*

1. **Home Depot**: Hampton Bay; Husky (lifetime warranty on tools); Behr (consumer reports top-rated); Ryobi; Rigid; Workforce; Glacier Bay; Thomasville Cabinets; G.E. (water heaters); Homelite; and HDX.

2. **Lowes**: Kobalt; Allen+Roth; Blue Hawk; Style Selections; Project Source; and Harbor Breeze.

3. **Walmart**: Sam's Choice; Great Value; Equate; Mainstays; Ol' Roy; and Special Kitty.

4. **<u>Target:</u>** A New Day; Goodfellow & Co.; Project 62; Joy Lab; Cloud Island; Up & Up; and Cat & Jack.

5. **<u>PetSmart:</u>** Great Choice; Authority; Top Paw; Top Shoppe; and Whisker City.

## BRAND LOYALTY

With proprietary brands, each retailer can establish their own *unique brand*. Thus, it creates a niche market for the customer. In essence, you are capturing market share and generating increased consumer demand for your private label products while simultaneously dictating the evolution of your assortment selections. Consumers can become fiercely loyal to their retail brands. Once they **REALIZE** that your proprietary brands are equal to or superior to their previous national brands, their retail dollars will flow to your registers. Another distinct and impactful advantage is your ability to thwart the byzantine process with national brands while supplementing the private label environment with SKUs that: provide a better/lifetime warranty, lower price points, increased product features/benefits, and sterling product performance.

Retailers are then able to retain "more control" over their product assortment and are no longer at the mercy of the national brands that sometimes contain rigid "dictums" on rules of engagement with their products. Customers are becoming extremely smart and savvy with their hard-earned dollars. In fact, they are willing to share them with retailers that are providing alternative products that are exceptionally crafted and deliver increased value.

**ENVIRONMENTAL ACTIONS**

Another potent differentiator for retailers is their commitment to the environment and the acknowledgment of their impact on mother earth. The millennial population (among others) are seriously disquieted about the surplus of retailers who are oblivious regarding their influence on the planet. Many retailers are grappling with consumer concerns regarding their lack of sustainability, Eco-friendly patterns, and their overall careless actions. Many retailers are seriously affecting the environment with some choosing (the minority) to address these issues. Consumers are now gravitating towards sustainable, green, and organic products and are now demanding that their retailers of choice implement these procedures. They are rewarding the stores and manufacturers with their wallets who operate by using environmentally friendly methods and green principles.

One of the key indicators of an organization's commitment to sustainable building practices is the Leadership in Energy and Environmental Design (LEED) certification, which is one of the most acceptable green building certification programs (Green Business Certification Inc, GBCI) used worldwide. "It includes a set of rating systems for the design, construction, operation, and maintenance of green buildings, homes, and neighborhoods that aims to help building owners and operators be environmentally responsible and use resources efficiently." (Wikipedia.org, 2020).

The LEED certification program has a four-level rating system: Buildings can qualify for four levels of certification: **Certified:** 40–49 points; **Silver:** 50-59 points; **Gold:** 60-79 points; or

**Platinum:** 80 points and above. The LEED 2009 performance credit system aims to allocate points "based on the potential environmental impacts and human benefits of each credit." (Wikipedia.org, 2020). The LEED Rating Systems make up a *voluntary program* meant to objectively measure how sustainable a building is in several key areas: impact on the location and surrounding environment, energy efficiency, building materials used, and water proficiency.

## RETAIL SUSTAINABILITY PRACTICES

Consumers are demanding that retailers adopt and implement the latest sustainability practices. Henceforth, it is essential to integrate sustainability into all aspects of your retail business: merchandising/supply chain, marketing, environmental impact, and energy consumption/usage. *Retailers should adopt a eudaimonia attitude (a moral philosophy that defines right action which leads to well-being) towards sustainability that will ingratiate their organization with their patrons through positive intentions regarding the environment.* Customers are looking for **environmental transparency** from their retail establishments while they are factoring in this information to be more ethically conscious of their purchasing decisions.

## MERCHANDISING/SUPPLY CHAIN PRACTICES

For the retailers that are fully devoted to becoming an environmentally friendly organization, their commitment starts with ensuring that the products they sell are adhering to the strict Eco-friendly standards that are prevalent within the industry. It all starts with a clear message to your suppliers about the importance of transitioning into a retailer that will be top of mind when it comes to the environment and sustainability best practices. Your suppliers will require a certain time frame to adjust and acclimate to your desired sustainability wishes, which should be given to them with the understanding and expectation of 100% compliance by your drop-dead time frame.

The guidelines should be achievable (and given with adequate notice), which could specify that: all their products will be 100% sustainably sourced, a reduction in greenhouse gas emissions, and zero discharge of hazardous chemicals within your timeline. In addition, all retailers should renegotiate supplier terms and agreements to reflect the expectant changes to their entire supply chain. They should contain provisions "built-in" to establish auditing procedures, meeting sustainability commitments, feedback intervals, and penalties for noncompliance or missed deadlines. Communication, collaboration, and engagement with your supply chain are the key components to a successful long-term relationship that will benefit all parties involved (retailer, customer, supplier, and the environment).

## SUSTAINABLE MARKETING

Sustainable marketing is meeting the needs of consumers, businesses, the environment, and society now and in the future through socially and environmentally responsible marketing actions. It calls for socially and environmentally *accountable actions* that meet the present requirements of consumers and businesses, while also conserving or enhancing the capability of future generations to meet their needs. Environmentally committed retailers must choose between short-lived economic gains or long-term ethical behaviors that will translate into increased market revenue for their stores. This creates a quagmire for retailers who might be

**ONE QUARTER** away from missing earnings and projections. They will have to answer and

respond to their shareholders and wall street (public corporations only) for their financial results.

**However, there is a win-win scenario available through proper karmic actions i.e. what you**

**send out to the universe, you will receive back proportionally in return.**

A strong sustainable marketing concept will encompass both the immediate and the future

needs of its customers, company, and the environment while staying true to the core ethics and

values that define each retailer. I have always admired and respected the retailers who have

chosen to implement sustainable marketing programs **BEFORE** the financial numbers have

started to diminish due to societal pressures. Integrity is about "doing the right thing all the time,

not just when someone is watching." (C.S. Lewis). Sustainable marketing is costlier than in

traditional marketing programs. Contrary to this, sometimes you cannot put a price on morals

and protecting the planet for future generations to enjoy.

## ENVIRONMENTAL IMPACT

With all the sustainability programs, Eco-friendly products, marketing programs, and green

awareness being promoted or implemented, each retailer must guard against "green-washing."

Green-washing is ("a compound word modeled on "whitewash"), or "green sheen." It is a form

of spin in which green PR or green marketing is deceptively used to promote the perception that

an organization's products, aims, or policies are environmentally friendly." (Wikipedia.org,

2020). Your *environmental impact* is the proverbial "putting your money where your mouth is"

axiom and how your company is affecting the environment is the litmus test for your actions.

If your company is giving tongue-in-cheek to environmental remediation efforts, your

customers will most certainly find out (especially in the digital age we live in). They will

probably boycott your stores, as well as start social media campaigns to spread this information

far and wide to expose your disingenuous ways. In general, most retailers are not as heavily

exposed as some other industries; at the same time, some retailers carry a myriad of products

(fertilizers, paints, automotive batteries, etc.) that if not properly stored and disposed of, could

significantly impact the environment.

## ENERGY CONSUMPTION/USAGE

In all retailers, energy consumption/usage is affecting the environment which contributes to

the global warming discussion. Energy is expended for the basic store operations throughout the

day/night. Thus, the biggest offenders are lighting, heating/cooling, refrigeration cases, and

electronic displays. According to the United States Department of Energy (DOE), retail

buildings account for the largest energy costs of any commercial sector in the country (Shah,

n.d.). Utility bills in retail buildings are measured on energy consumption and peak demand;

however, the demand charges are based on the highest rate of electrical use. Electricity tends to

be most expensive during peak hours when the demand for energy is the highest and the electric

grid is bordering on its maximum capacity.

The retailers who are focused on increasing their ability to maximize their green presence while also reducing their carbon footprint through their energy-efficient lighting options, solar energy programs, and smart energy management protocols will surely *capture market share* and establish their brand as an innovative leader within the retail space. Customers are increasingly looking at brands and retailers to adopt more sustainable practices. For the retailers that are hesitating to embrace green practices, they will most certainly find themselves scrambling to recover.

There has been a seismic shift from the digital age consumer versus the customer of bygone eras. The younger generations are starting to fully understand the pivotal negative impact that many retailers are involved in with their capricious behaviors towards our environment. These self-conscious individuals realize that we are at a **CRITICAL MASS** with our environment and it is up to their generation to reverse these pervasive and destructive actions that are affecting future generations to come. Their civic responsibilities have gone into overdrive with their objective being to preserve the planet at all costs. They are speaking with their mouths and their wallets while many retailers are experiencing the brunt of their message.

## BECOMING GOOD STEWARDS OF THE ENVIRONMENT IS CRITICAL

# **<u>SECTION FOR NOTES</u>**

# CHAPTER SIXTEEN: DIFFERENTIATION, PART TWO

## PRICING MENTALITY

The pricing of goods and merchandise quality can become *a major differentiator for a retailer* when it becomes a mantra with a strong commitment from the CEO down to the entry-level associate. It appears that in some retailers, you must sacrifice price for quality. Ultimately, this confounds the consumer. They are seeking both an aggressive and fair price, as well as a product that has superior quality. I know it sounds like every customer "wants their cake and still be able to eat it as well." Yet, there is common ground for each retailer to provide a fair price while offering quality products for their patrons.

Retailers are usually going to struggle with their pricing strategies because they are subjected to pricing wars from competitors and stiff opposition from online players. As a result, this causes market fluctuations among many categories. There are numerous pricing strategies utilized by both big box retailers and smaller independent shops to coexist within their niche: vendor pricing, competitive pricing, psychological pricing, bundle pricing, and anchor pricing. Each retailer has the opportunity to differentiate themselves from others by their dedication and unwavering assurance to pricing their products according to the market.

## VENDOR PRICING

Some retailers utilize the manufacturer-suggested retail price (MSRP) option for a proportion of their assortment mix and this strategy *kind of levels the playing field* when going head to head with the big-box brick and mortar stores. This approach (usually executed by smaller stores) will alleviate pricing wars and help preserve their gross margins while simultaneously protecting their profitability. The major *disadvantage of this strategy* is the dearth of tractability the retailer has to adjust to market conditions. Henceforth, if it has a surplus of inventory and consumer demand is weakening, then this may prevent a reduction in price that would allow for the quick sale of any excess inventory. In addition, it does not afford the retailer the luxury of cementing their differentiation (no distinct advantage) from its competitors.

## COMPETITIVE PRICING

Competitive pricing strategies are ubiquitous among retailers today; the methods range from subtle and diminutive to disingenuous and nefarious to capture market share while increasing top-line revenue. Most customers want to believe that a retailer is being transparent and ethical with their pricing methods. However, there are plenty of examples of retailers employing the bait and switch technique (a dishonest **marketing tactic** in which a retailer advertises a very attractive price on a product that is in short supply and will run out of immediately, which is meant to attract customers).

Is your company known for being the lowest price in town or a price leader among your competition? Each retailer must decide how they are going to approach the competitive pricing conversation and what measures they are going to utilize to attract new customers while preserving their existing loyal consumer base. Having a *strong and consistent price match guarantee policy* will ensure your company is heavily entrenched in safeguarding your customers from overpaying for their purchases by providing them with a safety net just in case they have overpaid.

Part of the competitive pricing strategy is to always evaluate your product quality versus your competition. Sometimes, the consumer is not aware of your superior product quality while being confused by the disparity in pricing that is evident from your competitors. In the home improvement segment, there is a cascade of pricing swings among categories: an interior door is priced at $39 and a similar interior door is priced at $79. However, the $39 door is **HOLLOW**, and the $79 door is **SOLID**. Through persistent employee training, the associate can *accurately explain* to the customer the reason for the price difference.

## PSYCHOLOGICAL PRICING

There are many gradations that a retailer can explore when it comes to psychological pricing stratagems. One of the more popular examples is the **"Weber-Fechner Law of Pricing,"** which states that the noticeable difference between two stimuli is directly proportional to the magnitude of the stimuli. For example, if two different products have their price increased by $1, i.e. a pack of light bulbs went from $2.99 to $3.99 and a pair of pants went from $69 to $70, then most people would accept the pair of pants as acceptable. This is due to the fact that they are already anticipating spending $69; henceforth, one more dollar is not that much. However, the same group of people will have an issue with spending **THE SAME DOLLAR** for the pack of light bulbs!

In this scenario, the customer is experiencing **LOSS AVERSION** which "refers to people's tendency to prefer avoiding losses to acquire equivalent gains. It's better to not **lose** $5 than to find $5." (en.wikipedia.org, 2020). The $1 increase on the pack of light bulbs has a *psychological financial impact on the consumer,* versus the same $1 increase on the pair of pants; adding a dollar to the price of an <u>inexpensive item</u> will make us feel more pain than adding a dollar to an <u>expensive item</u>. Conversely, removing a dollar from an inexpensive item will give you more immediate pleasure than subtracting the same amount away from the price of an expensive item. The Weber-Fechner Law states that approximately 10 percent is the average point where customers are stimulated to react to the pricing fluctuations.

## BUNDLE PRICING TO REDUCE PURCHASE PAIN POINTS

Price bundling is a pricing strategy used in marketing in which the company combines several products or services and then retails the bundle at a single price, rather than charging assorted prices for different products or services. This pricing strategy is very effective in reducing the inventory of slow-moving SKUs while driving top-line revenue throughout many categories. Bundle pricing can have the advantage of increasing sales more than standard a la carte pricing. Examples include bundling all four steps in a fertilizer program, computer-printer-software bundle, and television-DVD player- sound system, etc. Bundling can have an ancillary effect of increasing *demand for new products that were bundled* but are products that did not exist before the price bundled products.

There are disadvantages to price bundling for which each retailer should be aware of. Firstly, there are usually discounts taken to entice customer transactions that can cause an erosion of gross margin, which will impact profitability levels in these specific segments. Secondly, there is the possibility of customers abandoning their previous loyalty to other brands within your portfolio; thus, it results in the cannibalization of your popular brands. Finally, how your organization handles the customer returns of a single item or multiple items within the bundle. All three of these disadvantages must be taken into consideration while you are executing the bundling pricing strategy within your stores.

## ANCHOR PRICING

Anchor pricing is another strategy to utilize when attempting to highlight your value proposition and competitiveness of your products within your niche. Anchor pricing is a shared cognitive bias that uses an **ANCHOR** (usually a higher-priced item) to set the parameters for your perception of the product's price. Furthermore, it includes the customer's tendency to heavily rely on the first piece of information presented when making purchasing decisions. A product is truly never *inexpensive or expensive* as everything is considered relative. People love to compare when valuing products and having an anchor price affords them the opportunity to do just that.

Let's look at a couple of anchor pricing examples. You have a grill with all the "bells and whistles" for $1000. You also have a similar grill with fewer features for $500. The average customer will make their decision to purchase the $500 grill using the anchor-priced grill

($1000) as their beacon. Thus, it makes the $500 grill look like a bargain in comparison. Conversely, the opposite side of the coin is to offer a lower priced item ($300 television) with bare-boned amenities. Then, offer a ($375 television) loaded with additional features. Henceforth, you have created a value proposition for the customer, i.e. for only $75 more, I can purchase a television chock full of amenities.

Anchor pricing also assists in alleviating "paralysis by analysis" in the decision-making process for many customers as individuals are naturally indecisive by nature. Another piece of advice to understand about anchor pricing is to be sure to create a compelling narrative surrounding your good-better-best pricing strategies. If your goal is to increase sales of the "better" product within the good-better-best scenario, it is imperative to explain the perceived value to your customers, i.e. the lawnmower is not too expensive or not too cheap. However, it is just right for the benefits and features listed. This is also known as the "Goldilocks Principle." Just like the fairy tale, the porridge was not to hot and not too cold; it was **JUST RIGHT**.

## DO YOU STAND BEHIND YOUR PRODUCTS?

Another gigantic issue that is contributing to the "Retail Apocalypse" is retailers who are tightening their return policies while creating stricter rules for their customers to legitimately exchange or refund their items. Compounding this crisis are managers who have become the *right fighters in the organization* and whose mission is to **PROTECT THE COMPANY** from any and all returns. There is a direct correlation between retailers who have ultra-strict return guidelines with the retailers who are subsequently experiencing diminishing total company revenue. We discussed return policies in chapter five *(Revenue Deterrents),* and I felt it was imperative to revisit this prevalent concern among many major retailers.

*What is severely missing from the retail return processes is the human element.* Empathy is supposed to be implemented when there is a legitimate return issue i.e. a manager is called to the returns desk to assist a customer and instead, regurgitates the **EXACT SAME VERBIAGE** as the returns associate. The frustration for the customer is twofold; they must patiently wait for the manager to arrive. Then, *they are enumerated the retailer's return policy with no regard for them as a customer and or the extenuating circumstances involved.* Customers in today's economy have a superfluity of retailers from which to choose; it is the same retailers who have strict returns policies that are slashing jobs and closing stores that cannot seem to figure out what is going on.

Consumers want to allocate their dollars to organizations that will stand behind their products which allow them a reasonable time frame to return/exchange their items without being questioned like they are a criminal. I completely understand that retail fraud has dramatically increased from decades ago. However, the customer's perception (remember only 2% of customers are acting fraudulently with 98% acting honestly) is that they are being unfairly subjected to harsh return policies that are unwarranted. I know that wardrobing (the practice of buying, using/wearing, and then returning a product) is usually executed on clothing or electronics for a refund. While it is a widespread practice, without some wiggle room for your honest customers, you could be alienating your customers and they *will* take their business elsewhere.

Retailers need to establish a fair and flexible return policy that will allow your leaders to have some autonomy and malleability to satisfy your customers during the return process. Remember, not everyone is attempting to deceive you. The numbers suggest that (again, only 2%) of your customers are engaging in the practice of attempting to defraud you. Most customers will be understanding of a 60-90-day return policy on non-electronics/seasonal items and will be okay with certain specific guidelines (provided they are explained during their shopping experience). On the other hand, it is the unforgiving, intractable, and unsubstantiated policies that will infuriate them.

Some retailers offer a "lifetime warranty" on their products: Home Depot offers a lifetime warranty on their Husky tools; Lowes offers a lifetime warranty on their Kobalt tools and Shinola offers a lifetime warranty on their watches. Unfortunately, most of the organizations that offer a lifetime warranty on their products do not have a large footprint of retail locations and their revenue is generated predominantly through their E-commerce platform. People will pay a "premium" for products that offer a lifetime warranty. Primarily, because of the dependability factor (if anything happens to the product or it becomes damaged, it will be repaired or replaced free of charge) and the peace of mind that follows with that product guarantee.

## EXEMPLARY CUSTOMER SERVICE

The "Gold Standard" for any great retailer is its ability to execute exemplary customer standards daily which are consistent with their guidelines. During the 80s and 90s, there was an overabundance of retailers *who lead by example with their service levels.* They exemplified this core attitude by their daily interactions with their guests. Somewhere in the mid-2000s, this service mantra began to fade into the background in favor of self-checkouts, automated kiosks, increased visual electronic communications, and self-service stations. Many retailers bought in "hook-line-and-sinker" to this new age of servicing their guests by **NOT BOTHERING THEM** during their shopping excursion unless they absolutely had no choice, otherwise.

Many executive leadership teams became fascinated and enamored with the new shiny toys they were given while slowly beginning to succumb to the "less is more paradigm" and began to lose focus on the core values of customer service. The **NUMBER ONE COMPLAINT** I hear from customers is that they cannot find an associate to assist them. Many retailers do not even have brochures anymore, as they want their customers to go online and review their videos and specifications (again, losing the opportunity to engage with an associate). *We have already covered the huge advantages of increased revenue through assisted customers versus the disadvantages of lost revenue from unassisted customers in chapter eight (Revenue Generation, Part Two).*

Exemplary customer service means walking the customer to their destination and assisting them with their queries or handing them off to another associate. In addition, greeting each customer with an "open-ended question" e.g., *What can I help you find today? What brought you in today? How may I assist you?* or, *What project are you working on?* Each associate/manager must seek to understand the customers' needs while providing sufficient information to satisfy the customer. They must always maintain the attitude of **THERE IS ALWAYS A WAY.** Service is about attitude and commitment while doing whatever it takes to delight the customer through a myriad of resources within your arsenal: call another store for an out-of-stock item, offer free delivery, markdown a more expensive item and always thank them for their business.

Business, as in life, is a cyclical process and most retailers are chasing the online/E-commerce/self-service frontier. **While this emerging section is important, more customers are going to crave human interaction the more technology increases.** Customers are demanding the return of good ole fashioned associates to engage with during their visits. If retailers are not careful, then they will wind up alienating their core customer base in favor of the latest technological advances. *There must be a healthy balance between the relationship with technology and engagement with your patrons.* This crucial dynamic is approaching a "seminal tipping point" which is one of the major reasons retailers are struggling.

I understand that everyone wants to use the **AMAZON EFFECT** as their crutch. Despite this, retailers must get back to basics and start taking care of their customers. In chapter nine *(The Power of Engagement, Part One),* I spoke about the Manage by Wandering Around (M.B.W.A.) approach; if the executives and store team leaders are listening to their customers, then they will hear a *resounding call for additional* associates to assist them with their questions and concerns. Amazon is fulfilling some major requirements for people shopping for merchandise with their huge assortment product mix, their prime membership with two-day next-day or same-day-delivery, customer-friendly return policies, and their aggressive pricing.

The retailers who are intimately connected with their business understand that they can *mostly replicate* the similar things that Amazon is doing well. They must invest in their infrastructure, logistics, fulfillment, employees, and the most important piece – they must stop being in denial about the competitiveness of Amazon, or the fact that they are being labeled as an **AMAZON PROOF** segment of retail. A bully only responds to strength. You must fight fire with fire in order to remain competitive with Amazon. Most retailers possess *Amazon's kryptonite,* the ability to have face-to-face interactions with their guests, and establish that <u>emotional bond</u> we already spoke of in chapter five *(Revenue Deterrents)*. This, overall, is a massive advantage over a digitally native company.

There may come a day in our not too distant future where employee interaction is not warranted with your guests. Yet, that day is not today. "Best-in-Class" retailers are going to have to approach Amazon from all angles and plan their attack accordingly in order to remain viable in the digital era. It continues to bewilder me that so many retailers have basically abandoned their customer service commitments within their stores. I continue to hear that retailers are doubling down on their service levels. However, it sounds like tongue-in-cheek because according to the customers, it is not manifesting in their stores. It appears that many retailers are gravitating towards the latest and greatest technological advances at the expense of alienating their customers.

I would encourage more retailers to move away from an **INSULATED MANAGEMENT CULTURE** (where the only messages are coming from the top and are being regurgitated among all the other managers with no new or innovative ideas being expressed). This is because of leaders and employees fear of committing career suicide or being exiled. I would recommend starting to pursue and acquire leaders from different industries who possess valuable insights (which is what retailers need right now more than ever), instead of the tried and true method of **ONLY** recruiting leaders from the same industry.

The technology companies are famous for their talent acquisition strategies. They are fanatical about finding top-tier talent outside their specific industry. Throughout my retail career, I sought out people from all different walks of life. Many of these individuals possessed *diverse backgrounds* because I knew I would be able to teach them the product knowledge required. **I had fantastic success with military personnel, farmers, firefighters, and stay at home parents**. However, many times individuals from the same industry I would have a laborious time instructing them on work ethic, attitude, approachability, people skills, and overall persona. I notice many retailers like to stay within their comfort zone when bringing on new leaders, while they are severely underestimating the talent and different perspectives other sectors have to offer their company. Sir Richard Branson states: "It's all about finding and hiring people smarter than you, giving them good work, trusting them, and then getting out of their way."

The brightest and most "innovative leaders" (Steve Jobs, Richard Branson, Mark Cuban, etc.) always looked for top-tier talent in any industry; they were excellent at understanding human behavior. Steve Jobs was quoted as saying: "he would target people he was particularly inspired by, and then relentlessly pursue them." According to Jay Elliot, former Apple Senior Vice President, Job's strategy for hiring A-list players: "**Define the Requirements, But Don't Be Rigid.**" Steve always had a very clear grasp of the need. Yet, at the same time, he was not at all rigid about what qualifications for he was looking. Sometimes his choices surprised me when he saw something in a candidate hardly anyone else would have seen -- something that told him, "This is the right person for the job." (Artisan, n.d.).

Mark Cuban is famous for saying, "Anybody who reduces my stress becomes invaluable to me. I never want to get rid of them." All three men (Branson, Jobs, and Cuban) have an **INNATE ABILITY** to recognize superior talent *in any industry*. They can envision that individual working for their company while adding tangible value immediately with their experience. Exemplary service is achieved first and foremost by hiring and retaining the best talent available and then getting out of their way. I would suggest that the C-Suite teams approach this mentality of acquiring individuals with **TRANSFERABLE SKILL SETS** with a passion, dedication, and commitment while communicating this concept to their hiring managers, human resource managers, and recruitment professionals. Leadership is leadership, integrity is integrity, and character is character wherever you work.

## SECTION FOR NOTES

# CHAPTER SEVENTEEN: ORGANIZATIONAL CULTURE, PART ONE

## FIVE MAIN ANCHORS OF ORGANIZATIONAL CULTURE

Organizational culture is the **EIGHTH PILLAR** within the manual. It is a system of shared assumptions, values, morals, and beliefs, which governs how people behave in organizations. Retail business is truly a human endeavor and having a positive workplace culture makes for cheerful/satisfied employees. The organizational culture of any company is completely understood *by its actions, not its words.* Every person (associate, leader, vendor, or customer) will immediately sense the atmosphere created either positively or negatively by this credo - by your actions, not your words. *It consists of a symbiotic, synergistic, and invisible, yet tangible thread, that binds all people in the organization together as a family.*

Organizational culture has **five main anchors** in which it expresses itself:

1. The ways the organization operates its business.

2. Core values that are never negotiated or diminished by internal/external pressures.

3. How you treat your customers, employees, leaders, and vendors.

4. The extent to which autonomous behavior is allowed in making decisions, developing innovative ideas, and personal expression.

5. Are employees committed to achieving corporate objectives?

## HOW DO YOU CONDUCT YOUR BUSINESS OPERATIONS?

The **first anchor** within organizational culture is how you operate your business. According to author Jerry Sternin and his book, *The Power of Deviance: How Unlikely Innovators Solve the World's Toughest Problems:* "It's easier to act your way into a new way of thinking than think your way into a new way of acting." (Sternin, n.d.). Your operational mindset will determine the environment which your employees/leaders are working in; this will, in a large part, determine their behaviors. Retailers that have established an organizational culture of empathy, compassion, collaboration, inclusion, and superior ethical standards will usually have an atmosphere that is comprehensive and exudes a "lead by example mentality" that infiltrates every level throughout the entire company.

To fully champion a pervasive, positive culture within your organization, the impetus must start from the very top of the company (the CEO) i.e. "a fish stinks from the head down." This individual must become a beacon of light to empower others within the company to **ALWAYS OPERATE** from a place of honesty, integrity, inclusion, and ethical practices no matter the current circumstances or the projected outcome. Karma is defined as "the spiritual principle of cause and effect where intent and actions of an individual (cause) influence the future of that individual (effect)." (Wikipedia, n.d.) The Law of Attraction states that "like attracts like." This energy can either be used constructively or destructively depending on the predominant thought processes of an organization.

Organizational **KARMA** is how the *intentions of the company* (employees/leaders) generate the results the business can expect to receive. Positive/altruistic intentions usually lead to long-term successes while negative/deceptive intentions can *create* short-term victories. However, short-term victories are not sustainable in the long run. The energy created from these intentions must be returned. Consequently, **what goes around comes around**. One of the best examples of leading by example with organizational culture was Bernie Marcus, the former CO-FOUNDER/CEO of Home Depot. He was a very influential person within the company - not just because he was the CEO, but because he was *emphatic* about always taking care of the customer. He had a saying that created a laser-like focus for all employees to follow: **"IT IS MY MONEY TO SPEND."** Henceforth, he demanded that every employee, regardless of title or rank, lived and breathed the values of the company every day.

The quote of Bernie Marcus' about "his money to spend" was said to alleviate the financial pressures of operating a store/district versus the juxtaposition regarding customer satisfaction. In addition, this quote was emblematic of his true character. It gave the employees and leadership team the guidance and support they needed to remain true to his vision and organizational culture standards. There is a story I wanted to share that completely captures Bernie's philosophy on company culture. Bernie was playing golf with a customer who had gone to The Home Depot to purchase a new faucet since his was leaking. The customer said the employee had diagnosed that the customer needed a new **GASKET**. It only costs $1.50, which he bought instead of buying a $139 faucet. The customer was explaining to Bernie how his company is going to go out of business with this type of employee behavior.

The customer could not believe how Bernie was smiling from ear to ear after hearing about his story. Then, he asked Bernie about his peculiar reaction to losing a $137.50 sale. Bernie explained to the gentleman that what this associate did was **EXACTLY** how he should have treated you. We never want to mislead or deceive our customers about the products they need to purchase. Bernie asked the individual how *he would have felt had he found out after purchasing the $139 faucet that all he needed was a $1.50 gasket???* The customer was aghast when he heard Bernie's response, to which he then realized that he was absolutely correct with his assessment of the associate. Bernie used to say that we want our customers to shop our stores for **LIFE**. We are not in the business of soliciting the quick or unnecessary sale which could easily jeopardize the entire relationship with the customer.

## CORE VALUES NEVER DIMINISHED BY INTERNAL/EXTERNAL PRESSURES

The **second anchor** is that your core values are never altered by anything. Rather, they are set in stone and are meant to remain rigid to weather the tumultuous retail landscape. The actions that are repeated by your executive team (especially the C-Suite team) will permeate throughout your entire organization like a brush fire. Behaviors are the most powerful determinant of real change and to effectuate organizational change the dominant behaviors must be altered and adjusted to reflect the vision of your company. The timeless expression to describe this is **"BE THE CHANGE YOU WISH TO SEE."** Through the principle of the trickle-down effect, your employees and leaders will start to *emulate the behaviors of their senior leadership teams* and this will correspondingly result in favorable actions for most individuals. Transparency, authenticity, and sincerity from the senior leadership team are the *three main actuators* that are required to execute tangible behavioral transformation throughout your organization.

Now that we have addressed the C-Suite executives and their commitment to lead-by-example while they live and breathe the organizational culture they desire, the prominent behaviors (that are selected to alter) of the rest of the organization can be molded through the acronym **Q.A.R.O.T**: Quantifiable, Actionable, Repetitive, Observable, and Tangible. *The catalyst for change is to focus your energies on the most important behaviors (your pillars or values) that you want to change and then allocate the necessary resources to address those specific behaviors assiduously, a.k.a. "the sweet spot."* Many retailers want to solve every problem. They think that you must completely concentrate on every behavior to achieve success. Unfortunately, this stratagem will not be effective if everyone in your company is required to be proficient in every behavioral category.

Employees are very impressionable by the actions of their senior leadership team. They will figure out with lightning speed if your messages about corporate culture are genuine and ethical, or if they are *considered tongue-in-cheek*. Does your retail operation consistently operate with integrity, ethical behavior, honesty, trustworthiness, and compassion? Do your values adjust or fluctuate, depending on your financial situation? Are your convictions to corporate culture tenuous at best when your backs are against a wall? The upper echelon of retailers has aligned their corporate mission and values within the framework of operating their business with the customer, employee, manager, and vendor in mind. These retailers are extremely **CONSISTENT** with embodying their values within every interaction.

### HOW DO YOU TREAT YOUR EMPLOYEES, CUSTOMERS, AND VENDORS?

The **third anchor** is regarding how your organization treats all the individuals working for your company, shopping your stores, and partnering with your stores. In chapter ten *(The Power of Engagement, Part Two),* we spoke about showing empathy for your employees which is a solid foundation to build upon. Moreover, each retailer has intermittent periods of dalliance with the appropriate methods of treating the employees with respect, dignity, and kindness. Then those periods began to fade into the background as the *pendulum swings back to naughty town* as season approaches, a shortage of help is experienced or, there is a change in the leadership team (store, district, division, or C-Suite). Numerous managers revert back to the **OLD WAYS** of mistreating their employees and utilizing their superfluous fear-based tactics to garner results.

Many retailers that I worked for had the mindset of taking care of the customer (rightfully so), which is where most of the resources and energy were allocated. *Conversely, I never understood why the customer was more important than the associates, managers, or vendors that all worked together to provide for the customer.* I would always ask my superiors **WHY** everyone else in the company was considered inferior or unworthy of being treated with respect, decency, empathy, and compassion. I continually received the same answer: the customer pays your salary; and, without them, there would be no careers for any of us.

I completely understood that the customer is the **LIFEBLOOD** of your organization and that they deserve the best service you can provide. However, when did operating a retail business become an example in dealing in absolutes e.g., all or nothing, them or us, lopsided attention, and disproportionately treating one side versus the other. My superiors sometimes became infuriated with me because of my line of questioning which negatively impacted my career advancement. Nevertheless, my platitude was always the same. I always believed in my heart that **EVERYONE** deserves to be treated with homogeneity; there should never be favoritism for one side or the other. My superiors (and not all of them) were an intransigent audience and my message was being misinterpreted as disrespectful, unappreciative, and as a double entendre.

I remained true to my convictions apropos everyone in the organization should be treated equally and with the same respect and kindness regardless of their position, title, or rank. Because of my radical mindset (at the time), my stores were consistently in the upper echelon for revenue metrics, customer satisfaction surveys, and most importantly, extremely high employee satisfaction/morale. My peers and other districts managers would continually seek out my advice on how I was able to unswervingly maintain superior KPI's even through economic headwinds, declining consumer disposable income, and continual organizational changes.

When I explained to them my thought process of treating customers, associates, managers, and vendors with the exact same level of respect, attention, dedication, and empathy, most of them were non-believers. They remarked: *You are doing something else or you are hiding something.* To which I replied: *My intentions generate my karma and when I am treating everyone the same way, I can expect to receive the identical vibration in return from everyone involved.* Thus, I am **CREATING THE ENVIRONMENT I DESIRE**. The message is pretty unassuming in nature and many people *do not believe it* because of the simplicity in its design. I would often hear off-handed remarks (it can't be that simple, he has nicer customers, or he is just lucky) when I was explaining this perspective to my peers. **TREAT EVERYONE YOU MEET/WORK WITH HOW YOU WANT TO BE TREATED.** That is how simple it is!

### AUTONOMOUS BEHAVIOR

The **fourth anchor** is the extent to which autonomous behavior is allowed in making decisions, developing innovative ideas, and allowing personal expression within your organization. Autonomy in the retail sector (at any leadership level) is having the freedom of choice in making your decisions with confidence from your superiors to incur mistakes. Also, without having oppressive energy (spoken or unspoken from a superior) constantly hovering around you in which to critique or condemn your pronouncements. Autonomy in the retail sector is generally considered an "unacceptable practice" because of the deluge of regimented corporate structure/accountability that is placed upon the stores. This outdated temperament severely inhibits the store leader's ability to positively influence their environment and to fully express their creative inspirations.

Every day the headlines are talking about the "Amazon Effect" or the "Retail Apocalypse." It's how the retail sector is doomed, due to the retail sectors' *dearth of nimbleness to react and adjust* to the major online players or changing consumer preferences. Every time I read one of these headlines, I become bemused because the retail operators have the resources and

capabilities to thrive and succeed in the digital world, i.e. they have over 200 years of experience

and practice in dominating the retail landscape. However, because of **confirmation bias**, *a*

*phenomenon where individuals filter everything they experience through the perspective of*

*confirming their beliefs* they do not process the **ACTUAL INFORMATION**, but rather only the

information that is congruent with their views.

This obstinate behavior has had a stranglehold on many executive leaders in the 2000s. If you

study the top technology organizations, you will find a very successful blueprint that is being

implemented. There is no harm in "cherry-picking" from other companies that have an

efficacious operating strategy. One of the most powerful attributes the technology companies

employ is their understanding of the *positive impact autonomy has on their organization.* They

encourage autonomous behavior while rewarding their teams for exemplary results. If you read

their press releases, they openly admit that a lot of their top revolutionary ideas come from teams

of skilled associates who have full autonomy to achieve their goals. I completely understand that

a technology company is different from a retail organization. Nevertheless, the concept of

autonomy is being implemented with enormous success.

In the retail segment, a "dichotomy exists" that permeates the sector with regards to

autonomous behavior. You constantly hear that we give our leaders the freedom to express their

ideas and they have a degree of autonomy to achieve their goals. Yet, whenever these leaders

attempt to exert their autonomous behavior (or allow their associates this freedom), they are met with skepticism, intolerance, and are indirectly told to focus on the business acumen. You cannot speak out of both sides of your mouth, i.e. we encourage autonomy from our leaders and then criticize them for "wasting their time" focusing on pipe dreams or innovative ideas.

A common thread existed as I look back on my most memorable ideas. I was immersed in a comfort zone provided by senior leadership that afforded me the opportunity to attempt new projects. In addition, I received complete autonomy within my allocated resources while I obtained the full support and confidence from my superiors to stumble or make mistakes without retribution. There were some guidelines that we agreed upon such as: weekly progress reports, ensuring that I maintained a reasonable sense of balance towards my store manager obligations and responsibilities, and I didn't violate any company policies or protocols.

With this autonomy, I felt **EMPOWERED AND CONFIDENT** that I could achieve anything. In addition, with this new-found sense of support, my stores achieved new heights. I am extremely proud of:

1. Bringing "Gorilla Glue" to the Midwest Division (piloted the first SKUs at my store which sold extremely well) at The Home Depot.

2. Spearheaded bringing in the "Lodge Lighting Collection" to the Midwest Division at The Home Depot.

3. Helped spread the efficacy of the "Silent Salesman" in every store in which I worked.

4. Reached *watershed moments* with the "No-Limit Starbursts" in every store in which I worked.

5. Achieved a number one ranking (out of 1600 stores) at The Home Depot for new HIL credit accounts two weeks in a row while competing against stores with seven times my annual sales revenue.

6. Achieved a #4 ranking out of 1200 stores at PetSmart for charitable pet donations.

*Throughout my career, I noticed a prevailing trend that occurred every time I presented new or innovative solutions that were successful; I was given full autonomy. I could thrive and succeed in this exciting environment which led to fantastic ideas. As a result, it had a ripple effect on many of the stores within the company.*

I understand that there are certain predominant "impediments" to allowing autonomous behavior to flourish within the retail sector. The **first** major obstacle is a *loss of power and control* that is felt by superior leadership. Unfortunately, this feeling of forfeiture directly affects their EGO. As we know, there are very large egos running rampant in some leadership ranks. The **second** hurdle is *fear,* which manifests in the lower manager "outperforming" the boss and this individual *perceives* that they will look incompetent or ineffective. The **third** hindrance is the ability of the superior leader to *outwardly display confidence* in their subordinates, which is difficult for some leaders since they feel it would diminish their ability to lead.

All three of these reasons stem from an outdated modality of retail leadership that was implemented by managers for over a century (and to preface, not all leaders believe in ruling with an iron fist). There still exists (in some retailers) a mindset that you must be feared and unapproachable to lead others. Moreover, this will give you the raw energy to command your troops (per se); this is similar to other sectors that have an obstinate hierarchical structure which is constructed in stone. Associates and managers alike are demanding that their leaders have faith in them. They also seek leaders who entrust them with autonomy while treating them with respect, kindness, compassion, and empathy. Or, they are going to go elsewhere to obtain these attributes from their leaders.

## EMPLOYEES COMMITTED TO ACHIEVING YOUR CORPORATE OBJECTIVES

The **fifth anchor** is the commitment from your employees in achieving corporate objectives even through tumultuous periods while receiving their full devotion to the organization. This anchor is a *strong indicator* of how pervasive and impactful your organizational culture is being perceived and received by your teams. The retail organizations that have constructed a strong cultural foundation are built upon trust, empathy, inclusion, and caring for their associates. They will receive full support from their teams on a consistent basis in achieving corporate objectives (even some that are considered highly unlikely).

In some retailers, the company culture is "fractured and divided" throughout the organization. There are empathetic leaders who can **OVERCOME** the unpredictable cultural issues that arise throughout the company within certain divisions or districts that are implementing their own agenda and not the corporate agenda. These retail leaders will circumvent the geographical propaganda or misinformation that is diluting the corporate culture. They are highly skilled in the art of focusing their teams on the original corporate message upon which the culture is based.

In every retail organization, there are always plenty of *mavericks or outliers that will stoop to unethical measures to achieve results; and, in the short term, they will achieve their goals.* However, as we discussed earlier in this chapter that what you sow you will reap, i.e. **KARMA IS UNDEFEATED**. What is needed in every retail organization is **GATEKEEPERS** of the corporate culture. This should start with the C-Suite executives and start to filter down through the ranks to the store managers and their associates. Each store manager is *solely responsible* for the efforts and results of their store. They cannot focus on other stores/districts and their culture throughout the company.

Strong organizational culture will establish an environment of ethical consistency that is experienced throughout the **ENTIRE COMPANY**, i.e. each district, regardless of geographical location, will be operating identically to other districts throughout the company. Each retailer desires for their employees to be 100% committed to achieving corporate objectives. Likewise, these objectives must be achieved with integrity, transparency, honesty, and ethical behavior. Otherwise, the objectives just become a means to an end, while creating a slow erosion of the organization culture.

There are a few retailers who have very strong organizational culture within their company which can be felt in every store throughout the chain. These retailers provide a retail spectacle that encompasses their employees/leaders all behaving in unison (just like a beautiful symphony). The employees have a pleasant attitude, a willingness to go above and beyond, display a moral compass in their daily interactions, and have an infectious sense of integrity in everything they do. These retailers are defying the odds by achieving their corporate objectives consistently through a pipeline of committed employees who genuinely care about the organization, due to the fact that the company sincerely cares about them. Per Sir Richard Branson: "Train people well enough so they can leave, treat them well enough so they don't want to."

At this point in the chapter, I know most of you are asking the question, *why did I leave out* the anchor about the methods to incentivize your teams and how to reward your customers? Well, the myriad of ways to reward your employees are expansive and deserves more than one chapter to fully explain.

# SECTION FOR NOTES

# CHAPTER EIGHTEEN: ORGANIZATIONAL CULTURE, PART TWO

## METHODS TO INCENTIVIZE YOUR TEAMS

The **sixth anchor** of organizational culture is the effective methods your company utilizes to incentivize your teams. Dr. Phillip McGraw always says: "people do not do something unless there is a payoff." This sentiment dovetails into the overabundance of methods available to motivate and compensate your employees. According to a Gallup study, "less than a third of employees in America are highly engaged at work, and more than a quarter are highly disengaged." Let that information sink in for a minute… This means that roughly 40-50% of your staff are either slightly engaged or moderately disengaged.

According to the Gallup studies, employees who are engaged equates to, "having an opportunity to do what they do best each day, having someone at work who encourages their development, and believing their opinions count at work." In addition, disengaged employees are more likely to miss work, spend company time unproductively, consume more store resources, and are open to new career opportunities. We spoke about the power of engagement in chapters nine and ten *(The Power of Engagement, Part One and The Power of Engagement, Part Two, respectively)* with one of the most effective ways to ensure your teams are engaged is to provide an environment that rewards productivity. It affords employees opportunities to enhance their career trajectory and embraces employee collaboration. People want to feel like they are working for a retailer that cares about people and will recognize their associates/leaders when they achieve their goals.

## SOCIAL RECOGNITION

All employees regardless of sex, race, color, age, or creed will enjoy being rewarded for their hard work, achieving certain financial metrics, and being part of a successful team that offers incentives for their performers. Social recognition is designed to acknowledge achievements and encourage workers to develop strengths in key skill areas. Offering *sincere praise and validation* when employees show real talent will continue to enhance the organization's success. Most employees crave recognition and admiration from their peers and especially their superiors. Humans have an innate desire to receive recognition (whether they state it or not) while they are motivated from inner rewards of feeling appreciated and recognized.

Social recognition can come in many forms: a sincere **THANK YOU** for a job well done, a letter of congratulations (usually a written notice on a company scripted form), merit badges, soda/candy coupons, preferred parking spot, a shout out on the company "intranet," and employee of the month accolades. Every retailer I worked for had some sort of social recognition programs. However, most of the time, the process was intermittent at best and downright forgotten at worst. *These sparsely used recognition opportunities do not consume many store resources, yet they provide an excellent platform to recognize your employee's hard work, dedication, and store achievements.* They can really make a difference in the employee's confidence and their loyalty to your organization. I have witnessed servant retail leaders who became fanatical about recognizing their associates in the most public store/company forums possible, i.e. praise in public and criticize in private. Furthermore, their teams were **always at or near the top for store morale**.

According to Dan Pink, author of the bestselling book, *Drive: The Surprising Truth About What Motivates Us,* what employees really want is: "Autonomy- the chance to be self-directed and independent at work; Mastery- the chance to be good at what they do, overcoming challenges and finding creative solutions; and Purpose- the chance to feel they are contributing to the greater good-to be driven from within to work toward a larger group goal." The M.A.P. strategy should be included in every associate's job description within any role at every retail establishment to ensure that all your employees have the **OPPORTUNITY** to feel appreciated and are not left out of the social recognition programs available.

We spoke about autonomous behavior in the last chapter *(Organizational Culture, Part One)* and positively contributing to the organizational culture within a retail company. The mastery piece must be instituted within every retailer to counteract the presence of employee stagnation while kick-starting the atmosphere of positive associate engagement. When employees are given the opportunity to learn and or master their craft, they will become much more driven, engaged, and stimulated to do their best work. People are instinctually compelled to continuously learn and grow throughout their retail careers. When given the opportunity, they will excel if the task/s are appropriately challenging, i.e. not too hard or not too easy.

Employee purpose is often an overlooked behavioral component because of the temporal challenges that retailers face. Most retail leaders (who really want to create this type of atmosphere in their stores) are overwhelmed and understaffed to fully provide an environment that fosters and embraces employee purpose. Purpose is what allows the associate to bounce out of bed in the morning to rush to work to make a difference in the outcome of the store/company. *It is an internal motivation barometer that the employee utilizes to measure their happiness and connectedness with their retail organization.*

If the employee feels a sense of purpose at their store, then the individual will be highly motivated, fully engaged, and will experience a higher devotion to something that is bigger than themselves. They will feel connected while being part of a company that is moving the needle in the right direction and is committed to their employee's sense of well-being and overall happiness. Purpose sometimes does not directly show up on the financial numbers because it is a *feeling of empowerment* that the employee is allowed to pursue, e.g., a charitable cause, community involvement, or passion within the store that fulfills their longing for connectivity.

## EXTRINSIC MOTIVATION VERSUS INTRINSIC MOTIVATION

There are basically two types of motivation your employees/leaders will exhibit within your stores: extrinsic or external motivation and intrinsic or internal motivation. **Extrinsic motivation** is defined as when employees/leaders are motivated to perform a certain behavior or engage in a specific endeavor to earn a reward (cash, trophy, or company perk). Or, it may be to avoid negative consequences. **Intrinsic motivation** is defined as engaging in a behavior that is personally rewarding because you enjoy it or find it interesting. There are major differences in the psychological mindsets between these two types of motivation and as humans, we all are programmed to seek out pleasure and avoid pain. Henceforth, if a **majority of your store teams are extrinsically motivated,** then you are going to experience some drastically inconsistent results.

## EXTRINSIC MOTIVATION IN A POSITIVE LIGHT

We do not want to discount the positive effects of extrinsic motivation within the workplace, as there are numerous advantages to this type of behavior. Examples include:

1. Employees working extra hard for an upcoming store visit seeking social recognition for an outstanding store tour.

2. Employees striving to beat their best revenue week to receive a pizza party.

3. Store leaders attempting to have their district take first place in a company-wide contest for bragging rights and district-wide picnic for all stores.

4. Stores implementing a healthy eating challenge, so employees can receive discounted gym memberships.

5. Employees/leaders achieving "stretch goals" to receive bonuses or company prizes.

There are specific times when extrinsic motivation (company-wide or at the store/district level) can become a trebuchet of change that will catapult your store/company to new heights. This can enable your teams to expand their comfort zones while allowing your employees/leaders to realize unprecedented achievements that were previously perceived as unattainable. The strategic paradigm I employed was to think and act like a "chameleon." This meant I would adjust and adapt to my retail environment while implementing and executing the appropriate behavior necessary to achieve our aspirations. An 18-year-old might want to become CEO whereas the 65-year-old values autonomy, scheduling, or balance.

Sometimes, when short-term immediate results were required in sales, credit, or KPI's I would offer certain "enhancers" to facilitate the necessary competitive nature needed for results. I would offer an extra day off with pay for the top associates who received customer complimentary letters (i.e. associate provided exemplary service and the customer wrote in to express their satisfaction). This would *reinvigorate the associates* on the importance of excellent customer service. Again, I want to reiterate that this type of motivation was **ONLY** utilized for short-term results and was **NEVER** used in place of good old fashion resourcefulness, hard work, or proper planning.

Many times, a retail store needs a freshly infused external motivational trigger to stimulate the competitive juices and get the employees "fired up" to achieve some monumental accomplishment. *This achievement can forever improve their confidence levels when approaching similarly perceived unachievable goals.* Success is a mindset and the most successful people have a regimented mindset that they utilize to approach their goals and aspirations. They build upon their previous successful achievements, i.e. my store just surpassed $900,000.00 in sales last week which has never happened before. So, now I am going for a cool $1,000,000.00 in sales this week.

## THE OVERJUSTIFICATION EFFECT

The usage of extrinsic motivational tactics must be limited in scope and repetition to *safeguard against the overjustification effect,* which is when an expected external incentive, such as money or prizes, decreases a person's intrinsic motivation to perform a task. "Researchers have found that when extrinsic rewards (such as money and prizes) are given for actions that people already find intrinsically rewarding, they will become less internally motivated to pursue those activities in the future." (Cherry, n.d.). Retailers must be careful with offering too many external rewards or *going to the well to often* to motivate their associates. Unfortunately, these retailers can suffer from the overjustification effect which can severely damage their employee's naturally instinctive intrinsic motivation.

Another detriment to providing an inordinate number of external motivators for your associates to become fully engaged is the chance that your stores/company might contribute to a *conditioned reflex,* i.e. contiguity (which means that any two ideas will get associated if they occur in the brain at the same time). If this atmosphere continues unsupervised, then it **COULD** start a fecund of behaviors that will perpetuate this unfortunate cycle. I know many retailers that are utilizing these types of external behaviors through incentives (coupons, discounts, and special sales days) to attract customers. At the same time, these retailers could be contributing to conditioning their customers to **ONLY SHOP** when there are incentives.

The overjustification effect can be utilized *excessively* by stores (to motivate the employees) or by the organization (to motivate the customers). The retail sector is at an economic crossroads at this time while most retailers are struggling to maintain market share and keep their heads above water. Moreover, can you blame the retailers for offering discounts and using other competitive strategies to lure customers and increase top-line revenue? There is a razor-thin line that exists between executing properly planned economic tactics to maximize your offerings or becoming the retailer who is precipitously damaging the long-term reputation of your company. By repetitively engaging in these short-term measures, you run the risk of diminishing/tarnishing your corporate brand.

## EXPLORING INTRINSIC MOTIVATION

As we previously explained in this chapter, *intrinsic motivation* is defined as engaging in a behavior because it is personally rewarding, because you enjoy it, or find it interesting. This type of motivation comes from **within the associate and is long-lasting.** In addition, this can propel your associates through boisterous periods your company is going to experience with grace and ease. A retail company with a strong commitment to providing an inclusive and rewarding atmosphere, which is built upon a solid foundation of organizational culture, will always have a loyal employee base. They will weather the storms of uncertainty because they are intrinsically motivated to come to work and excel.

Intrinsic motivation should encapsulate 95% of your employee's motivation. This will allow them to express their creative ideas and feel like they are a part of a team. The **first key driver** in ensuring your store/company is fostering an environment of intrinsic motivation is being able to sincerely align your corporate mission with your own employee's values. Is your company showing compassion for others? Are you caring for the environment? Are you exhibiting honest and ethical behavior in your interactions with others? The **second key driver** is to become enthusiastic about guaranteeing that the environment you provide your associates encompasses the three main motivational factors of autonomy, mastery, and purpose.

All human beings are intrinsically motivated to engage in certain tasks in their lives from which they derive pleasure and that **DO NOT** offer any external rewards, e.g., hobbies (sports, games, or activities), passions (painting, woodworking, or playing the piano) and aptitudes that make them feel alive and purposeful in life. I vividly remember during my retail days that whenever an immediate result was needed or required, most of my superiors would always implement the "carrot or stick" method to achieve certain results. The carrot or stick approach "is a metaphor for the use of a combination of reward and punishment to induce a desired behavior. It is based on the idea that a cart driver might activate a reluctant mule by dangling a carrot in front of it and smacking it on the rear with a stick" (Wikipedia, n.d.).

The carrot or stick approach is a fully executed form of extrinsic motivation intended to solicit an immediate and desirable result. This form of motivation can *create a hostile and competitive environment that will exclude some associates because of the raw energy exhibited and the perceived fear that is sometimes present with this method of motivation.* This type of approach primarily involves a "dealing in absolutes atmosphere" with regards to specified achievements or economic aspirations; consequently, creating a chaotic situation that will instill a feeling of animus in some of your associates. This approach can also obfuscate your store/company values, which could unintentionally equivocate some disingenuous tactics for achieving victory from your associates/leaders.

I rarely implemented the stick approach throughout my retail career. However, I would, in certain circumstances, utilize the carrot method to provide the impetus needed to realize herculean accomplishments. When used judiciously, the carrot method did bolster the confidence or self-esteem of my teams, i.e. achieved a number one ranking out of 1600 stores for HIL credit card accounts at The Home Depot for two consecutive weeks. The *antithesis of healthy confidence is hubris. I want to precaution against utilizing the carrot method too frequently to achieve desired results, even though it is extremely tempting during challenging economic times.*

I want to reiterate the importance of marshaling your motivational methods around intrinsic measures. These convictions must be aligned with your employee's values to ensure that they can tap into their own internal pool of energy to accomplish your organizational objectives. The extrinsic/intrinsic motivational protocols can become a "slippery slope" to navigate when retail leaders are facing tremendous pressure from their superiors to achieve financial metrics. This can challenge the integrity and resiliency of managers to stay committed to their internal convictions.

There were many times when I thought about "going to the well one more time" to achieve a certain outcome. On the other hand, *I realized the message I would be sending to the other leaders within my store.* Moreover, I would not be setting an appropriate example for them to follow. As a retail store manager, you cast a large shadow with **EVERYONE** in the store watching you and how you react to or handle intense situations. Do you say one thing and do another? Are you committed to your convictions until the stuff hits the fan? Do you radically

alter your intentions when faced with seemingly insurmountable circumstances? It is during

challenging situations that your principles are put to the test and the associates are receiving *their*

*guidance* from the store manager's actions. They follow what you do, not what you say. In

chapter nineteen, *(Organizational Culture, Part Three)*, we are going to discuss some creative

methods to reward your associates as well as your customers.

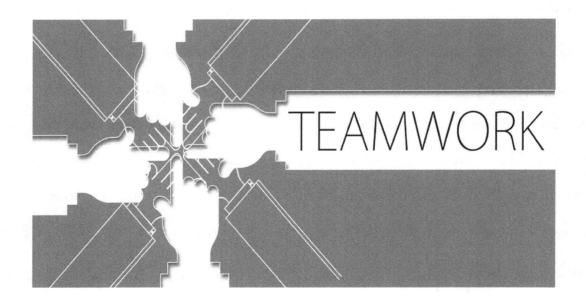

# SECTION FOR NOTES

# CHAPTER NINETEEN: ORGANIZATIONAL CULTURE, PART THREE

## CREATIVE METHODS TO REWARD YOUR EMPLOYEES

I wanted to further elaborate on the creative ways that retail companies (or any company) can utilize to stand apart from their competition in rewarding their associates. I have devoted three chapters to organizational culture because this pillar will determine the success of your organization and how your company will fare when experiencing challenging economic interludes. All ten pillars have their place within this manual. However, your organizational culture is the backbone of your company which creates the environment that will, ultimately, decide your long-term fate within the retail sector. There are numerous examples of stupendously successful retailers who faltered because their organizational culture was radically modified which sealed their vicissitudes of fortune.

## FOUR-DAY WORK WEEKS

One of the most effective and impactful methods I utilized to reward my associates was the implementation of the four-day workweek for some *full-time associates* in my retail stores. This option was a "voluntary" incentive that was offered to high performing associates (employees who received at least a meeting expectations review, but generally an exceeding expectations review, were punctual and reliable, achieved their monthly goals, and were consistently productive). This method was available during certain times of the year and was not considered a "permanent" schedule. Each associate completely understood, through a written document, explaining the process plus the details of the four-day work schedule. They were abundantly

aware that the schedule could be removed with advanced notice if necessary, which fortunately,

was an extremely rare occurrence.

I must address the pragmatic perception I had about the four-day work week when I first

heard about its implementation at another store. Immediately, *I was not a raving fan about this*

*concept in any sense of the imagination because of the perceived pitfalls associated with this*

*idea.* My retail mind began exploring all the conversations I was going to have about myriad of

possibilities and expectations from the associates regarding this program. How were we going to

staff our stores with adequate coverage? How is the program-controlled and monitored? What

are the criteria for being allowed to participate in this program? Are associates going to be

hopping mad when we ask them to come back to the five-day workweek, etc.?

After I gathered my thoughts and composure, I spent some time with the store manager of

another store who had already implemented the four-day workweek. I made sure that I

approached this concept with an open mind, I would seek to understand the benefits of this

program and the exciting, creative way to reward your high performing associates. All my fears

were premature and unfounded as I witnessed the program in action while speaking to many of

the associates participating to gather their observations. There were several highlights I gleaned

from the program which I would execute within my store that ensured a successful transition to

the four-day workweek.

I wanted to add some <u>precursory details</u> that will address some common questions about the program. The stores I implemented the four-day workweek program in had at least a 60% full-time mix and a 40% part-time mix, which afforded me the opportunity to flex up or down my store schedule to accommodate staffing requirements. To effectively execute this program, your retail establishment will need at least a 40% part-time mix to be able to react to your specific customer demands. Fortunately, most of the retail sector generally have at least a 40% part-time mix.

In addition, not every employee wanted to partake in the four-day workweek for various reasons: the scheduling would not work for their families, they did not want to work 10-hour days, or they enjoyed their schedule as it was. I was able to implement this program in numerous retailers without experiencing any staffing issues that negatively impacted customer service levels throughout the store.

The four-day workweek had certain protocols that had to be taken into consideration by the associates:

1. Their schedules were created for customer demand, not for their preferences. They could, however, request certain days off for specific reasons and we would attempt to accommodate accordingly, whenever possible.

2. Since the scheduling was extremely specific to customer demand, reliability and dependability had to remain exemplary.

3. The four-day workweek was a privilege that could be taken away (with advanced notice) for inconsistent performance or behavioral issues.

4. When it was time to revert back to the five-day workweek (with advanced notice), they would be accepting and positive about the change.

5. Each associate participating would read and sign a written notice outlining all the requirements to remain in the program with expectations and consequences.

My stores always received a huge morale boost from the associates who were partaking in the four-day workweek. This strategy fostered a deep sense of *gratitude and appreciation* from the employees for this amazing opportunity. This one available creative measure was a gigantic incentive for the **UNDERPERFORMING** associates to actively address their work performance issues. It became a driving force for tangible change for most of the full-time employees throughout the store.

With the four ten-hour shifts, the scheduling was inclusive of capturing and attaining positive "overlapping" of shifts which *compensated* for minor employee staffing infractions. This included: employee's running late for their shift by a few minutes, coming back from break or lunch a few minutes later, employees helping customers in another department working their way back to their home department, etc. The employees that were on the four-day work schedule were the positive example (for the store team) of what hard work, commitment, dedication, and productivity could allow you to achieve.

*The four-day workweek became a proverbial win-win for my stores as the top-performing associates were being rewarded for all their efforts. Moreover, the lower-performing associates were being motivated to improve their performance, and the balance of energy was being appropriately divided amongst the store team.* I enjoyed the autonomy necessary to be able to offer this option to the high performing associates. Accordingly, the program did not consume any extra pecuniary resources at my stores.

## COOKOUTS, PICNICS, & PIZZA PARTIES

The second creative method to reward your employees is to establish certain KPIs that have not *yet been realized,* which you know would be achievable if your team were to become galvanized and focused. Additionally, this provided a mild form of <u>extrinsic motivation</u> by offering a reward of a cookout, picnic, or pizza party when specific metrics were achieved. This form of **stimulus** does fall into the extrinsic motivational category and I do not recommend pulling this tool out of the toolbox too often. However, there is something about food, family, and friends that can bring people together. And, it can and will propel your teams to new heights.

During the earlier years of my retail career, I did not understand the positive impact of this form of **mild extrinsic motivation.** Our teams wanted to provide the necessary inducement required to achieve our financial numbers through the old fashion methods of planning, execution, ingenuity, and persistence. I was also fearful of *ringing the bell* too often to achieve our metrics, as I did not want to succumb to having to implement external motivational tactics every time we wished to accomplish specific objectives. Moreover, I felt inferior as a leader when I resorted to bribing the associates with food and parties which felt like cheating to me.

After I amassed aggregate of information from my peers, colleagues, and superiors, I realized that IF this form of external motivation was used <u>sparingly and strategically</u>, our store would be able to elicit two positive emotional anchors from the associates. Firstly, they would be *confident* about achieving our goals. Secondly, they would be responding *effusively* for the cookout, picnic, or pizza party. Anytime you can achieve positive emotional responses from your associates while aligning their motivation with corporate objectives, you will have succeeded in providing an inclusive and rewarding environment for your teams.

One final cautionary tincture about using this form of external motivation to achieve certain store objectives is to be extremely careful not to implement this impetus carelessly. This could *inadvertently create the foundation* for the "overjustification effect" to subtly creep in and replace your associate's intrinsic motivation. **Even when I executed this form of motivation judiciously, I was often approached by certain employees/leaders who wanted to receive an external reward <u>anytime</u> we were attempting to wade into unchartered territory.** I would then have to remind these individuals that we are performing our duties as employees for the company and that we **ALREADY RECEIVE** a salary for our efforts.

Overall, I found that when used appropriately, the external motivation of receiving cookouts, picnics, or pizza parties, was generally perceived from the associates as a well-intentioned reward for their hard work and dedication to achieving our store objectives. There is a native attraction for individuals to want to gather and consume food and drinks with their co-workers, peers, and leaders in a friendly atmosphere where they can interact and have a good time. During these prized occasions, I always noticed the intense bonding that took place, in addition to the burgeoning new work relationships that began to materialize. A good time for all!

## FLEX-TIME SCHEDULING

Another method of rewarding your associates is to offer a "flex-time" scheduling option that can be executed online through your intranet/internet portal or company app. A flex-time work schedule is an **alternative** to the traditional 9 to 5, Monday-Friday, 40-hour workweek. It allows employees to vary their arrival and/or departure times. Flexible scheduling is an awesome tool that can increase employee morale while assisting in alleviating work/life balance scheduling issues: e.g., associates caring for their families, day-care and babysitting concerns, ability to attend important family functions, schooling, or second job requirements. *Additionally, this program can provide employee's peace of mind with increased employee autonomy (this specific behavioral strategy keeps popping up because of the major importance it has on associate workplace satisfaction).*

The flex-time scheduling concept is usually implemented in conjunction with the remote work/telecommuting option at most companies because of the numerous organizations that wish to attract and retain top tier talent. Too many retailers are entrenched in the mindset of continuing established "outdated norms" within the retail sector when they should be looking to other industries to *cherry-pick* their most popular incentives for talent retention. Flex-time scheduling can work at all retailers large and small alike, provided that they institute some best practices while providing their employees with specific guidelines for proper execution. As with any new program rollout, it is critical to thoroughly explain in graphic detail, the expectations and nuances of the flex-time scheduling program to every employee:

1. All flex-time schedules are conducted through a bidding process that is based upon performance, availability, and staffing requirements of the store.

2. Certain scheduling slots will be allocated for tenured or knowledgeable associates to accommodate specific events e.g., customer clinics, special events, or unique programs.

3. All employees explicitly understand that their request is a request and is not guaranteed.

4. All employee requests must be approved by their department manager **AND** assistant store manager (store manager for department head requests).

5. Certain times and days will be **BLACKED-OUT** due to increased scheduling requirements: e.g., holidays, seasonal times, and major retail events.

6. Flex-time scheduling is a privilege and is not written in stone. Henceforth, management/company can adjust accordingly.

7. Zero tolerance for employee abuse or coercion/intimidation of other associates to achieve favorable scheduling slots.

The flex-time scheduling option can work cohesively and seamlessly within the retail sector, provided, the necessary guidelines are followed, and the entire store team completely understands the implications of this program. This concept is not readily accepted in the entire retail sector, yet. However, as companies like **Walmart** begin to implement this scheduling option, you will start to glimpse an *innovative model* that will pave the way for additional viewpoints from the human resources department as well as the executive leadership teams.

The retail sector is in desperate need of leaders that are open-minded, innovative, and *eager to embrace* the **NEW RETAIL ETHOS** that is permeating our society. Top-tier employees are in high demand right now and the retail organizations that have the best inclusive culture will attract and retain these individuals. According to the AARP, "61% of those who provide care for a family member older than 50 are also balancing employment, and half of today's workforce expects to provide care for aging family members in the next five years." (Fastcompany, n.d.). Flex-time scheduling is already being successfully implemented in other industries (technology, healthcare, and education) around the country, which is setting the bar extremely high for the retail sector to "join the party" and embrace the future.

## REMOTE WORK OPPORTUNITIES

When the average business individual thinks about careers that offer a remote working environment, the last sector they will conjure up in their mind is the retail sector. With the nature of the retail store and its complexities, dynamics, and extremely hands-on staffing model, telecommuting opportunities would appear conceptual at best or idiotic at worst. The basic idea of remote work is exactly spelled out in the name remote (e.g., faraway, distant, or far off). Moreover, how are the customers going to be serviced or assisted by an employee who is **NOT PRESENT IN THE STORE???**

If anyone would have mentioned the remote work concept to me twenty years ago, I probably would have asked them: *What planet are you living on?* or *Are you out of your mind?* However, there are some opportunities within the retail sector to *abolish this parochial idea.* If approached with the proper perspective, this can work tremendously well while providing a new way to reward your associates/leaders. Gallup estimates that active disengagement costs the U.S. $450 billion to $550 billion per year. In their study on remote work arrangements, they found that **ALL** degrees of remote work options showed higher levels of employee engagement than without remote work options. (Wong, 2020).

Let's discuss some areas of opportunity for the retail sector to take advantage of this expanding trend within the business world. First and foremost, with the technological advancements we have at our disposal (Skype, Zoom. Sqwiggle, or as a virtual assistant) staying connected and productive is easier than ever before. According to Forbes, "It is estimated that employers in the US lose $1.8 trillion a year in productivity. From distractions like water cooler gossip to excessive commuting, health problems, and more. Workers are finding it harder than ever to hit maximum productivity in a traditional office work environment." (Loubier, n.d.). Here is a list of the **distinct advantages** of offering remote work:

1. Increased productivity.

2.  Improved employee health and work/life balance.

3.  Increased employee job satisfaction.

4.  Reduced associate expenses e.g., commuting, fuel, and vehicle maintenance.

5.  Reduced company expenses e.g., the employee's not using electricity, not consuming company resources, and decreased equipment usage resulting in fewer maintenance costs.

6.  Decreased employee absenteeism.

7.  Ability to attract top-level talent.

Here is a list of the **perceived disadvantages** associated with remote work:

1.  Lack of collaboration with colleagues.

2.  Distractions at home or off-site location.

3.  Productivity issues and concerns.

4.  Unable to communicate effectively.

5.  The diminished ability for an individual to be involved with daily activities.

6.  Leaders fear their loss of power, control, and influence over their employees.

At the core of this controversial program is the propensity for many leaders to feel inadequate about their ability to **DIRECTLY** control and influence their teams with some of their employees working remotely. It is becoming a growing concern for many retail leaders to accept this positive, yet productive trend, while attempting to relinquish their steadfast beliefs that this is nothing more than pure *boondoggle* (work or activity that is wasteful or pointless but gives the appearance of having value). Many (but not all) executive leaders in the retail sector frown on associates/leaders who want to work remotely *when they could easily achieve the same workload at home or offsite for specific functions*. This viewpoint is an outdated mentality that is not allowing the retail industry to transcend and become strategically aligned with other industries.

At the corporate level, there are myriad of occasions when remote work could be offered: employee's working on a project, facilitating a meeting or conference call, planning a work assignment, or performing menial tasks that do not require an associate/leader to be "anchored" to a desk. This type of program could easily improve employee morale while simultaneously providing a proverbial win-win for both parties. The employee receives the opportunity to have increased work/life balance and the organization receives increased productivity while minimizing their associate usage expenditures. I have *rarely* heard about an individual who **DID NOT** want to participate in remote work or telecommuting opportunities within their company.

Now, not every associate can work remotely; however, **the main factor is determining which of your employees could work remotely and still be productive.** Newly hired employees might take some time to adjust and acclimate to their new roles. Some of your tenured and most experienced associates might need more time in the office or stores to be hands-on with certain projects or events. Employees who have recently transferred to different roles within the company will probably need a break-in period. *If proper discernment is used in selecting the appropriate employees to partake in remote work while communicating the* *expectations of the program to your teams, you should experience a fluid transition with minimal*

*problems or issues.*

During my retail tenure, I constantly heard my superiors and the corporate teams

**admonishing any individual who mentioned the remote work option for the retail stores.**

Every associate/leader needs to be there for the customers always with an all hands-on deck

mentality. I completely understood that the retail stores are completely different apropos

customer service levels, product fulfillment, product pack-out/pack down, and the daily demands

than other business sectors, e.g., technology, healthcare, or education, etc. However, I remained

confident that the retail stores **COULD** transition some of their associates/leaders to working a

<u>modified remote schedule</u> while still fulfilling their retail store responsibilities throughout the

week.

**I firmly believed in a "hybrid version" of remote work scheduling in the retail stores**

**that would accomplish and achieve all the desired results (financial, operational, and**

**behavioral) while brandishing this concept for others to follow.** There is a plentiful amount of

opportunities to implement a hybrid version of the remote working schedule within the retail

stores:

1. When associates/leaders need to write employee performance appraisals.

2. When associates/leaders need to prepare for a presentation or event.

3. Complete e-learning modules or classes to stay current with industry standards.

4.  When associates/leaders need to establish detailed summaries about their future growth opportunities to succeed or ascend managerial ranks.

5.  Creating schedules (remote working or standard).

6.  Taking conference calls or other business meetings.

When I mention a hybrid version of remote work scheduling, I am referring to a modified schedule e.g., only a couple of hours, ½ day or full day (not an entire week or multiple days in a week, etc.) depending on the nature of the occurrence. The **GIGANTIC ISSUE** that is prevalent with working in the retail stores is the scarcity of complete silence by the plethora of interruptions when an individual is attempting to focus on their objectives. Sometimes, an associate/leader needs complete and utter silence with zero interruptions for a specified period of time to achieve their aspirations. I can remember the *deluge* of interruptions and emergencies that would always arise when I was attempting to write a performance appraisal, coach another associate/leader, or forecast my weekly/monthly budget.

I understand that each new level of leadership encompasses increased challenges and responsibilities; however, all the great innovators and leaders always set aside **QUIET TIME** to just think or tackle their obstacles assiduously. It is darn near impossible to fully concentrate on important store issues, focus on innovative ideas, or prognosticate the future of your store when you are being inundated with constant interruptions that destroy your train of thought. This is where **remote scheduling** would become a *perfect solution* to these paramount concerns that all leaders (department heads up to the C-Suite) have concerning their quite time.

I was never given permission or allowed to execute **ANY** remote working schedules throughout my retail tenure (30 years!). I felt so handcuffed by my retail organizations for not affording me the opportunity to explore this amazing method which would establish a mutually beneficial and rewarding partnership for all parties involved. It is one of the few regrets that I have for working in the retail sector for so long. I did not continue to pursue this method of rewarding my teams. Instead, I succumbed to corporate malaise and peer pressure. *I would highly encourage all retail C-suite leaders to consider a hybrid remote scheduling option for your associates/leaders. Now is the time to embrace innovative ideas while accepting positive change that will reignite your employee's passion for your organization.*

## EMBRACING CHANGE IN THE RETAIL SECTOR

## **SECTION FOR NOTES**

## CHAPTER TWENTY: OMNICHANNEL CAPABILITIES, PART ONE

Omnichannel is the **NINTH PILLAR** in the manual. It is defined as denoting or relating to a type of retail that integrates the different methods of shopping available to consumers (e.g., online, in a physical store, or by phone) with a multi-channel sales approach that provides the customer with an integrated customer experience. *The demand for omnichannel fulfillment has been increasing exponentially especially during the Covid19 pandemic!* It is imperative that retailers consider integrated purchasing options to remain competitive within the retail sector. Customers are **DEMANDING** a fluid, yet seamless omnichannel encounter among all "touchpoints" that provides a more relevant, engaging, and consistent customer experience.

There is a gigantic chasm that exists between the retailers who are "all in" with their commitment to improving their omnichannel capabilities and the retailers who are *acquiescing to this emerging customer requirement.* Customers are starting to realize the power they wield which is becoming evident by the massive number of retail stores shuttering locations at a blistering pace. Omnichannel is **NO LONGER** a mild customer enhancement that will appease some individuals; it is burgeoning into a fully-fledged mandate that will determine the legacy and survival of most retailers. *One of the strongest indicators of a successful retail organization is its innate ability to remain nimble by reacting swiftly to market trends while maintaining an uncanny aptitude of prescience.*

The Amazon Effect is alive and kicking within the retail segment. This very real disruptive company is starting to capture ancillary categories within even the "highly touted" **AMAZON**

**PROOF BULWARK SECTORS** e.g., home improvement, off-price, and dollar stores. Amazon is an extremely poignant example of an organization that provides a holistic integrated omnichannel strategy that is fluid, convenient, and highly adaptable. Their vision is called the "Amazon Way" *which obsesses over customers, not competitors.* The reason I am spending some time speaking on Amazon and their superior omnichannel/E-commerce abilities is to showcase Jeff Bezos' (CEO of Amazon) impressive talent for not allowing an obdurate attitude to creep into his leadership style. This form of leadership style is immediately compatible with embracing transformation while still focusing on the <u>secular</u> aspects of retail. **ACCEPT-EMBRACE-EVOLVE!!!**

## BUY ONLINE; PICK UP IN-STORE

One of the quintessential anchors of a successfully integrated omnichannel platform is the Buy Online and Pickup in Store (B.O.P.I.S.) option that is mutating into a non-negotiable for most consumers today. Within the retail sector, consumers have an overabundance of choices with where to shop, and they won't necessarily separate their experiences from one retail organization to the next. Instead, most shoppers will judge all shopping experiences on an equal playing field. Henceforth, the retailers who provide a "best in class" omnichannel experience will effectively set the standard for the remaining retailers. Consumers are being inundated with *specific purchasing criteria* to receive free shipping or expedited shipping i.e. spend $79 or more or buy at least three items to bypass the shipping fee, etc.

The most successful retailers will offer their customers multiple choices for shipping options that will capture most customer requests. It is completely okay to have certain guidelines built into your shipping offerings. At the same time, <u>it is becoming the gold standard</u> to have a B.O.P.I.S. selection available for **MOST ITEMS**. *If your organization does not yet offer this option, this major oversight can severely damage your brand while simultaneously alienating your loyal customer base.* Right now, there is a small window for retailers to take advantage of with their ability to offer B.O.P.I.S. to their customers before Amazon has established a stronger brick-and-mortar presence (think Whole Foods, Amazon Go, Amazon Go Full Size Grocery Stores, and Amazon Book Stores).

Abandoned Cart Syndrome is a revenue killer within the retail sector which could be drastically minimized if every retailer would completely understand their customer's viewpoint, i.e. buy online/pick up in-store is becoming part of the **CONSUMER LEXICON** within the retail sector which is now being considered a requirement. Each customer is uniquely different in their tastes, selections, and choices. However, not providing a B.O.P.I.S. option will cripple your revenue stream while unfortunately forcing your customers to shop elsewhere. There are specific, tangible/financial reasons for some retailers who are unfortunately choosing to drag their feet with this option:

1. I.T. resources apportionment.

2. Infrastructure capital expenditures: Order Management Systems & Point of Sale Systems.

3. Refusal to accept new technology thus, holding onto "legacy systems."

4.  Regimented chain of command with inferior two-way communication.

5.  Inaccurate theories surrounding the forfeiture of shipping revenues.

6.  Increased store staffing/payroll budgets.

7.   The risk to reward ratios.

8.  Incomplete inventory visibility.

The predominant concern with most retailers surrounding the B.O.P.I.S. program is their Order Management Systems (OMS) requires a consolidated storehouse for inventory and orders which can leverage fulfillment centers throughout the organization. In addition, they need a **ROBUST POINT OF SALE SYSTEM** (POS) that can handle all the orders (through the various touchpoints) processed which flow into the OMS for a *complete view of the customer's orders across all channels.* A strong (POS) system will accommodate heavy demand by processing in-store pickups of products ordered online, as well as accept an order that will be supplied from another store or warehouse.

 Each retailer must fully commit to merging their online channel with their retail systems to provide a seamless experience for every customer. According to mi9retail: "69% of shoppers prefer to pick up online orders in-store to avoid shipping fees." (mi9retail, n.d.). In today's competitive marketplace, this should be a gigantic wake-up call for the retailers who have *procrastinated* with the buy online and pick up in-store program while providing the stimulus necessary to fully invest in their technological upgrades to remain relevant with today's consumers.

When retailers consolidate their financial reasoning with the capital expenditures for the buy online and pick up in-store program, they will clearly see that there is a myriad of benefits to the program. According to Retail Dive, "85% of shoppers surveyed said they have made additional in-store purchases while visiting stores to pick up what they already had bought online" (O'Shea, 2019). Retailers spend an *exorbitant amount of money on advertising and marketing* programs to attract customers to their stores, which can be accomplished (after the initial financial resources are accounted for) with the B.O.P.I.S. program. Furthermore, each retailer has **ANOTHER** opportunity to delight the customer while they are back in the store for another trip e.g., increased store revenue, improved customer brand loyalty, and enhanced customer satisfaction.

## BUY ONLINE; RETURN IN-STORE

The second available omnichannel service option for your retail guests *should be* the buy online and return in-store program (B.O.R.I.S.). It should go "hand in hand" with your B.O.P.I.S. program. This service option is considered sporadic at best or nonexistent at worst within the retail sector. Some retailers are still grappling to understand the concept of providing a smooth, non-confrontational, and pleasant return in-store process to every guest. According to Appriss Retail, "customers want their return to be fast and hassle-free, and they'll do anything to avoid return shipping fees or the time-consuming process of packing items into a box and shipping it out" (Retail, 2019).

There is a surfeit of hidden advantages to mastering the buy online and return in-store program. Retailers spend an excessive amount of their resources on attracting new customers into their stores while concurrently seeking to ensnare existing customers to revisit their stores more frequently. When a customer comes back to your store to return an item they purchased online, it is the retailer's fault about one-third of the time, e.g., the wrong item was shipped, variance in product appearance, or damaged item being received. Henceforth, by providing a cohesive (B.O.R.I.S.) process, you can possibly *mitigate the consequences of a failed online interaction while satisfying your customer,* i.e. turning a negative customer experience into a positive customer experience. Moreover, just like with (B.O.P.I.S.) you are creating an atmosphere for achieving additional revenue opportunities, increased brand loyalty, and substantial positive word of mouth advertising (for free) for your company.

Most consumers associate a retailer's return process with the customer service provided. Consequently, a retailer's behavior can **create an environment** where three of Aristotle's Laws of Association (there are four laws: the law of contiguity, the law of frequency, the law of similarity, and the law of contrast) can become ingrained in the customer's psyche. Through this *psychological process of association*, your customer's can **<u>PERCEIVE AND BELIEVE</u>** the following three laws about your return process:

1. **<u>Law of Contiguity</u>**: the principle that when two ideas or psychologically perceived events have once occurred in close association, then they are likely to occur in close association again. It is the subsequent occurrence of one tending to elicit the other.

2. **<u>Law of Frequency</u>**: the more often two things or events are linked, then the more powerful will be that association.

3.  **Law of Similarity:** If two things are similar, the thought of one will tend to trigger the thought of the other.

In chapter eighteen *(Organizational Culture, Part Two)*, we spoke briefly about the effects of contiguity and how it is a "conditioned reflex." This can be easily assimilated into your customer's consciousness, which if perceived as a negative experience, can have devastating consequences for your store/brand. If we ruminate about these three laws of association, then we will clearly see the aggregate dictates that each law creates a synergistic effect upon the other. Thus, it creates a monumental opportunity to strengthen your reputation with your customers by providing a seamless/hassle-free returns process. The returns process at many retailers is considered an adventure for many customers by providing inconsistent interactions for each guest.

The question I have for retailers is this: *if your **REGULAR RETURNS PROCESS IS CAPRICIOUS,** how are you going to treat your customers with a return which was purchased online???* Online returns at retailers are historically more challenging e.g., employee training is subpar, multiple complications with receipt information, repetitive nature of requiring a manager's approval, and length of transaction time. All retailers should focus their resources on providing an inclusive training program that is emphatic about ensuring their returns "modus operandi" is fully integrated with their online portal. *This critical segment of your business cannot afford to resemble a "cudgel" which can repel your loyal customers.*

Some retailers have third-party vendors that operate **synchronously** within their online websites. These offer their customers a myriad of additional product selections which enables the retailer to expand their reach. However, the major *customer issue* with these retailers that offer third-party vendors selections is, when the customer purchases an item from "your website" that is a third-party vendor item, the customer is **NOT ALLOWED** to return that item to a brick-and-mortar location.

The customer must work out the details of that return with the third-party vendor and that transaction is generally not a pleasant experience for the customer. There are numerous issues that can arise from dealing with these third-party vendors:

1. Communication from the seller is untimely or intermittent.

2. Customers can be forced to pay return shipping and must drop off the item/s at a delivery agent.

3. Sometimes, the customer must pay a restocking fee.

4. The customer might have to wait an inordinate amount of time to receive their new selection and or refund.

5. During this process, your company is **being connected** with this transaction, i.e. Law of Contiguity, Law of Frequency, and Law of Similarity, etc.

It would be in the best interest of retailers that house third-party vendors within their websites to espouse an "integrated system" for their customers that provides a seamless interaction for their guests. This encompasses *returns to any store from any vendor* on their website. If you read many of the customer retail review sites/blogs, you will hear the multitude of frustrated customers with this third-party vendor return issue. I have continually stated that retail organizations' return policies (online or store) can and will severely impact your credibility/livelihood with your customers. Customers are "shouting from the proverbial rooftops" that they have an inveterate perspective surrounding this particular dilemma.

Unfortunately, all retailers are going to be compared to Amazon for their superior returns process. All three laws of association (contiguity, frequency, and similarity) are constantly active in every customer interaction, which is being applied to your return procedures and (every area of your store). Consequently, it would behoove you to correct your (B.O.R.I.S.) processes promptly.

## MOBILE ACCESSIBILITY/COMPATIBILITY

Mobile usage over the past decade has skyrocketed and will likely continue intensifying as mobile technology maintains its ability to improve in functionality, portability, and convenience for its users. Many customers want to encounter an identical interaction on their mobile device when utilizing a retailer's app as they would from their desktop, laptop, or tablet ensuring a frictionless and engaging customer experience. Mobile is becoming the channel of choice for customers for interacting with products and services. *There are many retailers that have embraced the emerging consumer preference for mobile accessibility that customers are demanding in the digital age.*

Successful retailers have a mobile application that has ergonomic navigation. It mirrors their online portal while providing a synchronized experience on different mobile platforms e.g., android, IOS, windows, etc. *In addition, these retailers offer a responsive, yet immersive, website that functions robustly across all channels (especially the mobile channel) that presents a consistent customer experience.* Mobile application functionalities are being integrated by many retailers with their brick-and-mortar stores so that customers can place orders from their mobile devices, check product availability, purchase multiple items, and even place orders that can be picked up later in the day or at their earliest convenience.

## MOBILE DEFICIENCIES AFFECTING USER EXPERIENCE

While many retailers are embracing the mobile interface as an emerging technological necessity within their omnichannel strategy, there are still plenty of "retail laggards" that are not addressing their mobile inadequacies promptly. Here is a list of the most notable complaints from customers regarding their mobile website issues. (we will discuss the native mobile app in Chapter Twenty-One Omnichannel Capabilities, Part Two).

1. Major usability issues i.e. screen size requires adjustment to view items.

2. Compatibility concerns with different mobile devices e.g., android, IOS, and windows.

3. Page freezing while shopping.

4. Inconsistent search inquiries.

5. Latency with page load speed.

6. Advertisements blocking content.

7.  Problems encountered during checkout procedures.

The list of complaints above is a snapshot of what your customers "could be" experiencing while attempting to purchase products from your website from their mobile device. Any **ONE** of these issues can force your customers to become frustrated with the mobile process provided by your organization. This can create an *unsatisfactory environment* where they will "jump ship" and take their business elsewhere. I have personally encountered repetitive frustrations with many retailers who have not adequately addressed their mobile website experience. Furthermore, these issues slowly eroded my brand loyalty and consequently, compelled me to abandon that retailer altogether.

Inversely, there are some positive advantages to having a responsive mobile website:

1.  Effective indexing by search engines for better search results.

2.  Increased customer visits than with native apps.

3.  Easily accessible without having to download and store the native app.

4.  Fewer resources required to maintain i.e. maintenance, design updates, etc.

5.  Increased opportunities for "accessibility" from multiple mobile phones i.e. friends and family that do not want to download a specific retailer app.

I have always considered myself a **MICROCOSM OF THE MACROCOSM**. If this is happening to me, then how many other customers are experiencing an identical interaction? I want to "reiterate" my statement again about the exorbitant amount of resources in which many retailers are investing in advertising, marketing, and social media campaigns to attract new customers. They are aggressively seeking to entice existing customers to revisit their brand; yet, these same retailers are not **LISTENING** to their customers. *I learned early on in my retail career that an upset customer can provide a treasure-trove of valuable information about where your department, store, or company is failing to exceed customer expectations.*

Most customers will not inform you about their unsatisfactory experience, they will just take their business elsewhere. On average, one disgruntled customer will share their disappointing experience with twelve different people. What retailer can afford to consistently absorb this kind of negative feedback??? I am urging the C-Suite leadership teams within the retail sector to please visit your retail blogs, customer feedback sites, and website contact us-comments/feedback while listening to your store leadership teams upset customer "feedback correspondences." Only then can you implement corrective procedures immediately.

There is nothing more important in **ANY LEADERS JOB DESCRIPTION** than to ensure that each customer is satisfied with their in-store/online experience. If they are not satisfied, each leader should utilize all available resources to eradicate any foreseen impediments in a timely fashion.

# SECTION FOR NOTES

# CHAPTER TWENTY-ONE: OMNICHANNEL CAPABILITIES, PART TWO

### NATIVE MOBILE APPS

In particular, the millennial market is showing their preference for apps, mainly because of their desire for interesting and interactive experiences. The $64,000 question for most retailers is: *Should I have a robust/responsive mobile web experience for my guests, or should I invest in a "native" application and or should I invest in both???* In chapter twenty *(Omnichannel Capabilities, Part One)*, we spoke about the desire for most shoppers to have a seamless experience with their mobile website interactions. However, with native mobile apps from specific retailers, the user experience can become hyper-connected while providing a more immersive encounter for each customer.

According to Mobiloud.com, "over the course of 2019 their data showed that the average person spends 90% of their mobile time in apps vs. the mobile web. In addition, for the first time in 2019 people will spend more time with their mobile devices than they do watching TV" (Saccomani, 2019). I wanted to further dissect each advantage to fully express how all of the indicators can synergistically create an increased pleasurable experience for each customer. There is a *surplus of advantages* that native apps have over the traditional mobile website:

1. Ability to provide a "personalized" experience for each guest, e.g., push notifications for deals, coupons, and special events.

2. Page loading speed.

3. Personalized guest settings stored for convenience.

4. Strong loyalty programs equate to increased customer app usage.

5. Increased engagement from more loyal customers.

6. Higher conversion rates.

## ABILITY TO PROVIDE A "PERSONALIZED" EXPERIENCE FOR EACH GUEST

In today's digital world, mobile customers are craving personalization from their retail organizations of choice while demanding convenience, instant access to information, and the ability to explore options. Personalization offers relevancy that customers require when shopping in a world where the experience is progressively catered to individual preferences and prior behavior. Depending on the amount of data the customer is willing to provide, your company can begin to implement the custom personalization process to accurately anticipate and respond to each customer's tendencies. The *cornerstone* within the personalization process is **HOW MUCH DATA** will each consumer willingly divulge within your native app.

In-store "beacons," a.k.a. proximity marketing, are small, battery-operated wireless devices that transmit Bluetooth signals to nearby smartphones. This hardware communicates with customer devices, that have Bluetooth-enabled on their device, who possess the native app on their smartphone, and affords an unparalleled ability to communicate and interact with shoppers on a highly personal level. They deliver hyper-contextualized content to users based on their location within the retail establishment. Beacon technology can offer product suggestions, guide the customer around the store, and send push notifications for deals, coupons, and special events.

Many customers are becoming wary of providing too much data after the onslaught of retail data breaches that are proliferating our society. Retailers **MUST REASSURE AND GUARANTEE** their customers that the data they receive is going to be utilized in a safe, yet constructive, method that will allow the retailer to provide an increased interactive experience for each guest while safeguarding customers' sensitive information.

## PAGE LOADING SPEED

We live in a face-paced world where customer expectations are steadily increasing while their patience with page loading times is rapidly decreasing. There is a significant difference in page loading speed within the native retail apps versus the mobile website experience. **Page loading time is a major contributing factor in page abandonment.** As page loading time takes longer, abandonment increases exponentially. According to Hobo, "The ideal website load time for mobile sites is under three seconds. If Page Load Time goes from 1s to 3s the **probability of bounce increases 32%,** 1s to 5s **– the probability of bounce increases 90%,** 1s to 6s **– the probability of bounce increases 106%,** and 1s to 10s **– the probability of bounce increases 123%** (Anderson, 2020).

Your page load speed is *analogous* to wanting to test drive a Ferrari. When you get in the car, the engine won't turn over; yet, you continue to push the button anticipating the engine starting. How long would you continue to push the button to start the car before leaving frustrated??? This often-overlooked component can have devastating effects on your bottom-line while slowly

eroding your brand, reputation, and core customer base. Customers are demanding speed for

every interaction, not unlike the customer who spends one hour browsing your retail store

blissfully unaware of their time spent shopping. However, they become increasingly impatient if

they must wait a couple of minutes to check out. *SPEED IS KING; SPEED IS KING; SPEED IS*

*KING.*

## PERSONALIZED GUEST SETTINGS ARE STORED FOR CONVENIENCE

Consumers consider themselves more likely to buy when personalization includes purchase

history, recommendations based on previous purchases, and you know their name regardless if

the purchase is taking place online or in-store. Personalization is intended to simplify the

experience for the customer, which includes streamlining the pathways for customers to make a

purchase. Delivering personalized, hyper-relevant experiences that customers demand requires

committing the necessary resources to your native app to ensure that each guest's personalized

settings are stored for future visits.

The most successful retail native apps store their customer's preferences e.g., address,

contact information, preferred payment method, and shipping penchants. I know this might

sound remedial; still, simplicity and speed are the new levers of maximizing customer

engagement while combatting abandoned cart syndrome. I have heard horror stories from friends

and family members who were enthusiastic about purchasing through specific retail native apps.

Unfortunately, they decided to abandon their cart and shop elsewhere after the amount of time it took to "navigate" their way through the numerous roadblocks to check out.

Retailers *must streamline* their payment options, retain user settings, and increase the speed from cart to checkout in order to <u>eliminate friction points</u> that are major frustrations for their guests. *Anticipation, functionality, simplicity, and speed should be the most popular buzzwords surrounding your native app experience.* If your retail company is focused on these four buzzwords, while maintaining an atmosphere of active listening, your organization is probably in the upper echelon of providing a positive customer-driven experience.

## STRONG LOYALTY PROGRAMS LEAD TO MORE CUSTOMER APP USAGE

Retailers with strong loyalty programs have commensurate findings with increased customer app usage where customers can be identified in-store, keep track of loyalty points/stars, and get exclusive membership offers. Some of the most popular retailers with solid loyalty programs also have a robust and immersive native app, e.g., Kohls' "Yes2You Rewards;" Starbucks "My Starbucks Rewards;" and Sephora's "Beauty insider loyalty program." These retailers offer rewards for dollars spent on most purchases, in addition to increased points for specific items which can be redeemed for coupons, percentage/amount off, or free items.

Kohl's rewards their guests with one point for every dollar spent and, when the customer reaches 100 points, they receive a $5 off coupon. Starbucks loyalty program rewards its guests with two stars for every dollar spent using their native app or registered cards. In addition, they offer specific menu items that will have a certain number of stars attached for a specific action, i.e. 100 bonus stars if you purchase two mochas within two days; or, 150 bonus stars if you purchase a food or drink item three days in a row, etc. With Sephora's program (with over 10 million Beauty Insider members) you earn one point for each dollar spent, that can eventually be redeemed for free products or exclusive trips. Sephora utilizes tiered loyalty programs to distinguish its customers e.g., Beauty Insider, VIB, and VIB Rouge loyalty schemes.

Alibaba's loyalty program is called the 88 Membership Program. It delivers a personalized, convenient, engaging, and sometimes exclusive user experience for its members. "Creation of the 88 Membership program by Alibaba is its first foray into what it calls New Retail. It uses technology, interactivity, and a mixture of online and offline commerce to deliver efficiencies and enhanced services in shopping. Alibaba uses a proprietary algorithm that computes member points based on quantity and variety of stores visited, the goods they purchase, and their level of engagement within the app or website to generate a score or Taoqizhi.

Alibaba coordinates its members into three specific groups: Standard Members, Super Members who have a score of 1000 or more, and APASS Members who score higher than 2500. Depending on the group in which you are placed, you can qualify for extra data allowances from the Chinese mobile company Unicom, large discounts from participating brands, access to Marriott's global concierge service, or even a personal shopping assistant. Alibaba is leading the way with how businesses **CAN REWARD** their loyal customers for their patronage. Launched in 2018, the 88 VIP program has created immense growth opportunities for both brands and merchants.

## HIGHER CONVERSION RATES

So far, we have spoken about five major advantages to customer's usage of your company's native app. The final benefit is enjoying a higher conversion rate from your customers. All six native app advantages *segway nicely into what all retailers* (or businesses for that matter) want, which is increased revenue through "higher conversion rates." When retailers want to streamline the conversion process, the development of native apps proves more advantageous than through the mobile website. Conversion Rate Optimization or (CRO) should be at the apex of every C-Suite leader *to-do-list* because of the large financial ramifications it has on its bottom line. Retailers must ensure that users can easily switch from searching to browsing as it will increase conversion rates, drastically reduce bounce rates, and diminish shopping cart abandonments.

Retailers are facing an engagement dichotomy. On one hand, they want customers to utilize their native app to make purchases; however, they also want to entice customers to come into their stores. Smart retailers are using the app to do both by emailing customers information about their in-app shopping cart or wish-list items and offering in-store incentives/coupons to purchase their products. With the emerging movement toward customers wanting to have multiple choices for their mobile experience, it would be extremely **PRUDENT** for each retailer to invest in both a responsive mobile website and a native app to accommodate all your customer preferences.

## MOBILE EXPRESS RETURNS

We have already dissected the fact that the number one complaint most customers have with online shopping is the dreaded return process at many retailers. Customers know that returning an item and waiting for a refund, especially for a product purchased online, isn't always a

seamless process. Rather, it creates a sense of anxiety and trepidation among most customers.

Walmart is really starting to *listen to their customers* and have already begun to roll out its

**Mobile Express Return Program**. According to Walmart.com, the program is "an innovative,

industry-first experience that combines Walmart's more than 4,700 locations with the Walmart

app. "This November (2019), Walmart is adding Mobile Express Returns to its collection of

effortless shopping initiatives like Online Grocery Pickup, Pickup Towers, Mobile Express

Money Services and free two-day shipping." (Lady, 2019)

The process involves just two steps:

1. The customer starts the return using the Walmart App. They select the Walmart
   transaction and item(s) to return; then they follow the prompts to start the return process.
2. The customer finishes the return at the store where they can fast-track through the line via
   the Mobile Express Lane at the Customer Service Desk. They scan the QR code
   displayed on the card reader with the Walmart app. Then, they hand over the item to the
   returns associate.

Refunds will be credited to the customers' payment account as soon as the next day, and they

will not have to send their product through a delivery agent while waiting days for an online

return to be credited to their account. Walmart is also rolling out an innovative process within its

native mobile app which is called "Keep It." This feature will allow customers to **KEEP** certain

products (shampoo, household cleaning supplies, and cosmetics currently, with more items to follow) and receive an instant refund (credited back to the customer's original form of payment) on some purchases without having to return anything to the store.

The retail behemoth is also working to create a similar streamlined returns process for items sold by third-party marketplace sellers on Walmart.com. This has caused a flurry of misunderstandings from their customers (because they were unable to return **ANYTHING** purchased on Walmart.com through a third-party vendor at the stores). According to Daniel Eckert the SVP of Walmart services, "We recognize time has become the new currency in retail, as much as saving money. Therefore, we felt [Mobile Express Returns] was a growing expectation which we needed to address and do it well."

Walmart's aggressive viewpoint on alleviating customer anxiety/frustrations with their mobile express return process (averaging 30 seconds per return versus their traditional standard of five minutes per return) is how they are *separating the wheat from the chaff* from their competition. They are positioning their organization as the leader of the pack within the retail sector for maximizing each customer's time by radically diminishing the return time for customer online purchases.

This is a proverbial win-win for Walmart with their mobile express return program because most shoppers prone to returns are also the most likely to buy again. Henceforth, transforming an unpleasant process into a timesaving, seamless interaction will encourage the customer to purchase additional items.

# <u>SECTION FOR NOTES</u>

# CHAPTER TWENTY-TWO: INNOVATIVE CONCEPTS, PART ONE

Innovation is the **TENTH AND FINAL PILLAR** within the manual. It is what most retailers should be constantly cogitating about while, simultaneously, dedicating at least some of their resources to assessing their competition and "self-analyzing" their own deficiencies, weaknesses, and areas of opportunity. According to Merriam-Webster, the definition of innovation is "the introduction of something new, a new idea, method, or device." (Merriam-Webster, 2020). The retail sector is in the midst of a *chrysalis period* (major transformation) as the internet continues to change the way we purchase everything from light bulbs to groceries.

Within the retail sector, there is a huge fissure between the retailers who are actively embracing change and innovation in contrast to the proliferation of retailers who have become complacent, lethargic, and fiercely obstinate with the emerging technology that customers are demanding. **I am happy to see many retailers embracing change and innovation during the Covid19 pandemic**. In professional football, there is a saying for a cornerback that is covering a receiver: "If he's even, he's leaving." Retail translation: if retailers are *waiting around* for their competition to work out the kinks or go through the growing pains of innovative concepts before they adopt those ideas, then that retailer is going to secure <u>at least a temporary seat at the back of the bus</u>.

The most successful retailers are aggressively pursuing developing technology that will service their customers while assuaging their apprehensions over wait times, convenience, communication, or seamless interactions. *The digital revolution has changed the behavior and demands of consumers.* Pretty much everyone can ascertain **WHICH** retailers have missed the boat on innovation. These same retailers are shuttering stores, losing market share, experiencing diminishing revenue (quarter after quarter), and filing for bankruptcy. Inversely, the retailers who are on the "cutting edge" of accepting innovation as their *ally* are experiencing record-breaking financial numbers, opening new stores, capturing market share, and creating groundbreaking ideas and concepts.

Amazon is a disrupter for any industry it occupies because they obsessively focus on the customer, not their competition. Yet, they are constantly forging innovative paths that may appear "outlandish or ridiculous." However, they thoroughly enjoy voyaging into unprecedented territories while accomplishing their agendas. Amazon's success starts with their CEO Jeff Bezos who admits he has extreme tolerance for failure. All retailers can take a page out of Bezos playbook by embracing risk, creating a fiercely experimental culture (that will accommodate employee failure without fear of retribution), while having an unwavering belief in the ability to dominate your industry.

## SCAN AND GO TECHNOLOGY

Scan and Go is set to become retail's next celebrated disruptive technology. There are a couple of retailers that are starting to implement the "scan and go" technology in their stores today e.g., Walmart (Scan and Go), **as of September 2020, Walmart has decided to transition its Scan and Go service to Walmart Plus members. Using the Walmart app members will be able to scan their purchases as they shop and pay without having to wait in line.** In addition, Scan and Go has also morphed into Check Out With Me. The Check Out With Me option lets staffers check out a shopper anywhere in the store using a handheld device. Amazon (Amazon Go), and Kroger (Scan, Bag, Go). These two and a half retailers (Amazon is dipping their toes into the retail brick & mortar arena) are creating a "pivotal moment" within the retail sector as they are listening to their customers; customers hate waiting in long lines to check out! These retailers are grasping this concept that is giving consumers the option to shop their stores without interacting with a cashier. Kroger is aggressively pursuing this emerging technology that will assist in alleviating long check out times for their guests while providing a "viable" alternative for customers to pay for their purchases. Kroger plans to have its Scan, Bag, Go, technology in 400 stores by the end of 2018. Amazon opened its first store (Amazon Go) on the ground floor of its new headquarters on Seventh Avenue in Seattle with no checkout lines and no cashiers in January 2018. As of (July 2020), Amazon has a total of **26** Amazon Go stores located in four cities — New York, San Francisco, Chicago, and Seattle. There is a profusion of advantages to the scan and go technology that exists for customers and retailers alike:

1. Eliminates lengthy checkout lanes.

2. Streamlines the payment process.

3. Customers are in control of their transactions.

4. Establishes prime real estate for additional store products to be displayed.

5. Allows for reallocation of cashier hours to focus on customer-centric interactions.

6. Digital receipts reduce store expenditures on receipt paper.

7. Provides a seamless experience for the customers.

Walmart is becoming the quintessential "innovative leader of the pack" within the brick-and-mortar category because they are *obsessively focusing on entering new frontiers which will allow them to set the market, not chase the market like many retailers are doing.* Customers can either download the scan and go app, linking it with their preferred payment card(s), or use the handheld scanners located at the front of the store. Customers will scan items on their own as they walk through the store which creates a virtual cart. When the customer is finished shopping, they pay for their items through the app. Then, they proceed to walk through the Mobile Express lane which is situated at the front of the stores (for security purposes). Customers simply show their digital receipt to a Walmart employee (similar to Sam's Club or Costco) and they leave the store without having to wait to pay a cashier.

The Scan, Bag, Go, technology at Kroger is extremely similar in nature to Walmart's Scan and Go service, with the major discrepancy being that customers (at this time) **MUST** use self-checkout kiosks to checkout. Customers simply scan bar codes on items they will be purchasing either with a handheld scanner or via Kroger's smartphone app. When the customer has finished shopping, they will proceed to the self-checkout kiosks where coupons have been equated and a final total is instantly calculated. Ultimately, shoppers will be able to bypass Kroger's kiosks altogether and pay directly through the app.

As previously discussed, Amazon has already opened 26 of its Amazon Go innovative-cashier-less stores and is the company's first brick-and-mortar convenience store. The store concept is akin to a small neighborhood convenience store that carries an assortment of grab-

and-go items, e.g., salads, sandwiches, produce, meat, beer, and wine. Shoppers must download the Amazon Go app to their smartphone and scan it at a high-tech turnstile upon entering the store. Customers grab the items they want to purchase (which creates a virtual cart that is linked to the customer's account). Once they are finished, they simply leave the store whereupon their Amazon account is charged accordingly. The store is equipped with cameras, shelf sensors, and machine-learning software to help Amazon's computer vision system work efficiently.

Walmart appears to be going "toe-to-toe" with Amazon and it's Amazon Go store; it is piloting a program called **PROJECT KEPLER** which is an in-store shopping experience without checkout lines or cashiers. Project Kepler is coming from the secret Code Eight team, a part of their Store No. 8 tech incubator, which is rumored to be in the early stages of its infancy. On the contrary, the sentiment is full steam ahead for this project.

## POP UP STORES

In a fiercely competitive retail economy, many retailers failed to acclimatize to the changing retail market. Pop up stores are starting to gain traction within the traditional brick-and-mortar sector as an extremely cost-effective opportunity to execute a specific strategy for capturing increased revenue. Pop up stores can be opened as a "standalone unit" or within the four walls of another retailer. Kohl's opened in-store shops christened Amazon Smart Home Experience and staffed Amazon employees in 10 Kohl's locations in the Los Angeles and Chicago area. These in-store shops provided an immersive experience where customers could interact with (and purchase an assortment of) Amazon devices, including Amazon Echo, Echo Dot, Amazon Fire

TV, and Fire tablets. As of March 2019, Kohl's Corp. will expand to more than 200 the number of its stores offering Amazon products but will close the Amazon "smart home" shops it opened in 30 locations (Romell, 2019). *I applaud Kohl's for their ability to embrace <u>innovation and change</u> through their partnership with Amazon.*

Pop up stores used to be reserved for the struggling artist or the t-shirt vendor which were inaccurately cloaked in a *flea-market theme* that came with certain stigmas. There are no rules that are set in stone when it comes to the pop-up store concept. Numerous retailers are experimenting with multiple different formats determined by location, foot traffic, merchandise selection, and season. Pop-up stores can embody mobile food trucks, kiosks within malls, and pop-up sections within another retailer.

Here is a list of the distinct advantages of a pop-up store versus a traditional brick-and-mortar location:

1. Drastically less expensive (up to 80% cheaper) for the space.

2. Increased revenue due to location.

3. Improve brand awareness.

4. Effortlessly enter a new market and launch new products.

5. Minimization of risk with agile formats.

6. Enhanced personalization and customization.

7. Interactive space to gather product feedback.

With innumerable advantages for all retailers, the pop-up shop format should be in every retailer's **BEST PRACTICES MANUAL**. *This concept has an enormous amount of flexibility with minimal risk involved, while further offering a chance to broaden your brand in different markets that would have otherwise been impenetrable.* The Kohl's pop up shop format really is a win-win scenario for them that offered very minimal shortcomings. Consequently, it was a judicious and strategic concept to collaborate with, arguably, the number one innovative and disrupter of our time, i.e. Amazon.

## CUSTOMIZATION IS THE WAVE OF THE FUTURE

The retail sector was built upon the foundational principle of customizing products to match their customer's preferences. Conversely, as mass production of retail items through "mechanization" began to transmute the traditional method of how products were being produced, the time-honored *custom-tailored procedures* started to vacillate between both avenues. Finally, it became almost obsolete. The customization services retailers provided were then regulated to cobblers, tailors, artists, and **specific niches** within the retail sector.

In the digital world, we live in today, the customer is developing an insatiable appetite for custom made products that they are "expecting" their retail stores to provide for them. If retailers are unable or unwilling to assent, consumers are going to take their wallets to other viable, alternative options i.e. the smaller independent retailers who can capitalize on the customization niche. The **BIG BOYS** of the retail sector have traditionally been extremely slothful to react to emerging trends within the retail space. Recently, the Walmart's', Targets', Best Buys', Home

Depots', Lowe's', and a few grocery chains in the segment have started to exemplify (through leading by example on other pioneering fronts) the necessary innovative impetus to supplant their position in the digital race. Furthermore, *these major retailers must respond vehemently to this developing trend towards customers' preferences for customization.*

The innovative concept of using technology to create *bespoke products* is still in an embryonic stage at most big-box retailers. The customization method is another touchpoint where shoppers can intermingle with a brand, while data about each customer can be collected, which provides the retailer with information to further customize their product/experience. Retailers should approach the customization movement from the perspective of *REIMAGINING THE CUSTOMER EXPERIENCE* through the idea of on-demand manufacturing and 3D printing capabilities which will create an exhilarating new retail world.

### LIST OF RETAILERS WHO FOCUS ON CUSTOMIZATION

**SEPHORA** stands out from its peers with a robust *digital personal shopper* that specifically customizes product recommendations to a customer's exact skin type and tone, as well as her eye and hair color. PLAY! by Sephora is a subscription-based service which costs $10 per month. The customer receives five samples (five deluxe makeup, skincare and haircare samples, a collectible makeup bag, and a beauty bonus!) from experts that curate a selection of prestige products each month. So, you don't have to choose anything. You fill out your profile, subscribe to the service, and then, using the answers in your PLAY! Profile, Sephora's panel of experts determines which products are best for you. According to the Sephora website: "We know beauty isn't one-size-fits-all, so each month we choose which of these products we think are best for you, based on the answers you provide in your PLAY! PROFILE."

**ADIDAS** is focusing its efforts on customization of an individual's specific preferences (matching exact foot contours and pressure points) for their Futurecraft 4D shoes. As former company CEO Herbert Hainer states, "the company's products, services, and channels are designed with a consumer-obsessed mindset." Their core philosophy is creating engagement and brand desire within consumers today. For many years, Adidas has been on the *cutting edge* of innovation, implementing advanced technology for its products and within their stores to differentiate themselves from every other athletic retailer.

Adidas' ultimate objective is to allow customers to be measured and assessed in store for a perfectly fitted shoe that considers the user's gait, weight, and athletic aspirations. According to Adidas, "Imagine walking into an Adidas store, running briefly on a treadmill and instantly getting a 3D-printed running shoe." Adidas wants to use its 3D printing technology to *tailor-make soles for each and every customer*. The rest of the athletic shoe industry is going to have their work cut out for them!

**COACH** has it's "COACH CREATE, THE NEW DESIGN-IT-YOURSELF" program that caters to shopper's desire for personalized/customized products. Inside the stores, customers can watch their items come to life at a customization bar where a Coach Craftsman escorts them throughout the procedure with charms, rivets, hankies, and unique finishing touches. The process consists of three steps:

1.  **<u>Customize it</u>**- The customer chooses the bag, the details, the colors, and the placement. Coaches' craftsmen then create it for you.

2.  **<u>Accessorize it</u>**- Change a strap, add a bag charm, or add on a scarf. The sky is the limit for your creation.

3.  **<u>Personalize it</u>**- Add a personalized monogram to make it your own.

Shoppers can choose among nine points of customization, anything from the color and type of leather to the hardware metal. More than one million variations are possible.

Can you imagine walking into a Home Depot and asking for a special nut/bolt and, with their on-demand manufacturing and 3D printing capabilities, they make your desired item while you continue with your shopping? How about walking into a Target store and asking an associate to make you a "bespoke" sweater that perfectly matches your unique physical dimensions which you are told will be ready in 20 minutes? How about walking into a Dick's Sporting Goods store and asking for a custom-made golf bag that has a personalized monogram that will be ready in 25 minutes?

Customization is the latest innovative trend that will dramatically increase a customer's loyalty with your company. Why would your customer purchase an item elsewhere that **IS NOT CUSTOMIZED** to their specific predilections when they have the choice to customize??? This is the million-dollar question that **<u>ALL RETAILERS</u>** should be asking themselves if they are going to attempt to remain relevant/viable within the tumultuous retail sector that is experiencing a gigantic *digital transformation*. The retailers that fully grasp this concept will metamorphose into a uniquely competitive brand that can withstand the "peaks and valleys" happening with our economy while successfully navigating the disorienting retail sector.

## STORE WITHIN A STORE MODEL

The "store within a store concept" has some mileage on it throughout the retail sector with numerous retailers attempting to capitalize on this emerging trend in the past. However, through improper timing, unsuitable partners, or the necessary commitment required, the results were intermittent at best and disastrous at worst. This may not actually mean a *branded store*-within-a-store, but rather a portion of the floor space that is dedicated to offering different experiences e.g., restaurants, salons, tax services, etc. The S.W.A.S. concept is advantageous for all parties involved. The retailer offers optimal locations for vendors that it can charge higher rents, the manufacturer receives higher profit margins than it would through the traditional wholesale model, and the consumer receives lower prices and improved service.

The vendor of the store-within-a-store can offer lower prices, superior customer service, and adequate staffing (via partnership models only). They receive all the profits instead of having to apportion them with the retailer. Store-within-store retailers also benefit from exposure to a much larger customer profile than their stand-alone stores do.

Some specific benefits that make the store within a store collaboration a home run include:

1. SWAS become destinations, augmenting the retailer's appeal, and escalating foot traffic.

2. Defray costs and decrease overheads by subletting the space.

3. The revival of retailer's presence within the sector.

4. Not responsible for inventory levels, staffing, or planograms (applicable for partnership vendors only).

5. Enter a new market and launch new products (via a partnership or store-branded ideas).

6. It's convenient for shoppers and offers variety to the store selections.

7. Enhances store revenue through increased foot traffic.

**BEST BUY** is a strong example of a retailer creating collaborative arrangements that are successful with multiple partners by devoting space to 'showcase" specific vendors such as Apple, Samsung, Microsoft, Sony, Amazon, and Goggle. Best Buy fully understands the financial ramifications of partnering with blue-chip brands to further expand their customer reach. Best Buy does *staff these specific niche brands* with their own store personnel which provides a proverbial win-win scenario (for both partners). They strongly invest in employee product knowledge and are adept at explaining the technological information to consumers in a down-to-earth way that they can understand. Best Buy is delivering on endeavors to offer customers consultations and recommendations they can't find online, which is a key driver in its successful strategy to compete with its competition.

**J.C. PENNEY** is completely devoted to the store-within-a-store concept as evident with their successful partnership with Sephora. In retrospect, it leverages their strong reputation within the beauty sector to drive additional revenue to their stores. Each Sephora store within a J.C. Penney's clocks in with an average footprint of 2400 sq. ft., which is massive in scale compared to other highly visible SWAS alliances. Satish Malhotra, executive VP for Sephora inside JCP, stated that, "With our one-of-a-kind beauty collaboration, we are able to reach more markets where Sephora does not exist and introduce prestige makeup, fragrance and skincare brands that may not be available in many of these cities." **As of September 2020, JC Penney's future is uncertain due to bankruptcy proceedings.**

**LOWES** is not one of the deluges of retailers who come to mind when you think of SWAS models. However, they have sunk their teeth into the connected smart home device arena with the addition of an alliance with software-powered retailer b8ta. According to a Lowes press release, "Lowes is expanding its Smart Home powered by b8ta" connected-home shopping experience to 70 Lowe's stores nationwide. Each destination will feature a curated selection of top-rated smart home products that offer consumers onsite support from specially trained experts known as "b8ta testers." (Lowes Companies, 2017). The fully immersive section will feature 60 smart home products that include security systems, thermostats, cameras, lighting, and speakers. All SKUs are displayed out of the box to encourage hands-on play and enhance product knowledge.

**HOME DEPOT** is establishing an inveterate alliance with Tesla by opening small kiosks (in up to 800 locations) staffed by uniformed employees inside Home Depot stores. It will offer its solar panels and Powerwall electricity storage devices to customers. Home Depot is the nation's largest home improvement chain which will provide Tesla with a massive platform to showcase its products through an established retailer with strong roots anchored in the home improvement industry.

Home Depot receives increased foot traffic and the prestige of being the first retailer to partner with Tesla. Meanwhile, Tesla procures the opportunity to broaden their market reach, a reputed match made in heaven for both parties. Tesla's Powerwall ($6,000 retail price; however, prices can increase or decrease accordingly) is designed to store electricity that is either accumulated by a home's solar panels or purchased from the grid during off-peak hours. In addition, Tesla automobile owners can use the Powerwall as a fill-up station for their vehicle or supply power to a home in the case of an outage.

According to an article in USA Today, "Although the company makes traditional solar panels, Tesla also now sells innovative solar roof tiles that look virtually indistinguishable from traditional shingling and are meant to counter aesthetic concerns some homeowners have about placing large reflective black solar panels on their roofs." (Cava, 2018). The new Home Depot kiosks will sell only Tesla's traditional solar panels. Ambiguity still remains on whether the solar roof tiles would ever be offered at Home Depot.

Tesla energy specialists can recommend what combination of electricity storage units and solar panels will accommodate each customer's unique home configuration. The information will be based on using a consumer's home address to pull up satellite imagery that can estimate sunlight, shading, and other rooftop factors. After calculating the necessary factors, customers can receive a customized quote as well as arrange for a free at-home consultation. Home Depot is sharpening its "innovative chops" with the Tesla partnership through their aggressive attitude on collaborating with other businesses through an *interdisciplinary concept* that is mutually beneficial for both parties. **As of June 2018, Tesla will not renew its agreement with Home Depot to sell solar panels and battery packs at the retailer's stores**.

There's only so long a company can continue not making money, and that time has obviously come for Tesla. Elon Musk (CEO of Tesla) informed all employees of this decision while also announcing that the company was cutting 9% of its total workforce as part of a reorganization designed to reduce costs and help the electric automaker become profitable. *However, as of August 2020, Tesla has been profitable for all of 2020 and I can foresee Tesla revisiting this partnership with Home Depot in the near future.*

# **<u>SECTION FOR NOTES</u>**

# CHAPTER TWENTY-THREE: INNOVATIVE CONCEPTS, PART TWO

## INTEGRATION OF ARTIFICIAL INTELLIGENCE

One of the premier *mushrooming innovative trends* within the retail sector is the discussion surrounding the integration of artificial intelligence into the retail sector and how companies can best assimilate this technology without causing major disruption to their organization. When this topic is brought up, there are two executive/store sides that are approaching this technology from diametrically different viewpoints. On one side, individuals believe in implementing this innovative technology to keep pace with other retailers and to position themselves at the forefront of embracing change. Conversely, on the opposing side, people believe that this technology will totally disrupt everything they have known or which they have been accustomed to and will create the atmosphere for the slow demise of their career and or livelihood.

Artificial technology is the concept of machines completing tasks that have historically required human intelligence. According to RetailWire, "Accenture estimates that if stores invest in AI and human-machine collaboration at the same rate as top-performing companies, revenues would **climb 41 percent by 2022** and employment levels by 10 percent." (Ryan, 2018). Artificial intelligence will provide retailers with access to influential discernments before they are available to them, using cognitive interfaces in multifaceted systems, advanced analytics, and deep learning technology.

Artificial intelligence really consists of two distinct competencies: machine learning and deep learning. Machine learning can be described as giving computers the ability to learn without being overtly programmed. Machine learning adjusts in response to the data it is exposed to and through neural programming, which is an optimization algorithm. Therefore, it minimizes errors by constantly learning from newly acquired data. It generally attempts to make "solid guesses" with the data it has received. Deep learning is a subset of machine learning and is based on deep neural networks (similar to the human brain) which uses a cascade of multiple layers of data where each successive layer uses the output from the previous layer as input to formulate a "highly educated guess" based on the weighting factors.

## PRACTICAL APPLICATIONS FOR AI IN RETAIL

Artificial intelligence offers retailers copious advantages for practical applications within the retail space:

1. Image and voice recognition algorithms.

2. Deep learning to predict customer preferences.

3. Fraud detection.

4. Gesture recognition (which can interpret human gestures as commands).

5. Virtual mirrors (mainly used for apparel and accessories).

6. Virtual agents (which encompasses Chatbots).

7. Analyzing dark data (or unstructured data).

8. Marketing campaigns to increase ROI.

Many retailers are grappling with the idea of investing in artificial intelligence because they are entrenched within two main ensamples: they are waiting for other retailers to "work out the kinks" before they fully commit their resources and their apprehension over losing control through technological advances. There are other *ancillary perspectives* that are "in play" that are suppressing some retailers from pulling the trigger. Chief among them are executive hubris surrounding their ability to affect change through human efforts, believing their specific retail niche does not require artificial intelligence, and inability to allocate the necessary financial resources to be flexible and adaptable throughout the process.

Artificial intelligence can scale trackable interactions, marketing activities, and revenue exchanges into a single repository of insightful data that retailers can optimize for increased segmentation and personalization. Ultimately, the retail sector is mutating into a segment where the most successful retailers are becoming adept at creating customer experiences that are personalized, customized, and relevant. Artificial intelligence is another specific *technological tool* that when implemented and utilized correctly, will differentiate your brand from the competition. *The retail trailblazers are starting to separate themselves from the pack by loosening their inflexible viewpoints surrounding anchor methods of the past (legacy systems, outdated beliefs, and resting on their laurels) while staunchly embracing a myriad of opportunities available.*

### STAFFING FOR FOOT TRAFFIC NOT JUST REVENUE

Artificial intelligence can extrapolate complex data by measuring the ebb and flow of foot traffic within retail stores. There is a "growing trend" of retail stores starting to foretaste the surplus of financial advantages to factoring in-store foot traffic (among other touchpoints) when calculating store staffing models. Most traditional retail environments are characterized by unpredictable store traffic, which makes it difficult to provide consistent service quality, provide adequate staffing levels, and accurately predict projected revenue forecasts.

The latest trend focuses on a *comprehensive approach* that enables retailers to obtain aggregate labor requirements (through artificial intelligence algorithms). Therefore, exploiting store traffic statistics, point-of-sale numbers, previous historical data, and staffing information to formulate a more accurate picture for staffing efficiency. All stores throughout an organization would be assembled into comparable groups that address local/regional demographics, store layouts/size, store sales volume, and specific store nuances. According to Professor Rogelio Oliva who is the co-author of the book **Traffic-based Labor Planning in Retail Stores** along with his colleagues developed a data-driven method that helps determine optimal staffing levels. "Testing the method with real data, they found that it could increase sales performance for an apparel retailer by approximately 10 percent." (School, 2017).

The empirical data from the experiment was for an apparel retailer which, upon further experimentation, could potentially accentuate these findings within different retail niches. Maybe in a hardware store, the data would show a 15% increase in revenue, or in an electronics store could facilitate a 20% increase in-store revenue. The **germinal moment** to reflect upon is the mere fact that if the revenue increased just 10% for one apparel retailer, what are the ramifications for additional revenue for all retailers that are willing to adopt this perspective??? If we use the 10% increase as the benchmark for increased sales, what retail organization could consciously *turn a blind eye to the possibility of a 10% revenue increase* company-wide??? Here is where we should lean on the artificial intelligence platform (if your store/company has embraced this technology). AI can be a valuable resource to assist retailers with staffing models that are incorporating foot traffic into the metrics used for forecasting revenue projections.

## VOICE RECOGNITION TECHNOLOGY

With tech giants like Amazon, Google, Apple, and Microsoft heavily investing in the race to become the leader in voice technology, I portend that the retail sector will be a natural transition for this emerging technology. Voice recognition technology will assist customers within their retail stores, online, and with customer service inquiries. All the major tech players are "throwing their hat into the ring" to satisfy customer's ravenous desire for convenience to counteract their hectic, chaotic, and disorganized environments. The four most popular options for voice interface are Amazon's Alexa, Google's Assistant, Microsoft's Cortana, and Apple's Siri. Each player has made conversational interfaces more appealing with the omnipresence of smartphones, laptops, tablets, and computers all accommodating this technology.

According to comScore, "by 2020, 50 percent of all searches will be voice searches." (Jeffs, 2018). In addition, Smartphone speech recognition can write text messages three times faster than human typing. Voice interface is reaching a tipping point within our ethos as a large majority of customers are readily adopting and accepting this technology to streamline their lives. People are *gravitating towards* technology that will simplify their lives while freeing up time (analogous to automation) to focus on other priorities, passions, or past times. With the propagation of artificial intelligence-powered assistants, the retail environment is ripe for voice recognition technology to **augment their existing infrastructure**. Many "legacy brands are fragmenting" which is causing a massive structural reorganization that is, and will alter, the traditional retail space.

Voice interface can create a frictionless retail environment that will allow the customer to complete their shopping (in-store, online, or mobile device) by utilizing voice recognition software that will streamline their entire interaction. Let's project our consciousness into the near future for a hypothetical, yet very conceivable, environment. You walk into a hardware store and seek out an associate in which you ask: *Do you have any 56-volt lithium batteries for my lawnmower in stock?* The associate has an earpiece, phone, or tablet equipped with voice recognition technology that heard your question, that has immediate access to inventory levels (in real-time). It processes the information and communicates this information to the associate, who responds with, yes, we do on aisle 24; let me take you there.

Another customer walks into a department store looking for the perfect cocktail dress for an evening out with her husband. She visits a dressing room equipped with voice recognition technology and a virtual mirror, asking for a black cocktail dress. The virtual mirror scans her frame for dimensions, accesses inventory levels, and recommends the perfect cocktail dress for her. She absolutely loves the dress and agrees to purchase the item which she is told can be shipped to her home (by providing contact information). Or, it will be waiting at the front of the store. She can pay with the voice assistant then and there (or choose to pay through traditional means) and pick up her dress on the way out. Voice recognition technology has countless practical usages within retail stores which can enhance the interactions through their online portals to escalate the convenience factor for their guests.

As voice recognition continues to gain massive traction with consumers, it would behoove retailers to ascertain if their retail systems are fully capable of integrating with this emerging technology. With the soaring popularity of "smart speakers" flooding the market, mainly the Amazon Echo and the Goggle Home, the average consumer will have access to these speakers within their homes very shortly. The top impediment for successful usage of these smart speakers is their inability to understand more complex questions. The second most common issue with these speakers is the ability to understand the context for follow-up questions i.e. is that mattress available in king and how much does it cost? With the blazing speed of technology, these minor hindrances will be addressed and corrected transiently. The thundering question to be answered by retailers is: *Are your resources being allocated to construct the necessary infrastructure to accommodate the voice interface/smart speaker's environment???*

## SECURITY PROTOCOLS TO PROTECT CUSTOMER DATA

For artificial intelligence to work effectively in the retail industry, there must be a strong, safe, and secure collaboration between the retailer and customer with regards to the massive data that is being collected. Lately, every year we are exposed to information about the profusion of retail breaches that are inundating the retail sector with the same inevitable outcome: sensitive customer information was extracted from a retailer's website, servers, or mainframe.

The list of retail breaches in 2017: Saks, Chipotle, Brooks Brothers, K-Mart, Verizon, Whole Foods, Forever 21, and of course the shocker, Equifax is growing exponentially each year. At least 19 consumer companies reported data breaches from January 2018- November 2019: Macy's, Kay Jewelers, Adidas, Saks Fifth Avenue, Lord & Taylor, & Panera Bread. In 2020 retail breaches included: Walgreens, J-Crew, T-Mobile, and Claire's. Many of these breaches were caused by flaws in payment systems either online or in stores. These scenarios are being exacerbated by retailers who are **STILL EMPLOYING** legacy retail applications, inadequate infrastructure, and sluggish responses to mitigating/contesting the threat of cybercrime.

I completely understand that upgrading legacy systems to the latest cybersecurity measures is a daunting financial endeavor. However, this is one area of a retailer's business that **MUST RECEIVE** the necessary resources to combat the *"Blitzkrieg of cyber-attacks"* in the retail sector. Customers are putting their trust and faith in the retail sector (and others) to completely guarantee the safety of their sensitive information. Be that as it may, their trust is waning in the face of frequent security breaches that are becoming pervasive. What many retailers (and not all, some retailers **ARE** devoting the resources and dedication necessary to safeguarding their customer's data) are doing is waiting for an attack to occur before implementing any major changes to their security protocols. Retailers need to go on the offensive (institute a proactive not reactive strategy) and start implementing preventive measures **BEFORE** a breach occurs.

Another disingenuous tactic that some retailers are employing is attempting to "cover-up" the security breach until they have addressed and possibly, corrected the attack. This usually takes a considerable amount of time. Meanwhile, the affected customers are left out-of-the-loop during this process while their sensitive information is floating around on the dark web or being sold to criminals that are already utilizing their information for nefarious purposes. People are <u>inherently forgiving</u> when they are provided with all the facts in a timely manner while receiving a genuine and sincere apology from a person; or, in this case, a retailer for their transgression. Most people can admire and respect a retail organization who **<u>CAME FORWARD ON THEIR OWN</u>** without being forced to through outside forces demanding an explanation.

The key emotion for all retailers to exhibit before and after a security breach is empathy. Each retailer must put themselves in their customer's situation and realize the magnitude of the situation. Here is a small list of some of the pain and suffering a customer *could experience* after a breach:

1. Experiencing identity theft and the time/resources it requires to regain one's identity.

2. Loss of money which can cause an avalanche of adjuvant domestic issues.

3. The breach can affect the victims' families causing hardships to arise.

4.  Feeling violated by the retailer for a lack of preventive measures in place.

5.  Feeling anger towards the retailer for subjecting them to this trauma.

6.  Customers filing class-action lawsuits against the retailer.

7.  Exposing customers to potential ransomware situations.

8.  Customers deciding to never shop the breached retailer again.

9.  Permanent destruction to brand identity which will affect future revenue.

There is a "light at the end of the tunnel" for retailers in today's digital world. The good news after reading all the information surrounding retail data breaches is there are plenty of countermeasures that retailers can employ to ensure their data and their customer's information are safe and secure. Let's discuss some of the more popular methods available:

1.  Implement Cloud Access Security Brokers (CASB) which is a software tool that sits between an organization's on-premises infrastructure and a cloud provider's infrastructure. It acts as a "Bouncer" which offers an extension of protection from their standard security protocols.

2.  Adopt Cloud Computing Encryption Technology "Bring Your Own Key" (BYOK) which is a cybersecurity platform where users hold the encryption keys for their own cloud data.

3.  Expand encryption across all employee touchpoints e.g., laptops, computers, mobile phones, and servers to beef up security measures.

4. Increase opportunities for customers to pay with multiple financial platforms, e.g., PayPal, Android Pay, and Apple Pay to decrease P.O.S. fraud.

5. The company-wide espousal of Europay, Mastercard, and Visa (EMV) chip enable point-of-sale systems.

6. Install precautionary Distributed Denial of Service (DDoS) mitigation appliances which consist of dedicated hardware that squats in an enterprise's data center in front of the normal servers and routers which are specifically built to detect and filter malicious traffic.

As previously discussed, the ramifications of a data/customer breach are enormous for everyone impacted. Unfortunately, some retailers are not concentrating their efforts, resources, or preventative measures towards this intrusion while their customers are suffering the consequences of this gigantic oversight. Alarmingly, "Per Digital Commerce 360, retailers are not patching vulnerable web applications quickly enough, leaving holes for hackers to exploit. According to the 2020 DBIR, only half of the vulnerabilities are patched within three months after discovery. Sophisticated attackers know patches are unlikely to be applied" (Safruti, 2020).

At the risk of sounding redundant, I strongly encourage **ALL** retailers to commit the necessary resources to upgrade their cybersecurity measures to the latest safeguards available to ensure their customer's sensitive information is protected. I would like to give a loud "shout out" to **The Home Depot** for proactively investing the necessary resources into their cybersecurity programs. "Attivo Networks®, the award-winning leader in deception technology for cybersecurity defense, announced that The Home Depot® has been named an honoree of a **2018 CSO50 Award** from IDG's CSO Magazine." (Networks, 2018). The CSO50 Awards are bestowed on a select group of organizations that have demonstrated that their security initiatives have created outstanding business value and thought leadership for their companies.

## EVOLUTION BACK TO EXPERIENTIAL RETAIL

Consumer shopping patterns are evolving in the digital age which are requiring retailers to take a **HARD LOOK** at their core archetypes regarding customer engagement. *With the ubiquity of opportunities for customers to purchase their desired items online and have them delivered within a few hours, the most innovative retailers are coalescing the traditional brick-and-mortar shopping excursion with interactive and immersive experiences that will entertain and delight their customers.* Customers are demanding that retailers incorporate new experiences into their offerings by adapting their store formats accordingly. Shoppers are increasingly seeking a multisensory experience, i.e. an experience that stimulates all five senses while creating an emotional attachment to the brand.

There are many retail organizations that failed to notice the signs in the economy, e-commerce explosion, and changing customer shopping patterns. They continued adding new and ever more unprofitable stores. Ultimately, this created a saturation point that contributed to retailers cannibalizing their own stores. According to citylab, "The United States devotes four times more of its real estate square footage to retail, per capita, than Japan and France; six times more than England; nine times more than Italy; and 11 times more than Germany." (Florida,

2017). A re-correction is taking place within the retail sector as more retailers are shuttering stores, reformatting existing stores, and creating smaller formats to accommodate the changing retail climate.

**WE ARE OVER-RETAILED!** According to data compiled by the advisory firm Cowen and Company, "the US has about 23.5 square feet of retail space per capita, compared to 16.8 square feet of retail space per capita in Canada, and 11.2 square feet of retail space per capita in Australia. We simply have too many retail stores for our new retail environment" (Peterson, 2018).

Experiential retail is a concept that has its roots *firmly planted* in coercing shoppers back into stores to facilitate increased store visits that will encourage customer loyalty, maximize top-line revenue, and establish brand awareness within the ultra-competitive retail sector. Amazon is causing major disruption throughout the entire retail sector which is affecting traditional retailer's ability to **DIRECTLY COMPETE** with them. However, the number one advantage that brick-and-mortar retailers have that Amazon does not is a hands-on, engrossing, and interactive platform. In essence, stores provide experiences that cannot be replicated by an online consortium. Customers have always wanted to touch, smell, taste, see, and hear the products they are interested in purchasing. This is creating a *cyclical effect* whereby retailers are starting to return back to the sprouting stages of retail, i.e. when retailers provided all of these experiences authentically.

The permanent optimist within me concludes that this transformation will evolve into a more dynamic, inclusive, and entertaining proposition for the retailers who can adapt. *The universe, just like the retail sector, is fundamentally a concept of duality where each environment seeks to correct itself through adaptation to acclimatize to its intended balanced nature.* What does this mean for retailers who are struggling with adjusting to the changing retail landscape? What can legacy retailers do to stave off the bankruptcy proceedings? Here are some options for retailers to capitalize on the evolving experiential retail concepts:

1.  Provide flexible co-working spaces within stores/offices where it is appropriate to bring in fresh revenue.

2.  Movie theaters can rent out their theaters for alternative venues, e.g., comedy acts, business venues, birthday parties, etc.

3.  Home improvement stores can "carve out space" for popular cafes/restaurants. (Starbucks or a fresh concept maybe?). This increases their experiential experience offerings to customers and maximizes their time in the store, i.e. most people become impatient when they get hungry.

4.  Grocery stores can offer food and liquor bars with a sit-down atmosphere, instead of just a deli buffet to capture additional customers.

5.  Bookstores can transform their cafés into a beer and wine theme after a certain time, which will cater to a different clientele and increase revenue.

6.  Apparel retailers can install virtual mirrors (in the dressing rooms) to capitalize on the convenience factor and provide a seamless interaction for their guests.

An example of a poignant case study for providing an experiential retail excursion is Beerwolf Books in Falmouth, United Kingdom. By day it is a traditional bookstore that offers a broad range of literature, both new and secondhand that caters to mostly a younger crowd (students). However, at nighttime, it turns into a pub where they have a bar stocked with a range of locally brewed beers and cider. *The same bookstore transmogrifies into a different atmosphere during the evening which is tailored to attract a different crowd with its pub-like environment.*

Beerwolf Books is a prime example of how innovative retailers can strategize and reformat (during challenging economic conditions) to accommodate a different clientele within their own four walls. Essentially, maximizing their square footage into more productive and profitable retail spaces. Now, they are only offering beer and ciders at their location. On another note, with the addition of a wine selection and other mild spirits, a bookstore could reinvent themselves through the increased offerings into a **DESTINATION** with a unique, experiential interaction where customers would shop more frequently. Coincidentally, there is a bookstore "Books & Brews" in Indianapolis, Indiana that incorporates alcohol, wine, and spirits and is part brewpub, part board game library, and part used bookstore.

Retailers must have the courage to embrace new formats while lessening their "death grip" on *outdated/legacy retail mindsets* that are proving ineffective in the digital world. Dr. Phil has a perfect cliché for his guests when they are not achieving their desired outcomes with their <u>current behavior in their lives</u>, **"HOW IS THAT WORKING FOR YOU???"** This advice, which is raw and direct while cutting through illusions, is perfectly suited to any situation in your life. It can be a retailer who is struggling to maintain market share or a leader who is faltering with motivating their teams. It bears repeating again: **HOW IS THAT WORKING FOR YOU???**

## <u>SECTION FOR NOTES</u>

## CHAPTER TWENTY-FOUR: INNOVATIVE CONCEPTS, PART THREE

### CREATING WORK/LIFE BALANCE FOR YOUR LEADERS

Having experienced a long tenure in the retail sector (30-years total) with 20+ years as a manager/leader, the **NUMBER ONE** complaint among salaried leaders is the exhausting work schedule that is considered mandatory. Furthermore, it does not properly allow for adequate work/life balance. The retail sector is already notorious for having an undesirable schedule, akin to the restaurant industry, (nights, weekends, and holidays). Moreover, when you throw in the length of time per day (anywhere between 10-12 hours is the minimum requirement) that many salaried leaders are required to work, then you are creating an environment where most leaders will become *disgruntled and dissatisfied* with their careers. Over time, this will have a direct impact on each retail store. And, it will usually have negative consequences (exponentially) affecting the entire organization.

There is a new standard emerging among managers/leaders within the retail sector, in addition to other sectors, that individuals want to experience work/life balance in their lives and are not going to sacrifice their happiness for a slightly higher paycheck any longer. I never completely understood **WHY** if I chose to become a leader and assist others (associates, customers, and vendors) while accepting increased responsibilities, that I had to accept a decreased quality of life in exchange for my position. I would constantly ask: why must retailers *deal in absolutes* (all or nothing, i.e. if you want the position you must work the schedule) regarding the rigid expectations for their salaried leaders 50-55-hour **minimum work**

**schedules**? I have always believed in **"AN EVEN EXCHANGE OF ENERGY"** while constantly seeking out win-win scenarios for all parties involved.

During these question and answer sessions with upper management, I was bombarded with derogatory comments surrounding my lack of loyalty to the company, that I possessed a slacker attitude, or I did not have a strong work ethic. These statements were completely inaccurate, humiliating, unfair, and hurtful. I subscribed to the mentality of quality versus quantity with regards to my leadership style. It has always *served me well,* while allowing me to constantly exceed my metrics, consistently maintain high morale teams, and stay in the upper echelon for positive customer feedback. Most leaders feel that a 40-45-hour workweek would create a "Goldilocks Syndrome." It would allow each leader to have balance in their lives to spend with family and friends, pursue their hobbies, exercise, volunteer, and recharge their batteries.

Conversely, the 40-45-hour workweek should be **adjusted/increased** for peak seasonal times, x-mas season, or certain specific times for each retailer (and most leaders would not bat an eyelash for the increased workload). At the same time, the overall concept can/should be adhered to throughout the year. There are *three distinct viewpoints* surrounding most retailer's demur to implementing the 40-45-hour workweek for their salaried leaders:

1. Legacy mentality regarding good ole-fashion hard work requirements to be successful.
2. Trepidation about rocking the boat and having the innovative spirit needed to create the necessary changes to the outdated work schedule.

3. Fear over financial repercussions which include decreased revenue, increased staffing requirements, and lack of execution for company protocols.

## LEGACY MENTALITY REGARDING GOOD OLE-FASHION HARD WORK

Most people abhor change because of the "anxiety factor" that is created (going from that which is known, to an environment that is unknown). It is a deep-seated fear we possess as human beings. However, many innovative retail executives are embracing the new attitude from younger generations who are demanding that companies create a balanced work environment for all parties. I noticed a significant decrease in my energy and performance after becoming salaried and I did not understand why. After experiencing the salaried position for a while, I ascertained that most of my day was centered around problem-solving, handling customer/employee complaints, motivating/coaching associates, and implementing massive amounts of creativity.

Each one of these components requires additional energy (which I found out is not an unlimited resource) than your traditional associate responsibilities. Henceforth, I gleaned that each hour as a **high-performing leader** facilitated a sizeable increase *in energy expenditure.* This is why I felt completely drained at the end of my day. I surmised that if a salaried leader works a 10-hour shift, he/she might *feel like they worked* for 15 hours because of the increased energy expenditure that is experienced handling conflict resolution situations, putting out proverbial fires, and motivating/coaching their store teams. I used to live on caffeine, energy drinks, and energy pills (legally, of course) to have the energy to accomplish some of the herculean tasks that are expected every day in the retail stores.

The legacy mentality exists because of the increased work schedule that was created and needed in bygone eras. Those eras did not possess efficient technology, machines, or innovative techniques to achieve workloads. **We live in a digital world where technology is increasing our efficiency across all verticals which SHOULD be decreasing salaried leadership work schedules.** Unfortunately, a plethora of leaders still subscribes to the "must work hard to achieve success mentality." Moreover, this is showing in the lack of bench strength at many retailers, the extremely high salaried turnover metrics, and the precipitous drop-in excellent customer service within the stores.

## TREPIDATION ABOUT ROCKING THE BOAT

With the current state of the retail sector, many analysts are predicting a dystopian future for many well-established iconic retail brands because of many executive leaders' "austerity" towards embracing change and fostering a more inclusive environment for their employees. If you study the most popular legacy retailers, you will notice a severity of trepidation surrounding opposing viewpoints regarding store leaders work schedules, their requests for improved work/life balance, and flexibility to be involved in their family's lives, i.e. catching their child's soccer game or going to their son's basketball game. *Many store leaders feel like an oversized marionette with zero control over their personal lives because they decided to get promoted to the salaried level and improve their career advancement.*

More than ever, the retail sector is going to need **INNOVATIVE C-SUITE LEADERS** that are willing to aggressively challenge the status quo surrounding their salaried leader's schedules by providing them with fair, balanced, and flexible options. I have rarely encountered a salaried leader who said: "I love working sixty-five-hour workweeks and not being able to be involved with my family." I have seen younger leaders that are *newly promoted* who are still excited about the increase in pay, the new status of being a manager, and the nice perks that are included with salaried leadership while being mostly immune to the hectic work schedule. Unfortunately, after some time, with many leaders, the dissatisfaction starts creeping in. Furthermore, the manager starts to question the necessary trade-offs that are mandatory for the position while simultaneously deciding if the financial numbers, additional perks, and declining work/life balance are worth the sacrifices.

Unlike other industries, working a 55+ workweek in the retail sector is not only mentally exhausting but also physically demanding. Some leaders are on their feet for most of their shift - walking on concrete floors, loading extremely heavy items, and experiencing physically challenging tasks every day. I know many retail leaders who worked in the sector for decades who are now starting to experience the cumulative effect of the demanding work environment just like professional athletes, except that the retail store leader earns a pittance compared to the professionals.

These retail leaders will have to reconcile their physical pain and suffering for the rest of their lives, many of whom express extreme regret for the lack of empathy shown towards them from executive leadership for the difficult environment which they endured, as well as the severity of work hours expected. The time has come to change/reduce the work schedules of salaried leaders!

## FEAR OVER FINANCIAL REPERCUSSIONS WITH REDUCTION IN SALARIED STAFF SCHEDULES

The most "tangible fear" most retail executives possess is the *financial consequences* of reducing their salaried leader's schedules. This could encompass: a massive reduction in revenue, increase labor costs to compensate for fewer hours per leader, and disruption with executing company protocols. This specific hesitation from retail executives is buoyed only by an ingrained, outdated, and resistant attitude that is on **AUTOPILOT** with minimal empirical data to support their reservations. It is creating an environment of diminishing returns. The Law of Diminishing Returns is "an economic law stating that if one input in the production of a commodity is increased while all other inputs are held fixed, then a point will eventually be reached at which additions of the input yield progressively smaller, or diminishing, increases in output." (Hayes, 2020).

Many retailers are responsible for the very thing they are attempting to avoid; increased leadership turnover. In fact, it is becoming rampant within the retail sector because salaried leaders are *silently crying out for help* with regards to their current work schedule. These outdated work schedules are creating stress-related issues, family discord, relationship problems, health-related concerns, unhealthy eating habits, increased depression risks, and overall unhappiness in their lives. We need to reevaluate the work schedules which we are demanding of our salaried leaders while focusing our efforts on establishing work-friendly time frames that compensate for their leader's domestic pursuits. I have **ACHIEVED THIS WIN-WIN SCENARIO** with my teams, so I am speaking from personal experience about the efficacy of this method. **IT CAN BE DONE! IT CAN BE DONE! IT CAN BE DONE!**

My stores epitomized the concept of "quality versus quantity" with regard to salaried work schedules. *We were achieving and surpassing our financial metrics, receiving green status store visits from superiors, remained near the top for customer surveys, were among the elite for human resource related assessments, and were compliant with all company protocols.* Many studies reveal that most hourly workers reach a *productivity precipice* after working 50 hours per week. If the precipice is 50 hours for an hourly worker who is **not encumbered** with numerous stress-related responsibilities, then how many hours would this equate for a salaried leader **in retail**??? Leaders are inundated with increased job-related energy zappers, e.g., customer complaints, putting out fires (not real fires but store-related concerns), employee conflict resolution situations, coaching/counseling associates, and completing their own workloads.

I always believed in *empowering* my salaried leaders by providing them with work schedules of 40-45 hours per week (depending on the retailer and its annual revenue/size). This forced me to train them to become extremely efficient with productivity, think proactively, prepare extremely early, anticipate future issues while planning accordingly, and develop a competitive, yet inclusive, environment with their teams. I rarely encountered a situation when there was an important event coming up (store visit, seasonal preparation, new company initiative, or unplanned occurrence) where my salaried leaders **DID NOT** work extra to achieve our vision.

My salaried leaders were fresh, had work/life balance which afforded them the time to spend with their families, and were extremely grateful for the work atmosphere I created for them. My leaders were always willing to do "whatever it took" to get the job done while working with a positive attitude which spilled over to the rest of the store and became infectious for our teams. *Consequently, I always attained massive success with achieving/surpassing financial metrics, had zero salaried staffing issues, rarely had to ask the salaried leaders to step up, and experienced positive leadership morale* with <u>most individuals</u>. There are always a few **SLACKERS** who are selfish, not team-orientated, and attempting to buck the trend. Therefore, these managers are usually weeded out because of their own actions.

## HOW TO IMPLEMENT 40-45 HOUR SALARIED WORK SCHEDULES

Some people are asking **HOW** could I schedule my salaried leaders only 40-45 hours per workweek while still being successful with the day-to-day activities that are inherent in *operating a large retail store i.e. 60 million annually.* The first concept that I employed (with the approval of senior management) was to properly assess potential future leaders within the building. I would ascertain which department managers were interested and capable of moving to the next level/s within the company by imparting the "key carrier program" to the most qualified candidates. For this 40-45-hour work schedule to take flight, I had to first determine the staffing requirements upon which each store is dependent: annual sales volume, footfall, the size of store, average ticket, penetration by department, and seasonality, etc.

I always felt that my number one priority was to *develop future leaders* for each organization that would assist with leadership replenishment (turnover/churn over) while creating dynamic leaders for the future. Many stores/companies struggle with developing future leaders which are the lifeline of their business. If this is not properly addressed, it can create an environment of "diminished talent" to choose from when promoting leaders. The key carrier program is a positive experience for all parties involved. The department manager receives a promotion (with a pay increase) with increased responsibilities that affords them the opportunity to become (essentially) an assistant manager-in-training. The store wins because it is adding additional leadership coverage that will assist with customer service, employee engagement, and improved floor presence.

With each newly promoted key carrier, the "buddy system" would be in place to ensure the individual had the appropriate amount of time to *acclimatize to their new role*. This would **ALWAYS** include observing/shadowing how an experienced salaried leader handles customer/employee issues (to which they are privy, i.e. specific situations are for salaried leaders only). The key carrier program, when utilized correctly, will also dramatically increase your talent pool or **BULLPEN**. Many retailers are severely lacking in leadership depth in today's retail environment where most leaders are wearing a plethora of "responsibility hats" compared to decades ago.

To become a successful retail leader today requires additional training and experience than *ever before* in the retail sector, e.g., a digital world full of omnichannel situations, decreased staffing levels, and increased responsibilities are abounding which demand a brand-new skill set. With the retail landscape experiencing an unprecedented level of disruption, the retail leaders of the future will require additional training that has not been implemented yet while having to adjust "on the fly" with the current level of training they have, which is not idyllic.

The key carrier program, when executed appropriately, will create a fresh enthusiastic environment where all the associates can witness their potential career trajectory because of the descriptive leadership levels within the store that are attainable with the necessary performance. The salaried leaders will cheerfully assist with the training of the newer key carriers, which creates a mutually beneficial scenario for everyone involved. The salaried leaders can have excellent work/life balance in their lives and, as a result, the department managers that are selected can cultivate their career advancement effectively.

The overall effect on each store creates an inclusive environment where the salaried leaders have *sustainable* "positive morale" and are more than willing to work longer hours when necessary. Moreover, most leaders will express a fervent/grateful attitude towards the increased output, i.e. no grumblings or unpleasantness with the additional hours. The department managers have the opportunity to receive the required training towards becoming a salaried leader in their own store (or alternative store) which will **PRIME THE PUMP** for your future leaders. *This atmosphere of an even exchange of energy can be achieved when this program is executed* *properly for your salaried leaders to only have to work 40-45-hours per week.* Furthermore, other than certain times of the year or when unexpected situations arise, **THIS IS ACHIEVABLE** within the retail sector.

## HIRING/RETAINING MORE EXPERIENCED WORKERS

One of the most *detrimental changes* I have noticed within the retail sector over the last decade has been a "strategic corporate initiative" for <u>some hiring managers</u> (not all), of course, to retreat from hiring older workers in favor of younger workers to build the workspace of the future. I have also noticed an odious plan of removing older/experienced workers from the retail stores to accelerate their new vision. There is an avalanche of reasons for this new paradigm shift among hiring managers who are subscribing to outdated stereotypes. *Some hiring managers feel that older workers are more expensive, are intimidated by technology, are slower and unable to handle the physical demands of the job, lack the fortitude to be trained, and are stuck in their ways.*

It appears many retailers are "consciously obstructing their aspirations" because of what these hiring managers (and not all hiring managers, just to be fair to these hard-working individuals) are forgetting. While some of these purported reasons are true, there is a multitude of positive realities that are being overlooked. With unemployment at record lows, immigration policies tightening, and consumers' mandate for more knowledgeable workers, the workplace is changing faster than most retailers can adapt to with their current cultural philosophy surrounding hiring, retaining, and creating an engaging workforce.

Older workers have something younger workers do not and cannot have, which is good ole fashion experience. Experience takes time to accumulate and master throughout the years. Many retailers are starting to reevaluate their hiring methods, while at the same time realizing that mature workers can/will assist in re-balancing their stores to accommodate a healthy mix of younger workers and experienced workers. Mature workers have many favorable attributes that can contribute to any retailer's environment:

1.  Professionalism which probably took decades to master.

2.  Industry knowledge which is irreplaceable in the right niche; e.g., a retired plumber working at The Home Depot, a former electronic sales executive working at Best Buy, or a retired military captain working in leadership at Target.

3.  Reliability and dependability; i.e., many older workers do not miss work very often.

4.  Strong work ethic which was refined throughout the years.

5.  Actively engaged because they are happy with their jobs and most are making a conscious decision to continue working.

6.  Problem-solving skills that are usually exemplary because they have been applied throughout their working lives.

7.  Ability to work well within a team-orientated environment.

8.  Generally, drama-free and do not cause many frivolous workplace issues.

I would highly encourage all retailers to examine their current hiring practices while performing **EXIT INTERVIEWS** with candidates not selected (to gather pertinent information and to find correlations that exist). This will uncover biases, preselected judgments, or inhibitions your hiring managers are displaying regarding older workers. Many hiring managers will require a deprogramming to allow them to experience an epiphany about hiring older workers, while also altering their preconceived notions about this diverse, knowledgeable, and impactful age group (45+). Many hiring managers establish a *bulwark towards older workers.* This is grounded in non-factual precepts regarding this group of people when searching for specific job openings within their companies.

Some hiring managers are **ONLY LOOKING TO CHECK THE BOXES** for their job descriptions, while severely *overlooking a mature worker's transferable skill set, industry knowledge, work ethic, integrity, and professionalism.* Having worked for eight different retailers throughout my retail tenure, I have interviewed with (and spoken with hundreds of colleagues who have interviewed) many different hiring managers that exhibited these exact behaviors. Henceforth, I can personally attest to these practices remaining prevalent throughout the sector. The time has come for retailers to remove the shackles of the past for *consciously allowing ageism to exist within their organization* while championing an environment of inclusion and acceptance regardless of an applicant's age.

### INCONGRUOUS STANDARDS FOR REQUIRING COLLEGE DEGREES

There are some retailers who have strict requirements that prohibit or frown upon hiring any **EXTERNAL CANDIDATE** into their company (especially at the store level) that do not possess at least a four-year college degree. Unfortunately, this is inhibiting them from securing top-tier talent. Coincidentally, these same retailers are struggling to remain dominant within their specific niche in the retail sector. They are allowing individuals with "massive experience" and no college degree to matriculate to other retailers while creating a negative stigma surrounding their hiring practices with potential candidates. I have always found the adage of "four-year college degree **AND/OR** equivalent work experience" that will fully capture most potential candidates.

Many retailers are alienating retail leaders who possess a long history of successful retail leadership qualities that were garnered by decades of hands-on experience. These individuals chose a path that did not include a college education. However, the impressive skill set they have acquired was earned through the trials and tribulations of sharpening their retail leadership skills in the real-world through tangible examples instead of choosing the academic route. These retail veterans should not be discarded because they do not have a four-year college degree. Moreover, they should be embraced for their unique retail background that may provide your organization with innovative concepts and impressive standards of excellence.

Just to preface, I am a huge fan of college degrees and I fully support an individual's choice to further their higher education. Despite this, running a retail store/s as an assistant manager, store manager or even as a district manager requires an overabundance of soft skills, motivation, coaching/mentoring, foresight, adaptability, and real-world experience to become successful. I have seen and worked with numerous fresh out of college salaried leaders who had an impressive college résumé that could not hack it (due to no fault of their own). Mostly, because many of (not all) the courses they took regarding management, leadership, retail business training, and business practices were outdated, impractical and *were not transferable* to the retail store setting with the unique real-life challenges you are expected to handle.

Some colleges do not properly prepare you (unlike other industries where college institutions are outstanding with preparation, e.g., education, medicine, law, engineering, science, criminal justice, etc.) for the complexities that the retail sector will throw at you. Some college institutions need to revamp (or add to) their retail management curriculums to adequately prepare their students for the differences between academic knowledge and real-world knowledge. The current template is myopic, which is creating a **major disconnect** between *some colleges* and the current state of the retail sector. Subsequently, many students are not receiving the specific education that is/will be required for the transformation that is occurring in retail today.

<u>Academic knowledge</u> is based upon theories, statistical data, analytical perspectives, and *anachronistic methods* that are considered archetypal while missing the plug & play model that students require. <u>Real-world knowledge</u> consists of reading books from current retail individuals who are living and breathing the retail sector while offering hands-on/transferable skill sets that translate to the retail sector. In addition, I would suggest collaborating with contemporary successful retail leaders which could encompass standard guest lecturers that have tremendous retail experience, partnerships with local retailers, and possibly internships. It appears that some college institutions are going to have to reformulate their retail leadership curriculums (and or add a retail leadership program to their business school) to accommodate the rapid evolution that

is occurring within the retail sector. Hopefully, they will focus on flexibility, adaptability, and nimbleness to compensate for the *speed of disruption* that is becoming the standard.

## CONSISTENT STANDARDS FOR TWO-WEEK NOTICES

There are some *major discrepancies* with how retailers conduct business when employees/managers offer their resignation by putting in their two-week notice. It seems to be an unfair practice that is severely slanted in the company's favor. This forces the employee/manager between a "rock and a hard place" when they are transitioning to another stage in their professional life. Most states are considered an "at-will state" for employment. This means the employer or employee can sever the relationship with *no notice and for no stated cause*, unless there is an employment agreement between both parties specifically stating certain provisions, e.g., length of the contract, duration of employment, or proper protocols for separation.

Numerous retailers are subjecting their entire corporation to negative exposure, a scarcity of future candidates, and derogative stereotypes by how they are mishandling employees who desire to separate. I have witnessed an exorbitant number of individuals who have impressive character, strong morals, and high integrity. Furthermore, when they submit their two-week notice, they are **IMMEDIATELY ESCORTED** out of the building subjecting them to a humiliating and degrading process when they were attempting to do the honorable thing. This type of unprofessional behavior spreads like a brushfire throughout the retail sector while establishing a benchmark for this company. Even if only a small percentage of stores are acting this way, XYZ corporation will have a perception of negative organizational culture by mistreating their employees when they decide to separate.

Another unfavorable financial reality is that the employee **COULD HAVE JUST LEFT** with zero notice and started their new endeavor without missing a beat with their finances. However, quite possibly, they could have just lost two weeks' worth of salary which could be thousands of dollars *because they acted professionally*. **Conversely, when the employee does not provide a standard two-week notice, they are subjected to being called disloyal, ungrateful, unappreciative, lacking character, unprofessional, or untrustworthy.** Many retailers are creating an environment that is a *no-lose proposition for them* when it comes to two-week notices while unloading the full burden of risk onto the employee.

I have always thought that an organization/employee are characterized by their first impression and their last impression. In most cases, (not all, there are some unforeseen circumstances that are to be forgiven) this will be how people remember you. <u>This double standard needs to stop immediately</u>. This situation can easily be rectified by implementing a few concrete protocols surrounding separation etiquette:

1. When an employee submits their two-week notice, they are given the chance to fulfill this commitment with full pay.

2. If during this two-week fulfillment the employee does not maintain a professional and positive attitude while acting as a cancer for other employees, then the individual can be asked to leave immediately with no further obligation to compensate.

3. During this two-week fulfillment period, the employee is "expected to maintain" their standard level of productivity, i.e. no short timing it.

4. If the employer decides to separate immediately after receiving the individual's two-week notice, then the employee will receive the full two-week salary at 100% payout.

5. If the employee engages in any illicit, illegal, or inappropriate activities, immediate separation will occur will no additional salary commitments.

6. When an employee submits their two-week notice, human resources will conduct an **exit interview** (within the two-week time frame) to gather apposite information to determine the individual's reason/s for leaving while attempting to discern similarities that are becoming prevalent within the store/company.

7. Human resources conduct an exit interview on **EVERY** separating employee that did not provide a two-week notice.

We already spoke about organizational karma in <u>chapter seventeen</u> *(Organizational Culture, Part One)* with this being a glaring example of how **NOT TO TREAT** your separating employees. To restate, the basic definition of karma is what you put out to the universe, you will receive back in kind. Henceforth, if your company is treating individuals who wish to separate with unprofessional methods, what **DO YOU THINK** you will reap in return? *Many individuals experience massive guilt and anxiety with submitting a two-week notice or not submitting one due to the uncertainty surrounding the financial ramifications, being humiliated, possible indecent comments, or unfavorable treatment they could experience.*

True Servant Leaders understand that there are going to be individuals who will separate and pursue additional opportunities to further their professional growth. Yet, they will still handle these employees with class, professionalism, empathy, decency, and kindness. To recap from chapter one *(Talent Acquisition)*, **SEPARATING EMPLOYEES ARE STILL POTENTIAL CUSTOMERS.**

## <u>SECTION FOR NOTES</u>

## CHAPTER TWENTY-FIVE: CONCLUSION

### THE RETAIL APOCALYPSE IS HYPERBOLE

Throughout this book, I have presented a **ten-pillar strategy** for retailers small and large alike to implement within their organization. This manual can dramatically assist with alleviating many of the retail detriments that are causing a litany of retailers to drastically reduce their footprint, file for bankruptcy protection, execute employee layoffs, and radically alter how they approach their business model. There is a famous quote by the 18th-century banker Baron Rothschild: "The time to buy is when there's blood in the streets." My perception of this quote is that this *changing of the guard is forcing many retailers to adapt and innovate* with the opportunity to rise from the ashes with a stronger foothold within their respective niche while foraging into uncharted territories. This, in turn, will galvanize your employees, leaders, vendors, and customers.

I have the **UTMOST RESPECT FOR THE EXECUTIVE/C-SUITE RETAIL LEADERS TODAY**. After all, they are faced with the daunting task of evolving within an aggressive new arena that has never been witnessed before within the retail sector. The C-suite leaders are experiencing an all-out attack from every angle (Amazon, Omnichannel, younger generational shopping patterns, and digital curation) with no historical data to guide them. *This new retail arena is subjecting many retailers to confront a precipitous drop in revenue, decreased brand awareness, diminishing net income levels, and declining customer foot traffic.*

The year 2018 marks the 200-year anniversary of the first U.S. retailer---Brooks Brothers followed in 1826 by Lord & Taylor; then, Macy's was founded in 1858. Until the 2010s, most retailers followed similar successful strategies while the major difference (for success or failure) was the efficacy of executing those stratagems. **In today's digital world, the customer is afforded a cornucopia of choices when deciding WHERE to purchase their retail items.** This new arena is confounding many retailers with the acceleration of numerous innovative, immersive, and visceral experiences that are altering the retail landscape forever.

As I stated in the introduction of this manual, I believe that life and in retail, everything is cyclical in nature. Henceforth, we are experiencing an emerging new frontier that will crystallize into a fresh new retail sector that is befitting of a halcyon period from our past. The digital era is a *progenitor of the customer's desire to revert to a time when the retail sector was exploding with experiential touchpoints.* The ten-pillar system of Talent Acquisition, Talent Retention, Revenue Generation, Engagement, Merchandising, Store Environment, Differentiation, Organizational Culture, Omni-Channel, and Innovation **can assist any retailer by providing a proven successful blueprint to navigate the choppy waters retailers are experiencing today.**

The Retail Apocalypse has been described as all "doom and gloom" for the retail sector. However, in 2019-2020, many retailers (not all) will experience a readjustment period. This will **ONLY** happen **AFTER** they have finalized reducing their store footprint to manageable levels, increased their Omnichannel efforts, embraced new retail paradigms, relinquished legacy methods that are antiquated, and satisfied rapidly shifting customer expectations. The C-suite leaders within the retail sector have a <u>golden opportunity</u> to establish heuristic methods that will create an axiomatic bridge between legacy retailing of the past to the highly innovative, enthralling, and multisensory digital world of tomorrow.

Many retailers are communicating signs of optimism within the retail environment for 2018 and beyond with robust outlooks that are signaling the initial stages of the Retail Apocalypse demise. A brand-new retail landscape is emerging that will encompass a highly personalized, customer-centric world that is deeply rooted in artificial technology. Furthermore, it is broadening across many customer touchpoints that will usher in new methods towards complete customer satisfaction. There is an overabundance of retailers who are planning on *opening new stores* in 2018: Target (25), Walmart (25), Hobby Lobby (60), Dicks Sporting Goods (20), Ulta Beauty (100), Five Below (125), and Dollar General (900).

## FINALIZING THE PROCESS

I have provided ten pillars or *micro-verticals* throughout this retail manual. *Furthermore, when grouped together, through implementation, staunch consistency, and sterling execution, they will bolster your chances of creating a buttressed atmosphere that will remain "unaffected" by the recent detrimental retail environment that has claimed so many casualties.* I truly believe the retail sector is poised for a renewed alignment that will incentivize customers to continue visiting brick-and-mortar establishments. In addition, when combined with the digital enhancements that many retailers are investing the necessary resources towards, will create an engaging retail utopian future.

The content within this manual will "possibly" create some internal challenges for some executives, especially long-tenured leaders. It will force every individual to truly assess their current effectiveness of each pillar which will demand a completely **UNBIASED EVALUATION.** I am recommending a strategy that has always been effective for me when measuring my progress towards achieving a specific aspiration. I would only consider myself completely devoid or cured of a certain behavior/issue when it was "confirmed" by *my peers, associates, superiors, and if necessary, my customers.* This forced me to truly accept an honest introspection of a certain problem that I was experiencing by seeking feedback (for which I asked for absolute honesty yet fairness in their assessment) from my closest advisors.

This experiment was highly successful in altering my perspective towards achieving my goals. After encountering the brutal criticism which destroyed my self-inflated ego, I started to **EMBRACE THE HONEST FEEDBACK.** I knew this was instilling a sense of balance within me that was grounded in other people's notions of my behavior, performance, or effectiveness with my chosen endeavor. It is an extremely humbling experience to seek out your peers/superior's advice on your deficiencies. However, you will receive the necessary information you require to properly gauge your success. I would suggest that each leader implement a similar strategy when examining each one of the pillars within this book.

The **"EGO"** is a powerful tool in our professional/personal toolbox. It can propel any leader to achieve astronomical accomplishments when it is in *harmony within the individual.* On the other hand, when it is running rampant and unchecked, it can cause ignominious consequences for the individual and those working for them as well. Some leaders feel that when they have

achieved a certain "professional status" in their careers that they have acquired most of the

business acumen/knowledge they require. Henceforth, they do not seek out or solicit feedback,

accept other people's ideas, or feel the need to acquiesce their viewpoints. This is a crying shame

for many leaders because the greatest inventions or concepts usually are conceived from other

individuals who do not have a certain title or the massive professional experience/tenure of

others.

Some of the most impressive ideas I implemented throughout my career came from my

peers, customers, vendors, associates, and competitors for which I humbly and graciously

accepted. Moreover, *I would have never received these suggestions IF I was impervious to*

*change or considered unapproachable for new ideas*. I always excelled at executing and or

improving upon an existing concept for which I became fanatical about dissecting (to fully

understand it from all sides). I then continued to expand upon an idea/concept for the betterment

of our customers, employees, and bottom line.

I used to place post-it-notes of the behaviors I wanted to transform (that were communicated

from my superiors which required adjustment) on my bathroom mirror so that each morning (and

every night) I would review these notes and continue to address each day to improve my

situation. I would only take down the notes *after confirming* with a solid mix of individuals who

agreed that the behavior had changed. I took it to another level by soliciting feedback from my

peers (other department managers, assistant managers, or store managers as I progressed up the ranks) to further gauge my effectiveness with specific deficiencies. This process, which I continue to this day, is now executed in every part of my professional and personal life which continues to be a strong **BAROMETER** for any change or accomplishment.

It is my sincerest aspiration for each leader, department manager up to CEO, that has read this book from start to finish, that I have helped to improve your business acumen, increased your retail knowledge, and have provided you with an overabundance of different perspectives to effectuate positive change within your retail organization. I have thoroughly relished this creative endeavor which has become an effective outlet to communicate my viewpoints and insights regarding the retail sector. I hope that you have *enjoyed the journey* along the way. **THANK YOU** **FOR TAKING THE TIME TO ALLOW ME TO SHARE MY THOUGHTS WITH YOU.**

If you enjoyed this book and found merit within, I would be **HONORED AND GRATEFUL** if you could please leave a positive review on Amazon to increase exposure and assist others with finding this book. Thank you in advance for your time and consideration. I would love to hear your thoughts, perspective, and feedback. Please send your feedback to: jpmcnulty@newretailethos.com.

# ☯SUCCESS IS YOURS☯

# BIBLIOGRAPHY

(Anderson, 2020) https://www.hobo-web.co.uk/your-website-design-should-load-in-4-seconds/

Artisan. (n.d.). Retrieved from http://creative.artisantalent.com: http://creative.artisantalent.com/steve-jobs-about-hiring/

Cava, M. d. (2018, February 1). USA Today. Retrieved from usatoday.com: https://www.usatoday.com/story/tech/2018/02/01/tesla-solar-energy-kiosks-coming-all-800-home-depot-locationsnow-pitching-its-solar-products-home-de/1086956001/

Cherry, K. (n.d.). Very Well. Retrieved from Verywell.com: https://www.verywell.com/what-is-the-overjustification-effect-2795386

Covey, S. (2020, August 14). BraineyQuote. Retrieved from brainyquote.com: https://www.brainyquote.com/quotes/keywords/empathy.html

(Digitalcommerce360, 2020) https://www.digitalcommerce360.com/2020/05/20/amazon-triples-its-private%E2%80%91label-product-offerings-in-2-years/

en.wikipedia.org. (2020). Retrieved from Wikipedia.org.

Fastcompany. (n.d.). The future of work. Retrieved from Fastcompany.com: https://www.fastcompany.com/3058344/5-flexible-work-strategies-and-the-companies-who-use-them

Florida, R. (2017, December 19). CITYLAB. Retrieved from www.citylab.com:

www.citylab.com/design/2017/12/the-great-retail-retrofit/548753

(Hayes, 2020)

https://www.investopedia.com/terms/l/lawofdiminishingmarginalreturn.asp

Jeffs, M. (2018, January 8). BRANDED3. Retrieved from www.branded3.com:

https://www.branded3.com/blog/google-voice-search-stats-growth-trends/

(Lady, 2019) https://thekrazycouponlady.com/tips/money/walmart-automates-online-

returns-and-gets-ahead-of-amazon-for-a-minute

Loubier, A. (n.d.). Forbes. Retrieved from www.forbes.com:

https://www.forbes.com/sites/andrealoubier/2017/07/20/benefits-of-telecommuting-for-the-

future-of-work/#7a98fc2316c

Lowes Companies, I. (2017, November 7). Cision PR Newswire. Retrieved from

www.prnewswire.com: https://www.prnewswire.com/news-releases/lowes-collaborates-with-

b8ta-to-deliver-experiential-retail-that-simplifies-smart-home-shopping-300550679.html

Merriam-Webster. (2020, January 7). Merriam-Webster. Retrieved from www.merriam-

webster.com: https://www.merriam-webster.com/dictionary/innovation

mi9retail. (n.d.). The 3 Essential Elements of Click-and-Collect. Retrieved from

mi9retail.com: https://mi9retail.com/the-3-essential-elements-of-click-and-collect/

Networks, A. (2018, February 26). Nazdac Globenewswire. Retrieved from GlobeNewswire.com: https://globenewswire.com/news-release/2018/02/26

(O'Shea, 2019) https://www.retaildive.com/news/most-bopis-shoppers-make-additional-purchases-in-store/549068/

Perez, S. (2017, August 16). Tech Crunch. Retrieved from techcrunch.com: https://techcrunch.com/2017/08/16/amazons-private-label-business-is-booming-thanks-to-device

(Peterson, 2018) https://www.businessinsider.com/retail-apocalypse-is-still-in-early-innings-cowen-says-2018-10

(Retail, 2019) https://apprissretail.com/blog/is-your-boris-bopis-a-win-win-part-one/

(Romell, 2019) https://www.jsonline.com/story/money/business/retail/2019/03/05/kohls-earnings-rise-adjusted-basis-beat-expectations/3061911002/

Ryan, T. (2018, February 1). Retail Wire. Retrieved from Retailwire.com: http://www.retailwire.com/discussion/should-retailers-ramp-up-investments-in-ai-for-employees/

(Safruti, 2020) https://www.digitalcommerce360.com/2020/06/17/3-takeaways-from-the-2020-verizon-data-breach-report/

(Saccomani, 2019) https://www.mobiloud.com/blog/mobile-apps-vs-the-mobile-web/

School, M. M. (2017, December 4). MIT Management Sloan School. Retrieved from http://mitsloan.mit.edu: http://mitsloan.mit.edu/newsroom/press-releases/mit-sloan-study-finds-holiday-sales-could-increase-with-better-staffing-decisions-by-retailers/

Shah, P. (n.d.). PG&E. Retrieved from www.pge.com: https://www.pge.com/en/mybusiness/save/smbblog/article/how-retail-businesses-can-easily-reduce-energy-consumption-and-costs.page

Sternin, J. (n.d.). Good Reads. Retrieved from www.goodreads.com: https://www.goodreads.com/author/quotes/3461294.Jerry_Sternin

(visier, 2020) https://www.visier.com/clarity/reduce-employee-turnover-with-workforce-analytics/

Wikipedia. (n.d.). Retrieved from en.wikipedia.org: https://en.wikipedia.org/wiki/Karma

Wikipedia. (n.d.). Wikipedia, the free encyclopedia. Retrieved from en.wikipedia.org: https://en.wikipedia.org/wiki/Carrot_and_stick

Wikipedia.org. (2020). Retrieved from Wikipedia.org: https://en.wikipedia.org/wiki/Leadership_in_Energy_and_Environmental_Design

(Wong, 2020) https://www.achievers.com/blog/why-you-cant-afford-disengaged-employees/

# ABOUT THE AUTHOR

Jeffrey P. McNulty is currently the Founder & CEO of New Retail Ethos, LLC which assists retail organizations (regardless of size, scope, or niche) with alleviating and addressing common "Pain Points" through all facets of consumer insights, anticipatory intelligence, and retail research across numerous categories. New Retail Ethos services encompass increasing top-line revenue, addressing operational inefficiencies, providing innovative concepts that proliferate market share, imparting a proven system to drastically improve employee/customer engagement, and merchandising concepts that generate increased profitability.

Mr. McNulty is considered a "Hybrid" in the business world as he has 30 years' experience as a Retail Executive for The Home Depot, Lowes, Barnes & Noble, PetSmart, Shopko, Toys R Us, Publix Supermarkets, and Festival Foods as well as over 15 years of tenure as a Retail Market Research Analyst. He has conducted over 800 consultations on the retail sector throughout his career. Mr. McNulty has an Associate Degree in Retail Management from The University of Wisconsin Green Bay. Mr. McNulty can be contacted for seminars, classroom instruction, leadership venues, public speaking engagements, book signings, bulk book discounts, one-on-one tutorials, and advisory services at:

New Retail Ethos, LLC
P.O. Box 323
Wrightstown, WI. 54180
Business Contact:844-669-2888 or 920-888-2118
jpmcnulty@newretailethos.com
www.newretailethos.com
www.facebook.com/TheUltimateRetailManual
www.linkedin.com/in/jeffreypmcnulty

CPSIA information can be obtained
at www.ICGtesting.com
Printed in the USA
LVHW061054080121
676060LV00024B/246